Educating the Jewish Adolescent in the Teachings of the Religion and Culture of Judaism

Educating the Jewish Adolescent in the Teachings of the Religion and Culture of Judaism

AHARON KESSLER

VANTAGE PRESS
New York

This book was written by an experienced educator to tell people about the school of the Jewish community of Pittsburgh, Pennsylvania, established so that Jewish adolescents could learn who they are.

FIRST EDITION

All rights reserved, including the right of
reproduction in whole or in part in any form.

Copyright © 1997 by Aharon Kessler

Published by Vantage Press, Inc.
516 West 34th Street, New York, New York 10001

Manufactured in the United States of America
ISBN: 0-533-12081-0

Library of Congress Catalog Card No.: 96-90505

0 9 8 7 6 5 4 3 2 1

For my daughter, Penina,
and her husband, Marvin

Contents

Introduction ix

I. The Story of a School Where Jewish Adolescents Learn What They Are 1

Preface 3
1. The Amos Comay Program of Educational Enrichment—
    College Courses for Teachers—Pittsburgh, Pennsylvania 5

II. Jewish Identity 27

1. The Amos Comay Program of Educational Enrichment—
    College Courses for Teachers, by Patricia S. Feldman, Ph.D. 29
2. Judaism as Religion and Culture, by Eunice R. Baradon, D.Ed. 33

Bibliography 35

III. Jewish Adolescents Explore Their Identity:
    A Collection of Ideas and Sources 37

1. Preliminaries: About Educational Objectives 39
2. Introduction 45
3. Lecture I: Exploring One's Jewish Identity 53
4. Lecture II: Stages of Growth and Development 63
5. Lecture III: Why Should I Be Jewish? 68
6. Lecture IV: Concepts of Peoplehood 77
7. Lecture V: Identity and Identification of Certain Jews 84
8. Lecture VI: Summary of Ideas and Sources
    Responding to the Question, Why Should I Be Jewish? 88
9. Exploring One's Jewish Identity: Summary of Ideas,
    by Dr. Eunice R. Baradon 134

Bibliography 151

IV. Voices from Our Past: Moral Implications of Holocaust Literature, by Penina Kessler Lieber	153
Foreword	155
Preface	157
1. Memory and the Holocaust	159
2. The Literature of the Holocaust	164
3. The Moral Imperative of the Holocaust	176
Notes	180
Bibliography	181
Summary	182
V. The Image of the Historic Jew	185
1. Why This Bulletin?	187
2. Lecture I: Introduction to the Image of the Historic Jew	189
3. Lecture II: The Image of the Historic Jew	198
4. Lecture III: The Jew and History	203
5. Lecture IV: The Image of the Historic Jew in the Second Part of History	207
6. Lecture V: The Jews—First Martyrs in History	211
7. Lecture VI: Christian Theological Anti-Semitism	216
8. Lecture VII: Rehashing Ancient Prejudices	221
9. Lecture VIII: Jewish Martyrdom Challenged	227
10. Teaching Methods: Teaching Jewish Suffering as Martyrdom in the Jewish Secondary School	229
11. Martyrdom as Kiddush Ha-Shem	237
12. Jewish Attitudes Toward Christianity in Light of Christian Anti-Semitism	241
About the Author	243

Introduction

In *Educating the Jewish Adolescent in the Teachings of the Religion and Culture of Judaism*, Aharon Kessler analyzes Mordecai M. Kaplan's definition of Torah as a three-dimensional culture.

Mordecai M. Kaplan defines the three dimensions as a way of life or civilization process. A series of writings are the products of that process. The Torah is an instrument for transmitting it from generation to generation. In all three dimensions, Torah has one goal: to prepare the whole man for living his life as a human being to the full.

Aharon Kessler explains the meaning of culture and civilization as applied to Torah in contemporary Jewish thought and in the religion of Judaism. He goes further to explain the religion of Judaism and the ingredients that constitute the Jewish civilization: history, tradition in the broadest sense, contemporary Jewish society, Israel, Jewish ethics, and the objectives of Jewish education.

The realization in many communities throughout the United States of the limited status of American Jewish education resulted in an understanding of the need to create teacher-training programs, to revise textbooks, as well as to write new ones.

It was in 1950 that Pittsburgh examined itself. The Jewish Federation was awakened by its director, Dr. Maurice Taylor, for the need of a self-study. The American Association for Jewish Education was contacted. Two members of the faculty of the American Association were delegated to organize and conduct a study. They were Dr. Uriah Engelman, Director of Research, and Dr. Aharon Kessler, Director of Consultation to Bureaus and Communities.

In 1950, the Jewish community of Greater Pittsburgh, under the aegis of the United Jewish Fund, conducted a city-wide study regarding the status of Jewish education for the 4,000 children enrolled in the city's Jewish schools. The consensus of the 139 persons who served on the study committee and signed the document was that there existed a critical need to create a communal system of Jewish education for adolescents and older youth. On the basis of this recommendation, the College of Jewish Studies was founded and established by Dr. Kessler in 1952. It consisted of a High School Department and a Teacher Education Department.

The College of Jewish Studies, which opened in 1952, was recognized as an accredited school by the University of Pittsburgh. Twenty-four university credits in Hebrew language, Jewish history and literature were granted to graduates from the College of Jewish Studies. Also in the same year, Dr. Kessler was invited to join the graduate faculty at the University of Pittsburgh as a full member.

Thus, the Jewish Community of Greater Pittsburgh created the College of Jewish Studies as an answer to a need found through a self-study.

Aharon Kessler, prominent Jewish educator, received his Ph.D. from Dropsie College in history, biblical and rabbinic literature. In a span of two years, he moved the system of Jewish education in the city of Pittsburgh, Pennsylvania from an elementary level to a school of secondary education and a college of Jewish Studies.

Dr. Kessler focused his vision on the adolescent. "This age," he said, "deserves a 'great education,' which will give the growing adult a vision of achieving the values taught by his religion and culture." The author introduced the core curriculum, modeled after the core approach by Harvard University and Brooklyn College.

A rich body of literature was developed by Dr. Kessler, through which he guides teachers, students, parents, and board members toward dedicating their minds to the task of discovering the value of an effective Jewish education for the adolescent. Dr. Kessler has committed his ideas and experiences to two books: Educating the Jewish Adolescent in the Teachings of the Religion and Culture of Judaism *and* Judaism as Religion and Culture.

Educating the Jewish Adolescent
in the Teachings of the Religion
and Culture of Judaism

I

The Story of a School Where Jewish Adolescents Learn What They Are

Preface

Education can be viewed as a continuing struggle between the real conditions as they are and the ideal. The real conditions exist in the present. The ideal exist in the mind—what things should be or what one wishes them to be. To make the ideal real, the ground of the present must be conditioned to receive and incorporate in its growth the elements that constitute the ideal.

But the ground of the present is not always amenable to the demands of the ideal. The primary weakness inherent to change is resistance to the unknown. What is unknown can be a source of fear or tribulation to the inexperienced. How often do we in education hear the adage, "We haven't really done so badly in the past. Why take chances with the untried and untested?" In such instances, it is habit, not scientific curiosity or courage, that is speaking, and habit may easily become a formidable foe of progress.

Those who are involved in curriculum planning are destined to confront the struggles between the real and the ideal. Can such struggles ever be resolved? For an answer, we have to delve into the history of education and learn from the past what it alone can teach us.

1
The Amos Comay Program of Educational Enrichment—College Courses for Teachers

Pittsburgh, Pennsylvania
Aharon Kessler, Ph.D.
Chairman, Board of Overseers

Marvin S. Lieber, Esq.
President, School of Advanced Jewish Studies

> A school is meaningless without a curriculum, but it is more so when it has one that is meaningless. What things shall be studied and in what order? A system of education which avoids this question has lost its aim.
> —Mark Van Doren

> Our conversation is not about something casual, but about the proper way to live.
> —Socrates

The School of Advanced Jewish Studies is a beneficiary agency of the United Jewish Federation of Greater Pittsburgh. Dr. Eunice R. Baradon is dean and Dr. Patricia S. Feldman is director of student affairs and consultant to the college courses for teachers.

The Board of Overseers is pleased to announce that in response to numerous requests from educators and educational institutions, some of the texts and monographs listed in this bulletin will be made available—in limited quantities and for experimental purposes—to central agencies of Jewish education, teachers' seminars, and secondary schools.

To facilitate a better understanding of the structure and curricular objectives of the School of Advanced Jewish Studies (SAJS), and particularly the effectiveness of the publications as aids to teaching and learning, the following information has been added to the bibliography.

I. Structure of the School of Advanced Jewish Studies

Background of the School

The present School of Advanced Jewish Studies is an outgrowth of the former College of Jewish Studies (CJS) founded in 1952 by Dr. Aharon Kessler, who also served as dean of the school until 1985. Associated with the University of Pittsburgh as a member of the graduate faculty, Dr. Kessler taught courses in philosophies of education and history of Jewish education in addition to directing doctoral research in the Graduate School of Education.

Originally, CJS had two departments: a preparatory department for graduates from elementary congregational schools, and a department of teacher education for principals and teachers. The preparatory department consisted of a Hebrew division for students who desired to continue their Hebrew studies, and a Judaic division of social studies taught in English. These students attended CJS in addition to their regular school. The University of Pittsburgh awarded twenty-four academic credits in Hebrew language arts, Jewish history, and Jewish literature to graduates of the preparatory department.

By 1969 these two departments had undergone changes, and the College of Jewish Studies evolved into the School of Advanced Jewish Studies.

Evolution of the Preparatory Department

When CJS opened for instruction, it had an enrollment of eighteen graduates from one elementary congregational school. Each academic year the enrollment increased, and the number of dropouts decreased. At the time of this writing, the SAJS student body in the Hebrew and social studies areas numbers 307 adolescents, ages 13 to 17, whose parents are affiliated with Conservative, Reform, and Orthodox congregations, and also those who are nonaffiliated. Already full-time school students, these young adults spend after-school and weekend hours in Jewish studies. To qualify for graduation with a diploma, students are required to attend from 5 to 7 hours per week for a period of 5 years and maintain a high record of attendance.

Evolution of the Teacher Education Department

The purpose of the original CJS Teacher Education Department for principals and teachers was to deepen their knowledge of the subjects that constituted the curricula of their schools, and to broaden their knowledge of contemporary methods of instruction. In an address to the participants, Dr. Kessler explained that "in building a system of education, two programs of instruction, one for teachers and another for learners, should be instituted simultaneously. One without the other is incapable of fulfilling the objectives of effective education." The reason, he pointed out, "is that the strength of the teacher is the strength of the school, and the weakness of the teacher is the weakness of the school." In seminars and workshops that met weekly for fifteen years, Dr. Kessler taught the content subjects and Dr. Eunice Baradon directed experiments in classroom administration and evaluation of texts and methods of instruction.

Initially, central agencies for Jewish education throughout this country, Canada, and Israel were explored for curricula and instructional materials. Leading educators from the Jewish Education Committee of New York City were invited to report on new texts and methods of teaching Bible, history, Israel, music, and religion. After careful analysis of the materials gathered from outside sources, it became clear to the participants that in certain curricular areas there was a serious shortage of texts for students and source materials for teachers.

To alleviate the textbook shortage, Drs. Kessler and Baradon accepted the challenge of filling several gaps in urgent areas. Dr. Kessler authored two texts, one for the second-grade students entitled *My Hebrew Story Book*, and another for fourth-grade students, *The Humash Primer*. He also composed an *Analytical Reading Test for Prayers* and *A Four Year Curricular Outline of Prayers*. Drs. Kessler and Baradon coauthored three texts in English for the early grades, *The Home, The Synagogue*, and *The Community*. These works were immediately introduced in Pittsburgh congregational schools and in schools of other communities.

The needs in curriculum were addressed in several ways. Each new course of study was structured with several goals in mind. First, the material written for teachers was intended to help enrich their knowledge of subjects and ultimately broaden their students' knowledge. Second, the ideas and skills incorporated into the courses of study and taught by the instructors would aid youths to live as intelligent Jews, not only during their adolescence, but also during the rest of their lives.

To clarify these two objectives, Dr. Kessler posed two basic questions: "What should a teacher know of the Bible, history, and religion to prepare the child and adolescent to live an intelligent and active Jewish life as an adult?"; "What should a Jewish child know about Judaism after attending a Jewish school for a period of ten years?"

In looking for answers to these questions, Dr. Kessler turned to several sources. Recalling Thomas Jefferson's remark that "ignorant citizens cannot be governed democratically," Dr. Kessler confirmed his belief in the need for excellent Jewish education. Adding reinforcement to this belief was Israel's sage Hillel, who declared, "An ignorant person cannot be sin-fearing [pious]." As explained by Rabbi Samson Raphael Hirsch (nineteenth century), this quotation emphasized that "the ignorant person may attach significance to things which are actually without value; on the other hand, he may regard as unimportant matters which, in fact, should be viewed as most significant, and more often than not, he will fail to put his pious intentions into proper practice."

This necessity for education is indeed vital to Judaism much more than to any other modern religion, for Judaism is an intellectual religion and not a faith in the Christian sense. Israel's sages arrived at their doctrines by means of rational thinking; they did not legislate dogmatic conclusions. For the modern Jew, meaning and reason are essential to an acceptance of the religion, history, and culture of Judaism. Memory, nostalgia, and emotional attachments without knowledge and reason are insufficient to bind the modern Jew to Judaism. Thus, the central question became, "Are we preparing the young people who attend our schools to live intelligent and active Jewish lives as adults?"

Restated, the most pressing problem was how to create and maintain the kind of education that would be committed to enriching the lives of the teachers and students with intellectual, spiritual, and moral values whose roots are in authentic Judaism. The term *authentic* is used advisedly because much of Judaism, as it is practiced nowadays in our homes, schools, synagogues, and community agencies, may resemble authentic Judaism, but, in the main, however, it is a poor imitation of what Ahad Haam designates as "the sacred and eternal verities of the Jewish people."

Hence, the remaking of Jewish education required several new commitments: the formulation of realistic objectives; the development of source materials and instructional texts based on the objectives; and the reeducation of the teachers.

With its rededicated effort to prepare young people for living intelligent and active Jewish lives as adults, the College of Jewish Studies made the transition into the School of Advanced Jewish Studies in 1969. As the student body and faculty grew, the Department of Teacher Education underwent a drastic change. Unable to serve as a training facility for principals and teachers of the elementary schools of the community, it concentrated entirely on working with its own faculty and on supplementing the courses of study at SAJS with educational materials, particularly in areas where available texts were considered insufficient.

Dr. Eunice Baradon left her position as principal of a congregational school and came to SAJS as director of educational services, which included all facets of administration. She was assisted by Dr. Patricia Feldman, director of student affairs, who assumed the tasks of supervising the Judaic department, counselling students and teachers, and serving as consultant to the Teacher Education Program. Dr. Kessler, who served as dean, accepted the task of developing needed texts for teachers and students as aids to instruction and of teaching courses in faculty seminars.

With Dr. Kessler's retirement in 1985, Dr. Eunice Baradon became dean of the School of Advanced Jewish Studies. Dr. Kessler continues to develop texts for students and teachers.

II. Analysis of SAJS Educational Publications as Instructional Aids

Religion—The Psalms

Publication of a student text of the Book of Psalms grew out of the need to provide a religious experience in the classroom. Dr. Kessler's rationale in urging that such a course be included in the curriculum contained two ideas (1) In the United States, Jewish education is religious education; (2) The function of religious education is to provide knowledge about religion as well as opportunities for experience in religion. His reasoning agreed with that of William James, who said:

> If religion be a function by which either God's cause or man's cause is to be really advanced, then he who lives the life of it, however narrowly, is a better servant than he who merely knows about it, however much. Knowledge about life is one thing; effective occupation of a place in life, with its dynamic currents passing through your being, is another. For this reason,

the science [knowledge] of religions may not be an equivalent for living religion.

"In light of these ideas," Dr. Kessler continued, "it is the obligation of the Jewish school to include in its curriculum opportunities for teachers and students to share in some religious experiences." On the elementary level, schools conducted Sabbath services for their students, but on the secondary level such opportunities were found to be unproductive. This left the matter of providing religious activities within classroom time. The problem centered around what sort of activities could be accommodated within a classroom. Dr. Kessler decided on prayer, for, as William James said, "Prayer is the very soul and essence of religion. Prayer is religion in act; that is real religion." But, then again, what sort of prayer, and how was prayer to be administered in the classroom? The answer to these questions, Dr. Kessler explained, was obvious: "The Jews are the only people who have raised study to the height of worship. The Jews worship when they study and study when they worship."

One example of this attitude can be found by examining the content of the traditional Siddur. In addition to supplications, petitions, thanksgiving, and adoration, the Siddur contains nonpetitional quotations from the Bible and postbiblical literature. Another example is the manner in which Jews have always used the Book of Psalms. The one hundred and fifty psalms have served as religious experiences in various situations of life. They are cited in every kind of study and communion or conversation with God. Thus, it was decided for each class to recite (actually study) a psalm at the beginning of each school day. Dr. Kessler selected twenty-five psalms, to which he added appropriate commentaries. The text was published under the title *The Aesthetics of the Psalms*.

History

In structuring courses in history, Dr. Kessler raised the following questions: (1) "What should be our purpose in teaching Jewish history?"; (2) "How should Jewish history be taught?"; and (3) "What should the young adult derive from a study of Jewish history?"

The answer to the first question was almost self-evident. The most cogent reason for studying history was that the great truths that are embodied in Jewish history are the inalienable heritage of every Jewish child.

The answer to the second question was more subtle. Jewish history must not be taught as an isolated subject, but rather as part of a core program in which most or all subjects are treated in relation to a central theme. The theme, Dr. Kessler pointed out, was well expressed by Mordecai M. Kaplan in his definition of Judaism as a religious civilization: "Judaism as a religious civilization is to embrace that nexus of history, literature, language, social organization, folk sanctions, standards of conduct, social and spiritual ideals and aesthetic values, which in their totality form a civilization."

To the third question, the answer was more personalized. The young person or adult should find in Jewish history answers to questions, such as: "Why am I Jewish?" "What is my Jewish heritage, and why should I remain Jewish?" In other words, a youth should find there an acceptable definition of personal identity as a Jew and an intellectual understanding of the differences between being Jewish and being Christian. To explore this further, it meant a young adult should acquire an awareness of the sociological and cultural differences that separate the two peoples over and above their basic religious beliefs and theological institutions of faith and worship.

Still another objective to be derived by the learner from a study of Jewish history would be the discovery of the image of the Jew, i.e., the collective Jewish mind: when the people built the biblical society and the Second Commonwealth; how they adjusted to the communities in exile and dispersion; how they responded to the hostile as well as to the hospitable Christian environments; how they functioned as spiritual teachers, thinkers, and sufferers. In brief, in the historical image of the Jew, the young learner should be directed to find a personal Jewish identity. As a basic source to supplement the classroom texts, Dr. Kessler wrote the monograph *Peoplehood and Vocation*.

Torah

Dr. Kessler's introduction to the subject of Torah included this statement: "It is the obligation of the Jewish school to equip its students with a comprehensive knowledge of the meaning of Torah." The philosopher Rabbi Saadia Gaon (892–942) wrote, "Israel is a nation only by virtue of the Torah." The Mishnah quotes the sage Ben Bag Bag, who was a student of Hillel, on this advice: "Turn it [the Torah] and turn it for all is in it and grow gray and old in it, and turn not away from it, for there is no better rule for you than it."

Suggesting that students attending a secondary Jewish school be given a thorough knowledge of Torah would be an impossible objective. Rather, Dr. Kessler insisted they should be given a thorough understanding of what Torah is and the place of Torah in Jewish life. In teaching the Bible to adolescents, the following quotation from Mordecai Kaplan's writing, supplemented by rabbinic and modern quotations, became a guideline for the course on the Torah:

> Torah is a way of life or civilization process; it is a series of writings, which are the product of that process. It is an instrument for transmitting the Jewish way of life from generation to generation.
>
> The over-arching goal of Torah in all three dimensions is to prepare the whole man for living his life as a human being to his fullest potential.

Using this quotation as a basis of class discussion led to an analysis of such topics as, "Is Torah a book?"; "Has Torah relevance to contemporary life?"; "Why are there two Torahs, the written and the oral?"; "Is Halakhah also Torah?"; and "What is Aggadah?" The explanations given to each question included examples from rabbinic and modern sources. Subsequently, Dr. Kessler wrote a source book for teachers and students entitled, *Torah: A Three-Dimensional Culture*.

Judaism and Christianity

From its very inception, the curriculum contained a course of study in Judaism and Christianity. The content of this course dealt with the following nine topics:

1. What separates Judaism from Christianity? Is it only the latter's belief in Jesus as the Christ, or are there also other beliefs that make agreement between the two religions impossible?
2. Why did the Jews of the Second Commonwealth reject Jesus as son of God, Messiah, prophet, or rabbi?
3. Did Jesus create a new religion or a new ethic? Did he advocate abrogation of the Torah?

4. Why was Jesus crucified, and who was responsible for his death? Did Jesus die as a Jew or as a Christian?
5. Are there an available Jewish historical sources from the Second Commonwealth or from the Talmud that tell about Jesus?
6. What are the Synoptic Gospels?
7. How do the Jews and the Christians differ in their conceptions of monotheism, sin, salvation, and otherworldliness?
8. How should Jewish parents and teachers explain Christmas to Jewish children?
9. Were the birth, messiahship, and death of Jesus predicted in the Hebrew Bible?

The thrust of the central idea in this course of study focuses on the incompatibility of the "world views" in the two religions. In their efforts to convert Jews, particularly young adults, to Christianity, Christian missionaries mostly emphasize what they describe as the Jewish "misconception" of the divinity of Jesus. It is therefore essential for the Jewish school to broaden the gap of separation by highlighting the polarity between the two religions in theological, cultural, social, and moral ideas.

Dr. Kessler prepared two instructional monographs on these subjects. One, for younger children and adolescents, *Explaining Jewish and Christian Differences to Jewish Children* (published in Israel); and the second, *A Series of Lectures on Judaism and Christianity: Two Weltanschauungen* (world views), for teachers and older learners. He suggested integrating this course with courses in religion and history.

Religious and National Motifs in Jewish Festivals

In this course, the basic motifs in the major Jewish festivals are studied. The topics include the treatment of the spiritual and moral themes in the festivals; religious beliefs that are expressed in pagan, Jewish, and Christian observances of their respective festivals; religious and national motifs in the festivals of Passover, Sukkoth, and Hanukkah; concepts of the Covenant, freedom, and remembrance in the "pilgrimage" festivals; and *moadim*, appointed seasons.

The reason for comparing Jewish with non-Jewish festivals is to highlight the unique conceptions that Judaism communicates in its sacred occasions. For example, in paganism, holy days were observed as occasions in the lives of the gods. Similarly, Christianity observes its sacred days as occasions in the life and death of Jesus. In Judaism, however, festivals and holy days commemorate national-historical events in which God's presence creates an interlude in the ordinary functions of the universe and in human life. God, man, nature, time, and space become a unity, and spiritual energy pervades them. By recalling these events and God's share in them, the affairs of life are conducted differently before and after the holy days are commemorated.

To illustrate the national-historic concept, Dr. Kessler cited several examples. He explained the motifs in the three festivals of Passover, Shavuoth, and Sukkoth, which are ordained in the Torah as "pilgrimage festivals because on these occasions pilgrimages were made to Jerusalem." The central motif in each of these festivals is of national and religious significance. The national motif is expressed in the redemption of the nation from Egyptian slavery on Pesach. Prosperity of the land at the time when the soil produced the first fruits of the wheat harvest in combination with the motif of revelation in the receiving of the Torah at Sinai are celebrated on Shavuoth. The ingathering of the harvest, as well as God's protective care of the nation during their sojourn in the wilderness on the way to the Promised Land, is commemorated on Sukkoth. Thus, the religious motif that pervades each of these festivals is intertwined with the national motif. Hanukkah, the last festival (which is not mentioned in the Torah), also contains the two motifs. The national aspect is expressed in the Maccabean victory over the Syrian-Greeks and is commemorated by the candle-lighting ceremony. The religious aspect was commemorated by the rededication of the Temple after it was cleansed and purified of pagan defilement.

Attention is also given in this course of study to several other essential concepts. The Covenant (Berith), which is the dominating theme in God's relationship with Israel and Israel's loyalty to God, is studied. The importance of the Exodus as the basis for a total system of religious, ethical, and moral laws that facilitated the Israelites' opportunities to live in accordance with God's instructions is explored. And, finally, the "appeal to memory" in which the festivals, holy days, and fast days are to become memorials to the event is highlighted.

Dr. Kessler embodies these ideas in his monograph *Festivals of Freedom: Passover and Hanukkah*.

Anti-Semitism and Assimiliation

In this course of study designed especially for senior students, the topics of anti-Semitism and assimilation are studied. Dr. Kessler wrote a text entitled *The Fate of the Jews in the European Society*, in which he treated both subjects from historical and contemporary perspectives. It might be of interest to point out that in addition to the historical and sociological sources, this text contains ancient and contemporary Christian (Catholic and Protestant) sources explaining the reasons for anti-Semitism and assimilation and their effects on the Jewish people. The treatment of assimilation is also based on authoritative contemporary works by leading historians.

The following questions have been formulated as guidelines for the above topics: Why should the subjects of anti-Semitism and assimilation be taught in Jewish schools? Where are the roots of anti-Semitism to be found? Is anti-Semitism, in its current state, the result of social, economic, political, or religious factors? In which way does modern anti-Semitism differ from medieval anti-Semitism? What are the effects of anti-Semitism on contemporary Jewry?

What is meant by assimilation? What is the relationship between anti-Semitism and assimilation? How does assimilation differ from acculturation? What are the psychological aspects of assimilation?

Modern Jewish Literature

Three types of literature constitute this course of study: (1) The American Jewish novel; (2) the American Jewish short story; and (3) the literature of the Holocaust. "The purpose of teaching the American Jewish novel," writes Penina K. Lieber, "is to acquaint the students with a body of writing that reflects our roots in this country. These novels do not belong to another people in another place—they belong to us and our parents and our grandparents. They echo our past and predict our future."

In *American Jewish Fiction* (short stories), Max Nadel explains the value of studying the short story:

> Each selection deals with an experience or a series of experiences having a central theme and colored by the author's view of Jewish life in America and its values.... The class with the help of the teacher will make judg-

ments [of the world in which the characters live and work] first in terms of their own personal values and then in terms of esthetic, philosophical, moral, and ethical values which are considered absolute according to Jewish tradition and belief.

As Penina K. Lieber suggests, incorporating the literature of the Holocaust becomes essential because "the stories, dramas and autobiographical accounts would enable listeners to crawl inside the consciousness of this otherwise unimaginable moment and to participate in it as if they were actually there." She adds that "the vast moral and philosophical implications of the tragedy would be illuminated in light of our present Jewish existence."

The texts and collateral readings published on the Holocaust are as follows: *The American Jewish Novel* by Penina K. Lieber; *American Jewish Fiction* by Max Nadel; *Voices From the Past: Moral Implications of the Holocaust Literature* by Penina K. Lieber; *God in the Holocaust* by Aharon Kessler; *Blessed Be the Winds* (an epic) by Aharon Kessler; and *Analysis of the Historical, Literary and Psychological Implications in Bernard Malamud's Novel, The Fixer,* by Aharon Kessler.

Traditions That Serve As Guides for the Behavior of Past, Present, and Future Generations

This course of study designed for teachers was intended to raise questions and arrive at plausible answers on the following topics: How valuable are cultural or religious traditions fashioned in the past for generations that are removed in time, place, and intellectual achievements from those who established them? Does tradition have an inherent authority to veto behavioral patterns of future generations? How can ancient traditions be integrated into the lifestyles of future generations?

In a teachers' seminar, Dr. Kessler also suggested the following topics: Definition of *tradition* as the process of passing along the cultural elements from one generation to the next and their acceptance by future generations; the authority of former generations to impose their patterns of behavior upon later generations, and the readiness of the latter to keep the traditions alive by integrating them into their respective lifestyles.

In our contemporary Jewish society, the response of those who cherish their people's historical and cultural traditions is expressed in two distinct attitudes that reflect the views of the strict traditionalists and the modern traditionalists. Both traditionalists draw their attitudes toward tradition from rabbinic sources of the past, but each interprets the sources in accordance with his own world views. Explaining traditions to young people requires viewing them from both retrospect and prospect. Retrospect refers to the purposes that the traditions have served previous generations and their evolutionary development throughout the centuries. Prospect refers to the purposes they could serve current generations.

Dr. Kessler wrote the following monographs: *Teaching Tradition to Young People; Religion, a Series of Lectures* (published by the Institute of Jewish Studies for New Americans); *Festivals of Freedom: Passover and Hanukkah*.

Israel

The curriculum calls for teaching two courses about Israel. The first is taught in the eighth grade, and the second in the twelfth grade. Thus, SAJS students study Israel immediately upon entering the school and again in their last year. The reason for duplicating the study of Israel resides in the nature of the courses.

The first course is purely academic. It offers specific information concerning Israel as the land of the Bible and the historic homeland of the Jewish people; Zionism as the national liberation movement developed in the nineteenth century; the Aliyoth, the mandate granted Britain by the League of Nations over Palestine; the struggle for independence (1945–1948); the establishment of the state; and the current life in modern Israel.

The second course is more sophisticated because it deals with the status of the state: Israel's neighbors and the role they play in Arab nationalism; struggles between Jews and Arabs historically analyzed; the present power struggle of the great nations in the Middle East; Israel's Law of Return; political parties; cultural achievements and relationships between world Jewry and Israel. The basic text for this course is *Understanding Israel* by Amos Elon. In addition, Dr. Baradon compiled a supplementary manual of contemporary sources for both teachers and students.

In his seminars for teachers, Dr. Kessler raised several issues concerning the content of both courses. One issue dealt with devising a perspective of the topics upon which the course contents were to be structured. He urged introducing highlight information that attests to the positive aspects of the Jewish state, those aspects which contribute to the internal life of Israel's community, but also to the Jewish people and to the general human condition. He explained that it was necessary to select concrete examples that would help illustrate the diverse areas that comprise the political and cultural life of Israel. He further reminded the participants that in choosing materials for the courses, the textbooks would have to be supplemented with additional sources, such as concrete lesson plans, information bulletins, and monographs issued in Israel. The format of most textbooks, we have been told by David C. King, "Make them the wrong tool for the task of airing viewpoints or the reasoning behind them. Every issue is distilled down to a few information-packed sentences." Therefore, information must be sought in a variety of extratextual publications and prepared as collateral source materials. But first, an architectual blueprint for the most essential items to be selected had to be prepared. From such a blueprint, cognitive and effective structures should emerge. In a list of items to be included in all courses of study about Israel, Dr. Kessler proposed the following subjects. The depth and complexity would be age related. He titled the list "The Characteristics of the State."

1. Israel's population consists of over four million people; 83 percent are Jews and 17 percent Arabs, Druze, and others. More than half a million are native born, while others come from almost every country in the world. The 83 percent of the Jews are 26 percent of world Jewry.
2. Israel is a parliamentary democracy consisting of legislative, executive, and judicial branches and structured according to the principle of division of authority to ensure checks and balances within the system.
3. All citizens of Israel, regardless of race or religion, are guaranteed equality before the law and full democratic rights. Freedom of speech and assembly, of press and political affiliation, of strike and demonstration, as well as the right of the individual to vote according to his or her conscience are also guaranteed in Israel.
4. Israel's political parties represent all ideologies of its citizens, from communist to conservative-nationalist. All Israeli citizens over the age of eighteen may vote, and from age twenty-one to be elected to office.

5. Israel's parliament is called Knesset. It consists of 120 members. It elects the president and the speaker of the Knesset. It may dissolve itself and call for an election before the end of its four-year period. To become a law, a bill must pass three readings in the Knesset. The president, prime minister, and the minister responsible sign the bill into law.
6. Israel is an education-oriented society; one in every three Israelis is a student with about 1.5 million enrolled in some kind of educational program—a tenfold increase since 1948. Israel has compulsory free education of all children ages 5 to 16. The educational system consists of state schools (75 percent); state religious schools (20 percent); independent religious schools (5 percent); yeshiva schools; secondary and postsecondary; Arab/Druze schools (language in Arabic); state Druze schools. GADNA is a special educational framework of youth 14 to 18 sponsored by the Ministry of Education and Culture and Israel's defense forces. There are also professional and vocational schools and many universities.*
7. A special relationship exists between the Jews of Israel and Jews living outside of Israel (Diaspora). Over the last one hundred years, their common heritage has found expression in the rebuilding and restoration of the Jewish nation-state in the land of Israel.

The above outline is only a springboard to a more fertile ground of ideas. In developing a structure for the course of study, reference should be made to prophecies of the biblical classical prophets concerning the "ingathering of the exiles, rebuilding the nation's homeland and the nation."

Dr. Baradon assumed the task of building the structure. She spent several summers in Israel studying at the Hebrew University, and on her return put into practice much of the information she acquired there. Dr. Patricia Feldman contributed her skills in developing instructional materials for the two grades. Her work included revising texts, writing supplementary lesson plans, and creating a weekly newspaper for students entitled *We Are Concerned*. The efforts to enrich these courses with pertinent information has become an ongoing project at SAJS.

* The information cited above was gathered from Israeli publications.

Bible—the Former Prophets: Joshua, Judges, and I and II Samuel

Upon entering the School of Advanced Jewish Studies, students are introduced to the Bible through the historical books of Joshua, Judges, and Samuel. During their initial years of attendance in elementary schools, these students were not exposed to the Bible in the original Hebrew, nor to a comprehensive study of any biblical book in English. At best, they were acquainted with simple narratives about the lives of the patriarchs and Moses.

Because knowledge of Bible is a major objective in the SAJS curriculum, the problem of teaching this subject to adolescents lacking any real academic background must be resolved as early as the first two years of their attendance. In the Hebrew division, the first-year program calls for studying the books of Joshua, Judges, and Samuel in abbreviated and simplified Hebrew texts. In the Judaic division, the biblical texts are studied in English. In the ninth grade, the students are introduced to the Latter, or classical, Prophets. In 1972, Drs. Kessler and Baradon composed an English text of the Book of Amos, titled *The Book of Amos—an Encounter with Greatness*. The text had many virtues, as both teachers and students attested. But the historical framework and the actual prophecies cited in that text were insufficient for a comprehensive understanding of classical prophecy. Dr. Kessler, therefore, decided to supplement this text with several teachers' manuals as companions to the former prophets, and a more comprehensive text of the classical prophets, Amos, Hosea, and Micah. Dr. Kessler wrote (1) companions to the books of Joshua, Judges, and I and II Samuel; (2) *Historical Summary of the Popular Prophets from Moses to Elijah*; (3) *Analysis of the Classical Prophets: Amos, Hosea, and Micah*; and (4) *The Prophecies of Isaiah*.

The methodological approach employed in the biblical texts merges historical events with religious ideas. The events speak for themselves through biblical quotations, and religious ideas are communicated in the commentaries drawn from scholarly sources. In his introduction to the companions, Dr. Kessler explains:

> Teaching and learning the historical books of the Bible necessitate a perspective in which the historical facts and religious ideas are combined into one inseparable core. The prophetic historical books are actually structured in a core manner and have always been taught that way in Jewish schools. For numerous practical reasons, in modern Jewish schools, history and Bible are taught as separate blocks of knowledge. On the secondary

level of education, this approach is undesirable. When it is used, students may learn some facts and ideas but fail to see the relationships between history and religion as Judaism perceives it.

Prayer and Ethics

In a series of seminars, Dr. Kessler discussed prayer and ethics. He suggested the following topics for exploration: What is the nature of Jewish prayer?; What is the nature of Jewish ethics?; What have the sages meant by the statements that "man is a coworker with God in creation?"; How could man qualify himself to become God's coworker in creation of the better world?; How could ethics and prayer be integrated in the curriculum of the school?; What are some of the religious and psychological effects of prayer on the worshipper?; How did our ancestors pray for the better world?; Analysis of Sim Shalom; How the worshipper petitions God's help to qualify himself as His coworker in establishing the better world; Analysis of Elohai Nezor.

Dr. Kessler pointed out that the connection between prayer and ethics depends on the believer's God concepts. Obviously, the person who does not believe in God's existence, or that God is concerned with the way a person lives out life on earth, fails to see a relationship between prayer and ethics. The person may recognize some psychological effects of prayer on the worshipper but not as a dialogue between God and the individual. In that case, the nonbeliever views ethics only as a product of human reason. On the other hand, the believer in God's concern with humanity finds a life-enhancing communion with the divine. In other words, the believer recognizes a direct connection between prayer and ethics and accepts the moral values of truth, freedom, justice, mercy, and goodness as God's requirements of humanity. The believer does not reject the contributions of human reason to ethical values, but traces their source directly to God's authority. This is how Judaism establishes a link between prayer and ethics.

Although the Torah does not command prayer, it relates numerous instances of people praying and cites their texts. Some prayers are monologues in which the worshipper speaks to God; other prayers are dialogues in which the worshipper and God communicate with each other. Both forms have remained constant in Jewish worship. An examination of the traditional Siddur will show both forms.

The prayers in the Siddur are built on theological beliefs enunciated in the Bible, in the Talmudim, and in post-Talmudic sources. One fundamental belief derives from the assumption that God hears the worshipper's prayer (Shomea Tefillah) and responds to it in His own good time. This is the essence of the monologue type in which the worshipper establishes an intimate relationship with God. In the dialogue type, God speaks to the worshipper by communicating His teachings (Torah) to the person. The latter form is found in the Torah of Moses, in the prophecies in the Halakhoth and Aggadoth of the rabbinic sages, and in the historical events in which God intervened on behalf of His people, Israel. The Siddur contains both forms of prayer, the former as supplications and the latter as study. Thus, Jewish worshippers study when they pray and pray when they study.

The integration of monologue and dialogue prayers in worship made it natural for the stages to include requests for the establishment of the better world in which humanity would cooperate with God as His coworker. The two closing prayers in the Amidah (Shemoneh Esreh), Sim Shalom and Elohai Nezor, typify these kinds of petitions. In Sim Shalom, the petitioner prays for peace, goodness, blessing, grace, loving kindness, and mercy as God's gifts to the better world. In Elohai Nezor, the individual prays for divine help to become filled with salutary character traits so as to be able to serve as coworker in the establishment of the better world.

In this seminar, the six divine gifts stated in Sim Shalom are traced to their biblical, rabbinic, medieval, and modern sources and analyzed as ethical value concepts. Similarly, the character traits to qualify the petitioner for partnership with God, cited in Elohai Nezor, are traced to their sources in religious literature and analyzed as ethical value concepts. (This course of study is still in manuscript.)

The Contemporary Society: A Course of Study for Seniors

> For Desiderius Erasmus, the greatest scholar of his age, piety, scholarship, the conduct of life and preparation for civic responsibility were all indivisible parts of a complete education.
> —E.B. Castle

Speaking about his first four years at the School of Advanced Jewish Studies, Dr. Aharon Kessler said:

The projected curriculum calls for introducing the young student to a variety of subjects. The intent is to make the student at home with many basic events, ideas, and values in the civilization of the Jewish people. What would be the fruits of such an education? The young adult would know, to some extent, how Jewish leaders, prophets, sages, and poets have used their minds in trying to create a better world. Without such fundamental knowledge, the young person would be lost in the world he inhabits.

But the fifth year poses a problem. It is the year of their seventeenth birthdays, and their last year in our school. Intellectually and emotionally, these young people are more sophisticated than in previous years. The students are also capable of more balanced judgment and of making a synthesis of the ideas they have accumulated from their studies. The question is: How should the nature of the curricula in the fifth year differ from that of previous years? A reason for change is that most of these students will not only be graduated from SAJS but from their public and private high schools as well. The great majority of them will then leave their homes to pursue university studies at institutions in different cities.

In light of these factors, how does our school provide the senior students with courses of study that would give them an opportunity for concretizing much of what they have learned in previous years and help them prepare to lead active Jewish lives away from home? To do this, several sub-questions were asked prior to structuring the actual content: (1) Since individuals are unable to remember the vast majority of facts, concepts, and principles that they have studied over a period of four years, what would be the *most essential ideas and information* that should be emphasized during their last year? (2) What should Jewish young people know about Judaism as they face the challenges of a new environment without the support of a Jewish home and community? (3) How can our school help these young adults meet the new challenges in a realistic and satisfactory way?

Dr. Kessler's answers to the preceding queries formed the basis for the preparation of class texts and special materials. The answers were: (1) To acquaint the students in the fifth year with the kind of college environment they are about to enter through experiences of faculty members who had confronted similar challenges in their own days; (2) to select sophisticated ideas in Judaism for review and further exploration; (3) to identify the challenges they would face from within and without the Jewish community; (4) to present for serious consideration the possible effects of these challenges on personalities of students and to analyze authentic Jewish intellectual responses to them.

Once the primary objectives had been clarified, it became obvious that the major requirement was to present information, particularly in response to the last imperative. At the College of Jewish Studies some efforts were made in this direction, and later a fully structured program was developed at the School of Advanced Jewish Studies.

Drs. Baradon, Feldman, and Kessler cooperated in preparing a text for both teachers and students entitled *The Contemporary Jewish Society*. Among the subjects treated in this text are:

> Examination of the dangers to the Jewish people and to Judaism from without and from within. *Without* refers to anti-Semitism and *within* refers to assimilation, intermarriage, and apathy.
>
> Exploration of the essence and meaning of Judaism in the modern world. This includes a review of the views concerning these challenges by the religious movements: Orthodoxy, Reform, Conservatism, and Reconstructionism.
>
> Formulation of an agenda for Jewish living in our contemporary society.
>
> Comprehension of the concept of *Jewish peoplehood*—the ongoing role of the Jewish people in the history, culture, and religion of humankind and its unique growth and development as an evolving civilization for the contemporary Jew.
>
> Comprehension of the essence of religion—religion in general and the religion of Judaism in particular as it relates to human nature, identity, and a code for living a moral, ethical life.
>
> Acquaintance with intellectual Jewish thought. In this course, the philosophies of Moses Maimonides, Martin Buber, Franz Rosenzweig, and Mordecai M. Kaplan are explored.
>
> Acquaintance with dramatic moments in contemporary Jewish life: the Holocaust and its effects on Jewish society; Israel, and the effects of the Jewish state on Jewish society.

The texts and collateral readings in this course of study are:

Contemporary Jewish Society by Eunice Baradon, Patricia Feldman, and Aharon Kessler

Peoplehood and Vocation by Aharon Kessler

Torah: A Three-Dimensional Culture by Aharon Kessler

II

Jewish Identity

1.

The Amos Comay Program of Educational Enrichment—College Courses for Teachers[*]

Patricia S. Feldman, Ph.D.

Most teacher education and enrichment programs offered to those who serve as instructors in Jewish schools share several common characteristics. They are of limited duration, such as all-day workshops, or a short-term series of seminars. The stress is placed on method rather than on depth of academic content. Those who attend are "part-time" people whose formal Judaic background is usually limited to a few university classes rather than to those who have majored in a specific subject area inherent to the history, culture, and religion of the Jewish people.

Dr. Aharon Kessler, founder of the School of Advanced Jewish Studies in Pittsburgh, subscribes to the belief that if we intend to teach authentic Jewish ideas to children, those who have undertaken the task must be prepared to present more than the material found in textbooks. The teacher must have a wealth of Jewish knowledge that can be transmitted in the form of concrete concepts to young persons in any age group. These ideas can then become the foundation upon which the individual builds a literate and active adult Jewish life.

For this to occur, Dr. Kessler proposed that an entirely new approach had to be taken by establishing a series of ongoing courses to provide sophisticated and complex material for the adult learner. These courses contained a core of ideas to be incorporated directly into such classroom curricula as history, Bible, literature, and religion. Grade levels of students were not considered a factor, since the teacher would be taught how to take the primary concepts and present them in an age-appropriate fashion.

---

[*]This article was published in the December 20, 1984, issue of the *Jewish Chronicle of Pittsburgh*.

The preceding philosophical outlook became the driving force leading him to establish The Amos Comay Program of Educational Enrichment. This program allowed Dr. Kessler the opportunity for structuring and presenting a series of College Courses for Teachers, primarily for the social studies staff of SAJS.

Within the framework of the project, each participant receives incentive pay and is urged to select ideas culled from the lectures and written materials authored by Dr. Kessler. The response has been very positive, both from the standpoint of personal enrichment and from the perspective of educators introducing to teenagers authentic Jewish concepts that would otherwise not have been discussed.

The Amos Comay Program of Educational Enrichment—College Courses for Teachers has a number of component parts that make it practical, attractive, and innovative to the Jewish educational community in general, and to those who are directly involved, in particular.

It envisions a permanent two-year program of integrated academic content for teachers of Jewish social studies. Those who attend the weekly two hour, fifteen sessions per year will be granted the associate degree of master teacher. It should also be noted that a possible three-year program is currently being contemplated leading to the title of critic teacher.

Because of the scope and potential of the project, it was deemed necessary that a special board of overseers be invited to become directly and specifically involved in the Amos Comay Program of Educational Enrichment. The composition of the board includes rabbis, principals, and several lay persons. Among the duties of this board, chaired by Dr. Kessler, are: granting the master teacher certificates; suggesting areas that could be explored for development; judging the impact on feeder schools; promoting the concept of quality Jewish education; and finding ways to encourage area teachers to enroll in the College Course Program. The content for the first two years stresses the following transmissible and usable ideas in every presentation.

"Jewish Education Confronting the American Environment" has several objectives. First, the ways in which Jewish education can illuminate the ever-changing external and internal social environments and address the issues and problems that face the Jewish people today are clearly explicated. Second, specific knowledge is extracted from texts that will allow teachers to help their students structure their personal Jewish identities based on authentic historical, cultural, and moral developments in Jewish civilization.

The content topics in Jewish studies include such varied subjects as: "Definition of Identity; Experiencing Jewish Identity; fundamental differences between being Jewish and being Christian; Jewish peoplehood as vocation; Torah: a three-dimensional culture; and traditions that serve as guides for the behavior of past, present, and future generations." Dramatic moments in Jewish history stress the intellectual adventure of the biblical period and intellectual adventures of the Second Commonwealth.

A variety of sophisticated texts is required reading. Dr. Kessler's lecture notes and special monographs are made available to the participants.

In his opening address to a committee of rabbis and principals from the board of overseers, Dr. Kessler pointed out:

> If Jewish education is to maintain its integrity, we must begin to actively engage in teacher education. It remains a truism that the single most important factor in the success of any classroom is the teacher. SAJS can and should be at the forefront of a movement that will ensure that all children who attend a Jewish school receive the most effective Jewish education possible. We believe it to be most expedient and logical that we begin within our own staff and hopefully expand, at some future date, to help prepare a cadre of knowledgeable and dedicated teachers for other Jewish schools in Greater Pittsburgh.

In his lecture series titled *Religion*, the author, Aharon Kessler, meticulously traces the impact of religion on the individual and collective man from ancient times to the present. Throughout this text, he guides the reader from the general perspective of viewing religion as the dynamic civilizing force for all mankind to the more specific purview of the contributions that the Torah of Moses has made to the growth and development of the Jewish people. He explicates such elusive terms as *faith, worship, spiritual reality,* and *divine attributes*. By coupling numerous authoritative quotations with his own penetrating analyses, Dr. Kessler provides facts, concepts, and values needed to differentiate between God's religion and man's religion; to ponder the validity of various definitions of religion; and personally to probe history for insights concerning the impact that religion has had on the nations of the world.

Using an interdisciplinary approach that draws ideas and information from sociology, anthropology, and theology, Dr. Kessler shows the inherent logic of religion itself as a human need for a God belief, and the eternal verities in Judaism. Moving to contemporary Jewish thought, he constructs a succinct summary of the essence of Orthodox, Reform, Conservative, and Reconstructionist theological and philosophical thought.

This highly readable monograph is the third in a series of published lectures by Dr. Kessler devoted to material centering on the history, culture, and religion of the Jewish people. Each text deals systematically with one of ten identifiable ingredients of the Jewish civilization. While these monographs can certainly be studied as single, complete documents, taken together they constitute a magnum opus of the rich and variegated life of the Jewish people.

2.
Judaism as Religion and Culture

Eunice R. Baradon, D.Ed.

Culture has been defined as the total body of beliefs, behavior, knowledge, sanctions, values, and goals that mark the way of life of any people. Aharon Kessler adds that, in a broad sense, culture is defined as the way of life of the members of a society that includes ideas and habits which they learn, share, and transmit from generation to generation. Civilization generally means advanced or high culture. Thus, both culture and civilization contain beliefs, systems of thought, manners of living, customs, and traditions that are regulated by society as behavior.

In his booklet *Jewish Adolescents Explore Their Identity* Dr. Kessler writes that unless a student finds meaning in the history, religion, and culture of the Jewish people and perceives a relationship of his people's past and future, we cannot expect that the individual will develop a sense of Jewish identification and commitment.

David Ben-Gurion, the first prime minister of the newly established state of Israel in 1948, wrote of the two features marking the Jewish people as being unique and distinct from all other nations. These features were faith in the one Holy God and the emergence of the prophets who gave primacy to the moral and social values in the religious teachings of Judaism. He cited the visions of the literary prophets who, as far back as the eighth century B.C.E., preached of the supremacy of moral values and social morality such as social justice, righteousness, and equality of all nations. The prophets of Israel foresaw the age of redemption both for their own people and for all mankind in the distant future, in the "latter days."

These visions of the prophets must be taught to each generation of our adolescents. All subject matter dealing with the religion and culture of the Jewish people should be taught on the three levels of facts, concepts, and values. Special emphasis should be placed on helping the learner perceive the values inherent in Judaism and the individual's connection with these values. With the proper backgrounds, the teacher can be prepared to help Jewish youth understand why they are Jewish and why they should remain Jewish.

Bibliography

By Aharon Kessler:

Peoplehood and Vocation
The Fate of the Jews in the European Society
Toran: A Three-Dimensional Culture
Aesthetics of the Psalms
Festivals of Freedom: Passover and Hanukkah
Teaching Traditions to Young People
Companions to the Bible:
Companion to the Book of Joshua
Companion to the Book of Judges
Companion to I Samuel and II Samuel
Historical Summary of the Popular Prophets: From Moses to Elijah
Analysis of the Classical Prophets: Amos, Hosea and Micah
The Prophecies of Isaiah I & II
Explaining Jewish and Christian Festivals to Jewish Children
Two Weltanschaunngen (World Views), a Series of Lectures
God and the Holocaust
Historical, Literary and Psychological Implications in Bernard Malamud's Novel, The Fixer
Prayer and Ethics (Date of publication uncertain)
Lecture Notes from a Course of Study: Intellectual Adventures of the Biblical Period, given in college courses for teachers

By Aharon Kessler and Eunice R. Baradon:

The Book of Amos: An Encounter with Greatness

By Penina K. Lieber:

The American Jewish Novel
The Literature of the Holocaust
Moral Implications in the Holocaust

By Max Nadel:

American Jewish Fiction
(Also published by the Board of Jewish Education of New York)

III

Jewish Adolescents Explore Their Identity: A Collection of Ideas and Sources

I wish to express my gratitude to Dr. Eunice R. Baradon for her contribution of "A Teacher's Guide: Summary of Ideas," which is included in this monograph (pages 66 to 80), to Dr. Patricia S. Feldman for her interest in this manuscript and her literary contributions, and to Fay (Mrs. Nathan) Josephson for her meticulous and efficient care in preparing this manuscript.

1.
Preliminaries: About Educational Objectives

What Are Objectives?

Psychologists N. L. Gage and David C. Berliner (*Educational Psychology*, Rand McNally, 1979), pose the following questions: What are schools for? What is the academic curriculum? Why do students take American history? What is a given teacher trying to get her students to learn about American history? What is the purpose of a two-week unit on the colonial period? What is actually going to be studied in any particular class period? They explain:

> The questions deal with educational objectives. Objective means the same desired outcome, goal, aim, purpose, terminal behavior, and intention. . . . Whatever the scope of understanding—a nation's educational system, a school's curriculum, a course, a class session, a day's assignment, a one minute explanation—it makes sense to decide where we want to go before we start to move.

In 1951, soon after I arrived in Pittsburgh to establish the Council on Jewish Education, I invited Prof. Leo L. Honor of Dropsie College in Philadelphia to conduct a seminar for the local Jewish educators. Professor Honor opened his remarks with the following parable:

> How would you characterize a person who approaches a ticket agent at Grand Central Station and asks for a ticket? The agent inquires, "Where do you want to go?" The person responds, "Wherever the train takes me, there I want to be." Obviously, that person should not be regarded seriously. But isn't this exactly what we do in Jewish education? We are handed a textbook and told, "Wherever the textbook takes us, there we want our children to be."

In his analysis of the parable, Professor Honor spoke of the need to formulate clear and precise objectives for each lesson since it is only through specifically formulated objectives that a teacher can teach and students can learn.

Since this is a truism, it becomes incumbent upon us to ask if Jewish educators recognize the need for formulating objectives for all courses of study in the Jewish school. Unfortunately, too many educators do not follow this procedure. From the early days of this century, the literature devoted to Jewish education has been filled with general objectives couched in a variety of idealistic, obtuse, and sometimes practical language. They were universally directed toward expressing religious and nationalistic ideas and ideals. Almost always these objectives were related to the content of the curriculum; namely, they delineated significant religious and national events, narratives, rituals, laws, and ideas. The facts were to be taught to the Jewish child so that he would become knowledgeable of his heritage. Psychologists designate such objectives as *cognitive*. Cognitive objectives, they say, are "processes like knowing, perceiving, thinking, conceiving, judging, and reasoning." There is nothing wrong with cognitive objectives except that as educational tools they are insufficient to educate a person. In an educative process, cognitive objectives must be combined with affective objectives, which deal with feeling, emotion, attitude, appreciation, and valuing. When cognitive and affective domains are intertwined, behaviors show more involvement, commitment, and internalization than if either one domain were missing.

Cognitive and Affective Domains

In past centuries, the Jewish home and school shared the responsibility of educating the child and youth. The home provided the affective elements through living experiences, and the school provided cognitive knowledge that contained reasons and meanings for the behavioral experiences. For example, when I was a young child, my grandmother would awaken me early on Thursday mornings to take me with her on visits to well-to-do families where she collected alms for the poor. We then visited indigent families to whom she distributed the alms, each family according to its needs—"For making Sabbath," she would say. When I once asked her the reason for that practice, she replied, "That's what a Jew has to do. In Heder, you'll learn the reason."

The average contemporary Jewish home delegates the responsibility of providing the cognitive and affective elements to the religious school. To say that the school is incapable of fulfilling the demands is an understatement. Without the home, the school, any school, operates in a vacuum. Unfortunately, this maxim is not sufficiently recognized by many parents. The school's efforts to remedy the condition, either because of parental resistance or due to its own inadequate communication, has been forced to ignore the affective needs and concentrate on the cognitive only.

As it relates to the Jewish school, this means presenting selected subject matter of significance to the religion and culture, particularly in Bible and history, simplifying the material, and searching for suitable methods to communicate the material to the children. On the surface, this procedure appears to be educationally sound, but in reality it isn't for several reasons. Since the great majority of children terminate their Jewish education at Bar Mitzvah, and a small number at Confirmation, the knowledge they receive in the elementary school is on a juvenile level that is inadequate for young adults and adults. In addition, no opportunities are provided for affective influence. Furthermore, Jewish educators are under the wrong assumption about the significance of methods. In their desire to "perfect" methods of teaching, they overlook the teacher's need of a solid background in the context of the subjects they teach. They believe all that teaching requires is up-to-date methods suggested by educational psychology. Methods are certainly helpful tools in communication, but they are not designed to enrich the teacher with knowledge of the subject matter. As a case in point, method can be helpful in speeding up a student's reading of Hebrew, but it can't be helpful to a teacher who lacks knowledge of grammar to teach her students how to use the Hebrew language correctly. The same holds true of teaching history. Replacing the lecture method with the problem-solving technique can be a great improvement in many instances. But the teacher who lacks historical background is incapable of helping the students clarify concepts and values and validate the factual information under discussion.

Method is composed of three elements: The teacher's personality; knowledge of subject matter; and "knowledge of patterns of behavior (which includes skills) applicable to various subject matters, characteristic of more than one teacher, and relevant to learning." Learning is crucial because it refers to the student. This leads me to another consideration.

Education's Two Demands

Jewish education, like all education, must seek to satisfy two demands: transmission of the cultural heritage, and providing for the educational needs of children. As to the extent of heritage, it is safe to say that all four religious orientations in Judaism are more or less in agreement on the nature of their ingredients and what must be placed in the curriculum of the Jewish school. Differences do occur, however, in attitudes and emphasis relating to the scope and significance of the contents of one subject or another. For instance, some educators from the various orientations consider teaching Hebrew language arts of greater importance, while others prefer social studies. Some advocate biblical studies as a priority, others regard study of the Talmud as paramount. There are certainly differences in interpretations given by strict traditionalists, modern traditionalists, and nontraditionalists to certain historical events, divine revelations, and ancestral authority in matters of law and custom.

In the American system of Jewish education, these problems have been more or less resolved by having each orientator operate schools that emphasize and perpetuate its point of view. This answers the question of what must be taught as vital to the transmission of the cultural heritage. The second demand to provide for the affective needs in the children's education has not received sufficient attention from educational circles.

Education's Responsibility to Develop Individuality

Prof. E. A. Beauchamp of Northwestern University wrote long ago:

> It is part of our unique way of life to stress the development of individuality, and school programs continuously are called upon to meet the demands of individuals as they live in schools. Each person, young and old, is impelled into activity because of motives based upon his interests and needs. Some interests and needs are distinctly individual, others are somewhat common to people of equal age and similar cultural backgrounds. Nevertheless, each person must have opportunities to explore and satisfy these interests and needs. Perhaps it is correct to say that it is through recognition of the existence of interest and need patterns in school that teachers are able to motivate pupils to work in learning activities.

How does Beauchamp's statement apply to Jewish education? As seen above, the curriculum of the Jewish school system is built upon two assumptions. One is that cognitive knowledge is sufficient to produce factual information, emotion, and attitude. To a very limited extent, this assumption is true. But feeling, emotion, and attitude depend on more than knowing and thinking. The person must be sensitized so that he is able and willing to receive the knowledge and respond to it. This necessitates internalization. Psychologists put it this way: "The learner is doing something with or about the knowledge besides perceiving it. He responds to it by his willingness to accept it and finally has a sense of satisfaction of the response." The question that troubles me in response to this assumption is, How much and how often do children and adolescents in Jewish schools willingly respond to their learning experience?

How can the curriculum of the Jewish school be improved to infuse sensitivity from the affective domain into the cognitive? I believe that one way might be by reversing the process of curriculum building. Currently, curriculum building begins with the assumption that all a child needs to know to become educated in Judaism are certain factual information and ideas that tradition and precedent have determined. In other words, it is tradition and precedent that decide what, in their eyes, a Jewish child should know as a result of attending five or ten years in the Jewish school. Perhaps it would be better to reverse the process by asking, What kind of Jewish knowledge and how much of it would be most beneficial to the child's and adolescent's social and psychological needs by attending five or ten years in a Jewish school? This question should lead to several considerations, all dealing with the interests and needs of the child at various stages of his growth and development. Why is this important?

Let us begin with an analysis of the two primary subjects of Bible and history. The Bible consists of twenty-four books divided into three divisions: Torah, Prophets, and Hagiographa. These writings form a literature that spans a period of fifteen hundred years. Obviously, it is beyond the capability of any Jewish school to teach every biblical book, or one complete book, or part of any book in the limited time that is available to the children and the schools. To this problem must be added the difficulty of biblical content itself. For example, properly teaching the first book, Genesis, requires that the teacher have sophisticated knowledge of extrabiblical sources, such as archaeology and ancient history. A similar problem confronts the teacher of Jewish history. Jewish history is not only ancient history, it is the history of a people that has existed for close to four thousand years and, in the words of Simon Dubnow, is "a microcosm of the historical existence of mankind."

Since the study of history is divided into periods and each period consists of hundreds of years, how much information of each period can be taught in any Jewish school? Authors of history textbooks try to solve this problem by selecting information from several periods which, to them, is of historical significance. From a methodological standpoint, this approach is logically sound. But from a psychological view, the process of selectivity as it is employed in the textbooks is inadequate. In structuring courses of study in history, especially for adolescents, consideration should be given to their personal, present, and future behavioral needs. Historical events, concepts, and values should be selected on the basis that they contain both cognitive and affective elements and that they address themselves to such critical issues as, What should the events and ideas mean to the learner today and in his adult life? They should answer such questions as: What kind of being am I and how am I different from other human beings? and Why am I Jewish and why should I be Jewish? They should also respond to, What shall be my attitude toward other religions? and Are the Jews a race, religious community, or nation (people)? It should further contain definitions and causes of anti-Semitism, the effects of living in two cultures, and a host of other issues which, if they don't confront the learner at his present age, will surely occur to him later in life.

In the Jewish school, selectivity of content in social studies should be related to the psychological needs of the learner as he moves from childhood to adolescence and from the protective environments of his home and community to environments where his belonging to the Jewish people or his religion may be challenged. The aim of the two units of *Lecture Notes*, "Teaching and Learning History" and "Jewish Adolescents Explore Their Identity," which I have prepared for SAJS, is to stimulate the teachers' interest in the issues and suggest guidelines of response.

2.
Introduction

In a recent article titled "Cults and Jewish Identity," sociologist Charles Selengut posed the following question: "Who are the young Jews who join cults?" His reply touches on several aspects of the problem: The families they come from; their Jewish upbringing; the various reasons that led them to convert to cult movements; their attitudes toward Judaism; and other identifiable conditions.* I shall quote liberally from both the facts and the author's interpretations of the facts found within the context of the article. Following this, I shall relate this material to the content in this unit.

Extracts from Selengut's "Cults and Jewish Identity"

A. Backgrounds of the Jewish Cult Members

a. I conducted a study of 100 Jewish members of the Unification Church and the Hare Krishna movements in five American cities. The respondents came from social backgrounds similar to the bulk of American Jewry. The majority of the parents work in the professions, teaching, or the sciences or employed as executives and managers.... As other researchers have also noted, Jewish cult members generally come from upper-middle-income, at times, even wealthy family backgrounds. About sixty percent of those I spoke with graduated college, and over 85 percent had attended for at least two years. I also met members who had received doctoral degrees in the arts, sciences, and law.

b. Their Jewish Background and Education

Over 75 percent come from families who were formerly affiliated with a synagogue, and over 90 percent practiced such popular home rituals as the

---

*Midstream, January 1986.

Passover Seder and lighting Hanukkah candles. Only nine of the 100 Jewish cultists I spoke with attended synagogue or temple weekly or bi-weekly, but almost all of the families who were synagogue-affiliated attended sometime during the High Holiday season.... 50 percent of those interviewed had attended some type of supplementary Hebrew or religious school.... All but one described the Jewishness of their families as ethnic and cultural rather than religious.

c. The Respondents' Reactions to Their Jewishness

1. The holiday celebrations in my family lacked a conscious spiritual orientation. They weren't really religious. My mother would cook for Passover, we'd recite the four questions, and invite the whole family. On Rosh Hashanah and Yom Kippur we'd also invite the family....

2. The thing that bothers me most about my Jewish upbringing was that I didn't understand the meaning of things Jewish.... My Judaism had no understanding. We just did some things but it never seemed related to religious thinking.

3. We did many rituals at home but it was a very rational activity. I always thought my parents did it for the kids and not out of any real religious fervor. I guess that's typical of rationalist Reform Jews with whom their religion doesn't mean very much other than a kind of ethnic identification.

d. Professor Selengut's Comments on the Respondents' Statements:

It is important to recognize that the Jewish religious experience of those converts to cult movements was a kind of "cultural religion" emphasizing child-oriented and family activities. Such religiosity has the merit of providing some Jewish folkways for the home but it avoids the incorporation of religious norms and meanings into everyday life. The emphasis of such religio-cultural activity is the selective remembrance of an ethnic past without centering upon or necessarily acknowledging transcendental (supernatural) belief and religious authority. The families of many of the new converts enacted some religious rituals but such activity was unrelated to an active belief in the reality of God, a specifically imperative and intellectual and theological understanding.

Cultural or folk religion may, indeed, be the norm in contemporary Jewish life. Occasional attendance at synagogue services, involvement in Jewish charity fund raising, and the sanctification of major lifecycle events make up the content of Jewish religiosity for the bulk of American Jewry.

As Jonathan Woocher has pointed out, the religiosity of American Jewry is a kind of Jewish "civil religion, which, while binding the community together around a common core of beliefs, tends to deemphasize religious law and doctrine as it relates to everyday life."

B. What Percentage of Young Jews Have Converted to Cult Movements?

In speaking of cults, it is important to ascertain the total membership of the two cults that have attracted young Jews, including Jews for Jesus and others of that ilk. Professor Selengut, however, speaks of two Oriental cults, which he identifies as "new religious movements." I shall again quote from his study.

> According to all available studies of new religious movements, Jews are overrepresented, in proportion to their numbers in the total population, in American cult movements.... It is fair to say that although Jews make up only three (3) percent of the American population, about 10 percent of the current membership of the Unification Church and about 20 percent of the Hare Krishnas are of Jewish background....
>
> Most sociologists explain the high proportion of Jews in the cults as a result of an "oversupply of young Jews" without deep religious socialization and experience, viewing it as a direct consequence of the secularization of American Judaism.... A significant Jewish issue emerges from the study of Jewish cult members. In their experience even the "religious" activities of childhood—*Seder, Bar Mitzvah, Hanukkah lights, religious school,* perhaps *synagogue attendance*—were themselves transformed and experienced as non-religious cultural expressions. Put simply, the activities were not encounters with the holy; they were emptied of specifically transcendental meaning.

To the progressive Jewish educator, Professor Selengut's and other sociologists' research studies about Jewish youth who join Eastern cults and their conclusions are not new discoveries. They do, however, raise two questions: (1) What do the respondents' reasons for their alienation from Judaism tell us, not really about the religion of Judaism, but about the respondents themselves?; (2) Are their reasons characteristic of all Jewish young adults who are alienated in one form or another from Judaism and the Jewish community?

Although the statements are precise and clear, the implications require interpretation. It is obvious that the respondents' conflicts with Judaism arose during their adolescence or in the early years of young adulthood. These are periods in life when the person leaves his childhood identity and enters into a new kind of identity. In psychological language, it is said to mean a turning point, a crucial moment which may bring on an identity crisis. The effects of such a crisis vary with individuals. In the case of the respondents canvassed in the various studies, it caused them to lose what psychologists describe as "personal sameness and historical continuity," or "the sense of being at one with the community and history." Such effects are not limited to converts to new religions, but are characteristic of all those who alienate themselves from their community and history. The respondents indicated two distinct reasons for their alienation, both emanating from lack of knowledge and appreciation of Judaism. One was the lack of rational meaning, and the other the lack of transcendental reality. I seriously question the validity of the first reason because what kind of rational meaning had they found in the Eastern cults? It is more likely that their quest was for esoteric mystical thought and personal experience. If that be the case, then the respondents do not represent the bulk of alienated Jewish youth but are rather persons who possess strong dispositions toward religious mysticism and to strict religious discipline that they failed to find in their homes and religious schools.

Although the study does not identify the religious orientations of the families in which the respondents were raised, it is obvious that they were either Conservative, Reform, or nonaffiliated. It is doubtful that among those interviewed there were many who came from Orthodox homes. Professor Selengut points out, "Unlike most Catholics and Protestants who join the cult groups, the Jewish members claim that joining the cult represents for them a discovery of transcendental religion and the reality of a personal God-experience which they did not have in the Jewish community."

Both Conservative and Reform orientations are built on the principle that Judaism is an intellectual and rational religion that fosters tradition and change. Reform emphasizes the latter over the former, while Conservatism takes a contrary view. Orthodoxy is faithful to tradition and opposes any change that weakens tradition. It demands belief in a personal God and in His intimate relationship to the faithful.

Underlying factors that lead to alienation of Jewish youth from Judaism or from the Jewish community are not exclusively religious. No doubt lack of spiritual orientation in home life, which the first respondent claims, and lack of understanding "of things Jewish," cited by the second, are serious causes of alienation. But consideration should also be given to psychological and social factors in the lives of maturing youth, and especially those of Jewish youth.

As Erik H. Erikson points out,

> A state of identity confusion usually becomes manifest at a time when the young individual finds himself exposed to a combination of experiences which demands his simultaneous commitment.... Decisions and choices and, most of all, successes in any direction bring to the fore conflicting identity, or negative identity.... The loss of a sense of identity is often expressed in a scornful and snobbish hostility toward the roles offered as proper and desirable by one's family or immediate community. Any aspect of the required role, or all parts, be it masculinity or femininity, nationality or class membership, can become the main focus of the young person's acid disdain. Such excessive contempt for their backgrounds occur among the oldest Anglo-Saxon and the newest Latin or Jewish families; it easily becomes a general dislike for everything American, an irrational overestimation of everything foreign.... *(Identity and the Life Cycle*, W. W. Norton & Co., 1980.)

The last sentence in this statement should be of concern to Jews because the "hostility" that young Jews acquire when they lose their ethnic identity extends to their Jewish people and its religion and culture. This, surely, is one cause of alienation from Judaism and the Jewish community.

Jewish parents and teachers of adolescents in Jewish schools should give serious consideration to a second possible cause of alienation characteristic of minority groups who live in two cultures, their own ethnic culture and the dominant majority culture. This problem has received a good deal of attention from leading sociologists and psychologists. The late Kurt Lewin (director of the Research Center for Group Dynamics, MIT) has dealt with this problem as it relates to Jews and Jewish youth in great detail (*Resolving Social Conflicts*, Harper & Bros., 1948). To cite a few pertinent statements from his essay "Psycho-Sociological Problems of a Minority Group":

> It is one of the greatest theoretical and practical difficulties of the Jewish problem that Jewish people are often, in a high degree, uncertain of their

relation to the Jewish group. They are uncertain whether they actually belong to the Jewish group, in what respect they belong, and in what degree.... There are persons whose whole life-situation is characterized by such uncertainty about their belonging, resulting from standing near a margin of groups.

Such people, according to Lewin, stand near the margin of their own and other groups in an effort to cross the boundaries that separate the respective groups: "It is characteristic of individuals crossing the margin between social groups that they are not only uncertain about the group they are ready to enter, but also about their belonging to the group they are leaving...." Uncertainty creates conflict and "conflict creates tension, which leads to restlessness, unbalanced behavior, and over-emphasis in one or the other direction. Indeed the Jews are commonly characterized as being restless."

How does Lewin's theory affect the young Jewish adult? Briefly stated, from Erikson's analysis of the identity crisis we know that "identity confusion usually becomes manifest at a time when the young individual finds himself exposed to a combination of experiences which demand his simultaneous commitment." Jewish youth, even those who were raised in homes of strong Jewish consciousness or spiritual orientation, generally are unable to escape the conflicts of identity confusion to which they are exposed when they leave the protective environments of home and community and enter college. The uncertainty of belonging to the Jewish and non-Jewish groups and the culture shock from academic challenges are potent factors in their commitment to the new social and cultural lifestyles. "No wonder," writes Lewin, "that frequently a Jew may shift his attitude as to what the Jewish group means to him; and if he has lost faith in religion, or has lost belief in what he used to consider the special ideals or mission of the Jews, he is likely to show a strong tendency to break loose from the group altogether." It is indeed unfortunate that Jewish education has not given sufficient thought to the psychological needs of the adolescents in the curriculum of the Jewish school. Numerous reasons can be cited, some legitimate and others of shortsightedness, for this obvious attitude toward the post–Bar Mitzvah youth.

The subjects of identity crisis and living in two cultures as they affect the Jewish adolescents constitute the theme of this unit of *Lecture Notes*. The methodological approach is directed to three aspects: (1) comprehension of the psychological stages of growth and development of the youth at the ages of thirteen to seventeen when he attends the School of Advanced Jewish Studies; (2) projection of uncertainties about his membership in the Jewish people which he may encounter as a young adult and even as an adult; and (3) projection of courses of study as integral parts of the school's curriculum in which future uncertainties are raised and their answers presented for deliberation. The final goal, as Professor Jerome S. Bruner explains it, is for the student to master himself, discipline his taste, deepen his view, and challenge his curiosity.

The pedagogic approach is what is known as *problem solving*, in which the topic is presented as a problem for the students and teachers to explore and arrive at the correct conclusions. The following questions and problems have been posed and answered:

What am I?; What kind of entity?; Which kind of being?
Why am I Jewish?
Why should I be Jewish?

The format of the *Lecture Notes* has been designed to be used as source material for teachers who would recast the information into lesson plans geared to the age and comprehension levels of their students. With this thought in mind, I have delimited the scope and content of the topics to what may be considered classical explanations. These thoughts and ideas should serve well as a beginning, rather than an advanced or definitive study of such problems as the identity crisis of Jewish youth, why one is Jewish, and why one should be Jewish.

The literature dealing with these and similar problems that confront adolescents, young adults, and adults, not only in the American Jewish community but also in Israel, is extensive. To be Jewish and to remain Jewish is totally voluntaristic. Rabbi Arthur Hertzberg writes:

> Even the "sabra" [native born Israeli] can choose freely to leave for other shores and to forget both Israel and Jewish identity. That process is even more available in the Diaspora where the open society presents the individual Jew with insistent opportunities and temptations simply to leave his Jewishness without even making a decision to assimilate. The majority of the Jewish people now lives in Israel and in the Diaspora, outside the halakhah, with the religious tradition either in national memory and group experience or, to be more truthful and exact, to highly personalized senti-

ment. Under these conditions ... the question needs be asked: can the Jewish people survive?

In light of such consideration, it is all the more essential to supplement the classical explanations with information from more recent studies in teaching Jewish adolescents why they are Jewish and why they should be Jewish. Unfortunately, neither timewise nor staffwise could such an ambitious program be undertaken in the present day. The lack of time is self-explanatory. As to the staff, only teachers who are well versed in contemporary Jewish thought could be entrusted with such sophisticated subject matter. Therefore, I emphasize that these lecture notes are only a beginning.

3.
Lecture I: Exploring One's Jewish Identity

The subject to be discussed in the following pages is personal identity, with specific reference to Jewish identity. The importance of this subject in the context of orientation* will be self-explanatory as we proceed with our study. At this time, I believe it is necessary to clarify the meaning of the term *identity* as it will be used within the context of this unit.

For a shared definition of *identity*, I refer you to Erik H. Erikson. The following is a quotation from his essay, "The Problem of Ego Identity."

> As far as I know, Freud used it only once in a more than incidental way, and then with a psychosocial connotation. It was when he tried to formulate his link to the Jewish people that he spoke of an "inner identity" which was less based on race or religion than on a common readiness to live in opposition, and on a common freedom from prejudices which narrow the use of the intellect. Here, the term "identity" points to an individual's link with the unique values, fostered by a unique history, of his people.... The term "identity" expresses such a mutual relation in that it connotes both a persistent sameness within oneself (selfsameness) and a persistent sharing of some kind of essential character with others.

In my own usage of *identity*, the term will sometimes be related to psychosocial concepts while at other times it will refer to patterns of behavior as treated by sociologists.

Structuring a Course of Study

In discussing the creation of a course of study titled "Man," Prof. Jerome S. Bruner (*Toward a Theory of Instruction*, Harvard University Press, 1966) states:

---

*In the first unit of *Lecture Notes*, I have suggested that orientation sessions in social studies be provided at SAJS.

In describing a course of study, one must begin by setting forth the intellectual substance of what is to be taught, else there can be no sense of what challenges and shapes the curiosity of the students.... Unless the learner also masters himself, disciplines his taste, deepens his view of the world, the "something" that is got across is hardly worth the effort of transmission.

With this warning in mind, Bruner begins his course of the study of man as follows:

The content of the course is Man: his nature as a species, the forces that shaped and continue to shape his humanity. Three questions recur throughout:

>   What is human about human beings?
>   Why did they get that way?
>   How can they be more so?

.... We make every effort at the outset to tell the children where we hope to travel with them. Yet little of such recounting gets through. Much more useful, we have found, is to pose the three questions directly to children so that their own views can be brought into open so that they can establish some points of view of their own.

You might wonder why, in a discussion of content subjects and methods of teaching Jewish history, Bible, and religion, I preoccupy myself with the problem of identity. Some might even ask, "Doesn't identity belong in a course of psychology, or can teachers deal with it in the limited time that is available to them and to the students in the Jewish school?"

The suggestion to include in the curriculum of the Jewish school a course of study, or at least a series of discussions, which deals with Jewish identity derives from my experience with both the formal and informal teaching of adolescents. Knowledge of the Hebrew language arts and social studies is certainly effective in enriching a person's comprehension and appreciation of his cultural heritage. But a time comes in a person's life when he is confronted by challenges that relate to the very core of his own being. It is then that knowledge of his heritage without knowledge of his personal nature or self is insufficient. Such a time occurs in an adolescent's life when he leaves the protective environments of home and community and enters the open society of university life or the world of work. The challenges confronting young adults who come from families that live in two cultures is even more severe. Reaction to such challenges will depend upon the individual's assessment of his or her personal identity and ability to make rational choices between alternatives. For Jewish youth, knowledge of Judaism is one primary source for meeting such challenges. Conceptions of their own Jewishness is another. It should, therefore, be obvious that a school that prepares young Jewish adults to draw upon the sources of academic knowledge should also prepare them to meet challenges to their personal identity.

I shall once again quote from the writings of Erik Erikson on this subject. He titles his observations, "Time of Breakdown":

> A state of acute identity confusion usually becomes manifest at a time when the young individual finds himself exposed to a combination of experiences which demand his simultaneous commitment to physical intimacy (not by any means always overtly sexual), to decisive occupational choice, to energetic competition, and to psychosocial self-definition. A young girl may ... on entering college, meet young people of radically different backgrounds, among whom she must choose her friends and her enemies; radically different mores especially in the relationship of the sexes which she must play along with or repudiate; and a commitment to make decisions which will necessitate irreversible competitive involvement or even leadership. Often she finds among very "different" young people a comfortable display of values, manners, and symbols for which one or the other of her parents or grandparents is covertly nostalgic, while overtly despising them. Decisions and choices and, most of all, successes in any direction bring to the fore conflicting identifications.... On the other hand, any marked avoidance of choices leads to isolation and to an inner vacuum.

Erikson's psychosocial analysis needs no commentary. In Jewish education, those who have worked with adolescents also know other reasons contributing to identity conflict in young adults, particularly when they find themselves in bewildering situations on a college campus. Such experiences frequently lead to culture shock. Sociologists explain culture shock as "psychological and social maladjustment when individuals experience mental conflict as a result of living between two cultures and fail to establish organic unity between the cultures." Such persons are described as "marginal people who are in a state of mental conflict by reason of participation in two groups and are not fully committed to the values and standards of one or the other with whom they identify."

In my own experience, I have encountered Jewish students who admitted to suffering from culture shock. For example, on one campus a graduate of a yeshivah confided in me that he suffered from mental anxiety as a result of having read Frazer's *Golden Bough*. He said, "I feel as if I live in two worlds which I can't reconcile." On another campus, I met a young man who had changed his Jewish name to one he considered to be more "American" and refused to date Jewish girls. His answer to my inquiry as to why he had changed his name was, "I cannot live as a hyphenated person, Jewish-American. I wish to live as a whole American." In those days, incidents of this sort may have been somewhat unusual. Today, they are more common. Culture conflict too frequently leads to interdating, mixed marriages, and to the joining of religious or mystic cults.

When during a lecture concerning the curriculum of Jewish secondary schools, I suggested including a course of study on Jewish identity, I was asked, "Aren't high school youth too young to deal with the identity problem? They still live at home and are unaware of culture conflict." My reply was, "As high schools prepare teenagers scholastically for more advanced learning at college, it might also be wise to prepare them for the college environment where they will be exposed to culture conflict." Later, I found support for my suggestion in the writings of Erik Erikson. He writes:

> Adolescence is the last stage of childhood.... The individual subordinates his childhood identification to a new kind of identification... with dire urgency, they [the new identifications] force the young individual into choices and decisions which will, with increasing immediacy, lead to a more final self-definition, to irreversible role pattern, and thus to commitments for life. The task to be performed here by the young person and by his society is formidable; it necessitates, in different individuals and in different societies, great variations in duration, in the intensity, and in the ritualization of adolescence.

It should be noted that the problem of culture conflict among Jewish youth has not escaped the attention of the Jewish community. As early as fifty years ago, Avukah, the Zionist youth organization, was active on American campuses. Later, the B'nai B'rith Hillel Foundation developed elaborate religio-cultural programs for college youth. Their successful achievements, however, have been limited. I believe that the major reason for their limited accomplishments is due to the fact that they come too late in the lives of the young people. Neither the Hebrew nor the Sunday schools prepare their students to anticipate the challenges that await them at college. In addition, they do not motivate them to participate in Jewish experiences on the campus. The most propitious time to begin preparing a young person to meet culture conflict at college is during the early stages of adolescence.

Ideas to Think About: What is Identity?

According to Erikson, "Identity really means a necessary turning point, a crucial moment.... It is a sense of being with oneself as one grows and develops; and it means at the same time, a sense of affinity with a community's sense of being at one with its history or mythology." Lacking identity means "the loss of personal sameness and historical continuity."

William James defines identity as a "mental or moral attitude in which the person feels most deeply and intensely active and alive.... *A voice inside speaks to him and says, 'This is the real me.'* "

Erikson relates an interesting story about Sigmund Freud. In 1926, Freud spoke to a Jewish group in Vienna and said the following:

> What bound me to Jewry was (I am ashamed to admit) neither faith nor national pride, for I have always been an unbeliever and was brought up without any religion though not without respect for what are called the "ethical" standards of human civilization.... But plenty of other things remained over to make the attraction of Jewry and Jews irresistible—many obscure emotional forces, which were the more powerful the less they could be expressed in words, as well as a clear consciousness of inner identity, the safe privacy of a common mental construction. And beyond this there was a perception that it was to my Jewish nature alone that I owed two characteristics that had become indispensable to me in the difficult course of my life. Because I was a Jew I found myself free from many prejudices which restricted others in the use of their intellect; and as a Jew I was prepared to join the Opposition, and to do without agreement with the "compact majority."

Erikson adds the following comments to Freud's statement:

> Freud's "consciousness of inner identity" includes a sense of bitter pride preserved by his dispersed and often despised people throughout a long history of persecution. It is anchored in a particular (here intellectual) gift

which had victoriously emerged from hostile limitations of opportunities.

Erikson concludes "that the pride of gaining a strong identity may signify an inner emancipation from a more dominant group identity...." His statement may well be applied to Jews who acquire a strong identity of their Jewishness and also acquire "inner emancipation" from the negative forces of the environment enabling them to feel pride in their Jewishness.

Exploring One's Identity in a Course of Study

Taking Bruner's three questions in his study of man as models for an orientation course in Jewish Identity, I suggest exploring the following questions as problems for explanation:

What am I; What kind of entity; Which kind of being?
Why am I Jewish?
Why shall I be Jewish?

The first question was posed by Prof. Robert Nozick (*Philosophical Explanations*, Harvard University Press, 1981). He explains the reason for the question as follows:

> .... The self is a problem and puzzle to itself. Our desire to know our nature ... determines what alternatives we choose to live and be.... We each want to understand not only the kind we are, but also what constitutes our individual identity as a particular being of that kind.... If what we are is persons, we want to know what differentiates or individuates one person from another. Viewing ourselves from the inside, we also each want to understand ourselves as a particular one of these persons.

The preceding statements by Nozick ought to figure in our study of identity. For example, his thoughts bring to mind such concepts as:

> The self wants to know its nature and exactly to what the term *I* refers.
> It wants to know alternatives in choosing how to live and to be.
> It wants to understand the kind of being all people are.
> It wants to understand what constitutes individual identity.
> It wants to know what differentiates one person from another.

It wants to understand what makes ourself a particular one of those persons.

Problem I: What Am I? What Differentiates Me from Others?

For our purposes, I suggest that we treat these questions from a sociological rather than philosophical perspective. Sociology studies the processes and patterns of individual and group interaction with emphasis on human personality. It examines patterns of behavior, attitudes, beliefs, and value characteristics as products of individual and group experience within specific social and cultural environments. This approach can, without difficulty, be employed in our study of Jewish identity.

To the questions, What am I? and How am I different from others?, I suggest the following explanations:

I am a human being and a Jew.

As a human being, I am different from other human beings because nature has gone a long way to make each person different from any other person in the world. By different, I mean neither in our physical image nor in the moral sense of better or worse. I refer instead to the uniqueness of personality. An individual acquires his personality from two primary sources: his own distinctive human nature, and the continuous experiences produced by his cultural environment and social interactions. These are not only characteristics of individuals but also of groups.

As a Jew, I am different from other members of the society in which I live by reason of the fact that I live in two cultures: the dominant or majority culture, and the Jewish or minority culture. The Jewish culture is basically transmitted to me through my family and community. Living in two cultures does not make me less human nor an unusual kind of human being. It does, however, distinguish me in my interactions with others. This is because I possess cultural traits that my non-Jewish neighbors do not possess. Do these traits interfere with the dominant culture of the majority? Not at all. True democracy advocates "cultural heterogeneity [pluralism] with other minority groups maintaining their identity...which do not conflict with major values and norms of the dominant culture."

I recall an incident that illustrates the application of this principle in action. A foreign student at Columbia University lamented to his professor of English that he found it difficult to rid himself of his foreign accent. The professor replied, "Why do you want to get rid of your foreign accent? A person who speaks correct English with a foreign accent gives evidence of knowing two languages. This means that he has a plus where others have a minus." The professor's reply to the student illustrates a truly democratic attitude that applies to individuals who live in two cultures and find it difficult to harmonize the standards and norms of the cultures involved.

Jewish customs, beliefs, values, and patterns of behavior do not provide contradictory standards or opposing loyalties to the dominant American culture; in other words, they do not detract from the Jew's Americanism. They give, instead, evidence of enriching the Jew's life with spiritual and intellectual values. In brief, "the Jew has a plus" in his personality.

The following is a quotation from an address by Justice Louis D. Brandeis, delivered in New York City in June 1915 (*Brandeis on Zionism*, foreword by Justice Felix Frankfurter. ZOA, 1942):

> Let no American imagine that Zionism is inconsistent with Patriotism. Multiple loyalties are objectionable only if they are inconsistent. A man is a better citizen of the United States for being also a loyal citizen of his state, and of his city; for being loyal to his family, and to his profession or trade; for being loyal to his college or his lodge. Every Irish American who contributed towards advancing home rule was a better man and a better American for the sacrifice he made. Every American Jew who aids in advancing the Jewish settlement in Palestine, though he feels that neither he nor his descendants will ever live there, will likewise be a better man and a better American for doing so.
>
> Seton-Watson commented:
>
>> America is full of nationalities which, while accepting with enthusiasm their new American citizenship, nevertheless look to some centre in the old world as the source and inspiration of their national culture and traditions. The most typical instance is the feeling of the American Jew for Palestine which may well become a focus for his *declassé* kinsmen in other parts of the world.
>
> There is no inconsistency between loyalty to America and loyalty to Jewry. The Jewish spirit, the product of our religion and experiences, is essentially modern and essentially American. Not since the destruction of the Temple have the Jews in spirit and in ideals been so fully in harmony with the noblest aspirations of the country in which they lived.

The following quotations are from the writings of the sociologist C.

Bezalel Sherman (*The Jew within American Society*, Wayne University Press, 1961):

> In 1916, when ethnic minority groups were being pilloried as hyphenated Americans, John Dewey insisted on the international character of America. He wrote:
>
>> ... such terms as Irish-American or Hebrew-American or German-American are false terms because they seem to assume something which is already in existence called America, to which other factors may be externally hitched on. The fact is the genuine American is himself a hyphenated character. This does not mean that he is part American and that some foreign ingredient is then added. It means ... that he is international and interracial in his make-up. He is not American plus Pole or German. But the American is himself Pole-German-English-French-Spanish-Italian-Greek-Irish-Scandinavian-Bohemian-Jew-and so on. ... The hyphen connects instead of separates.
>
> Horace M. Kallen, the father of the theory of cultural pluralism, goes even further than Dewey. "The base of American democracy," says Kallen, "is diversity. American culture is founded upon variation of racial groups and individual character ... spontaneous differences of social heritage, institutional habit, mental attitude and emotional tone.... It is a symphony that comes to life anew with the playing of each orchestra. The ethnic groups are the instruments of the orchestra; and though each plays its own part, they all contribute to a harmonious whole ... each of which contributes something unique to the symphony."

The ability of Jews to live in two cultures by making a modus vivendi with the dominant culture is one of the unique features in history. The following thoughts from Bezalel Sherman's work sheds light on this phenomena:

When other groups emigrated, they were as leaves which social winds scattered to a foreign land; the tree from which they were blown remained rooted in the old territory. When Jews emigrated, it was not just leaves that were windblown, nor branches, but whole segments of the tree. From the time the Jews lost their national independence till the establishment of the State of Israel, the Jewish tree itself was uprooted. Immigrants of other nationalities sought new homes for themselves as individuals; Jewish immigrants were part of a people which was itself homeless. Others first became minorities in America; the Jews had for ages been a minority everywhere. For others, minority status was an exception; for Jews, the rule. The need to adjust to conditions of life in a strange country first became a problem for other groups only in America; for Jews, it was a problem they had to face uninterruptedly for many centuries. Others came to their new country with one culture; the Jews came with two cultures. One culture—their own—they carried deep within themselves, within their spiritual and psychic being. The other they bore upon themselves, like an outer garment. Each time they trod new ground, they changed their outer garment, but always they succeeded in retaining at least in part their inner culture.

The Jews were the only ethnic group that arrived in America with a past experience of being a minority. They were consequently able to skip that whole period of adjusting themselves to minority status....

Sherman attributes the following quotation to Robert Park:

The marginal man who is forced to live in two worlds and two cultures absorbed much greater experience of life and displayed a more flexible and greater capacity for adjustment than the man who lived under normal conditions. The marginal man is always relatively the more civilized human being. He occupies the position which has been, historically, that of the Jew in the Diaspora. *The Jews, particularly the Jew who has emerged from the provincialism of the ghetto, has everywhere and always been the most civilized of human beings.*

4.
Lecture II: Stages of Growth and Development

Problem II: Why Am I Jewish?

Before we discuss the topic "Why Am I Jewish?" I wish to digress for a brief moment and elaborate on the theory of identity as it relates to the adolescent. My intent is to seek a better understanding of Jewish adolescents with particular reference to the young adults who attend SAJS.

The age levels of the SAJS student body range from thirteen to seventeen. With few exceptions, these young people have had five or six years of Jewish schooling prior to entering SAJS. The elementary schools from which they came are not part of an organized system of Jewish education that provides a systematic curriculum. Because of this fact, SAJS cannot simply structure its courses on the assumption that a firm academic foundation has already been acquired. As a starting point, however, the age-related needs are taken into account. Since these students are adolescents, the first question that looms high at SAJS pertains to the objectives to be formulated for Jewish social studies. In other words, how our curriculum should harmonize the philosophical outlooks in Jewish history, Bible, religion, Israel, and the holocaust with the growth patterns of the adolescent's mind. I shall mention briefly selected characteristics of each age, hoping that the teachers will pursue more intensive study of this subject in *Youth, the Years from Ten to Sixteen* by A. Gesel, F.L. Ilg, L. B. Ames (Harper and Brothers, 1956), from which these quotations are taken.

Age 13: Thirteens live in the present, the "here and now," and the near future. There are some thirteens who become enchanted by faraway times and places, but most realize that "only the present can be lived"; "The immediate past is gone, and you can never get it back again."

Age 14: Fourteen expresses his global, inclusive thinking, even his concept of time. He expands in his thoughts to include the world. Most fourteen-year-olds have some conception of God. They do not think of Him as a person, nor very often as a spirit. Some at thirteen conceive of God as a "power over us" or as a "huge plant, factorylike, producing thoughts." Others conceive of Him as an "idea in people's minds." Still others are more vague and general in the concepts. They speak of "something that just is." They realize the inadequacy of the human mind and that it "cannot even get close to an explanation." Although at fourteen the individual is more than not a believer, he doesn't yet feel much influence of his beliefs on his behavior. He is not moved to pray as he did when he was younger. But he does think of the Deity as "something you could go for help."

Age 15: Fifteen is generally regarded as "an enigma." He shows many characteristics that neither teachers nor parents can easily understand. I have selected several characteristics from his school life that I believe should be of interest to teachers. "The mature traits of the fifteen year age period can be envisaged under three headings: (1) Increasing the self-awareness and perceptiveness. (2) A rising spirit of independence. (3) Loyalty but adjustment to group of home, school, and community."

> The psychological development of the individual is profoundly affected by the pressures of groups.
> Fifteen can be exciting to teach even if they are challenged in some new field. They ask many questions "why" and "wherefore". They are more able to think for themselves and are quick to pick up an error in a discussion. Fifteens learn quickly in new fields and like the stimulus of a new lecturer to give them fresh material or a new slant on some topic. They want to have an opinion and to have sufficient information for discussion. Religion and race are two of their favorite topics for discussion particularly if these topics are vital to their own experience. Fifteen tends to identify himself with the situation, the person, the idea. Fifteen has a more defined ethical sense.... He is capable of judging right from wrong, basically from his own "point of view" or his own individual standards.... Fifteen is as unsure of his ideas about the Deity as he is about death. He may solve his dilemma simply by saying he doesn't believe in God, and yet he hesitates. He says it's "kind of hard to say" or that he is "looking around for an idea of God."

Age 16: Fifteen was a necessary forerunner. The year prepared the way for the broader and more balanced integrations of the behavior of sixteen. With this advantage, sixteen displays greater self-reliance and deeper self-containedness. Wholesome self-assurance is his cardinal trait and a symptom of his potentials. He is more tolerant of the world in general. Sixteen lives in the present and looks to the future. Though some sixteens don't have a concept of God that satisfies them or can't grasp or figure out what God is, others are finding their way into their own religious reality. Sixteen has not yet built up a strong continuity of religious feeling within himself.

I also wish to direct your attention to an analysis of the adolescent mind by Erik Erikson. He writes:

> The adolescent mind is essentially a mind of the *moratorium*, a psychological stage between childhood and adulthood, and adulthood between the morality learned by the child and ethics to be developed by the adult. It is an ideological mind and, indeed, it is the ideological outlook of a society that speaks most clearly to the adolescent who is eager to be affirmed by his peers, and is ready to be confirmed by rituals, creeds, and programs which at the same time define what is evil, uncanny, and inimical. In searching for the social values which guide identity, one therefore confronts the problems of *ideology* and *aristocracy* [aristocracy in this sense may mean rules established by heredity or by the elite], both in their widest possible sense which connotes that within a defined world image and predestined course of history, the best people will come to rule and rule develops the best in people.
>
> In order not to become cynically or apathetically lost, young people must somehow be able to convince themselves that those who succeed in their anticipated adult world thereby shoulder the obligation of being the best.

Ideas to Think About

The predominant idea underlying the purpose of education in the Jewish school is to transmit the knowledge of the heritage of Judaism to the next generation. The idea is noble, and in past generations was also effective. Knowledge has many powerful forces at its command. Modern science has revealed the mystery of some of the forces and the manner of their operation and effects on the human mind. Other forces remain to be discovered. From what we know, it is certain that knowledge, to be effective, requires a particular environment in which to operate. The environment may be an individual person or a social group. In either case, one's knowledge must lead to action and interaction. When it remains dormant, it dissipates. This principle is of crucial importance in education. In psychological language we say, with John Dewey, that knowledge (or learning) should lead to change of behavior.

In most Jewish schools knowledge of Judaism is transmitted for the sake of knowing rather than for finding a means to apply what one has ascertained to conditions of the environment. By environment, I mean the self and/or community in which an individual lives. For example, rabbis and Jewish teachers are deeply concerned with the spiraling mixed marriage rate among Jews. They are equally concerned that the majority of Jewish university students are not conscious of their Jewish identity and estrange themselves from Judaism. Unfortunately, however, these same educators appear to be oblivious to the role they should assume in helping adolescents discover their religio-cultural identity.

The content subjects taught in Jewish schools are quite literally blocks of infantile, unconnected knowledge. As such, they are void of ideas, concepts, and, particularly, values. This discrete information remains lodged in the mind as dormant bits and pieces to be forgotten in a very short time. I stress *values* because psychologists tell us that "a value is an orientation toward a whole class of goals that are considered important in one's life." Do Jewish youth require "an orientation toward" an understanding of why they are Jewish and a conviction for why they should remain Jewish? Are blocks of infantile knowledge without values sufficient to answering these vital questions for succeeding generations?

Obviously, the statement by Erikson quoted above says something worthwhile that we can easily apply to Jewish education. To clarify the issue further, it is necessary to examine Erikson's commentary more carefully.

According to him, the adolescent is exposed to two world views: one is transmitted to him by the society in which he lives, and the other is idealistic. Both outlooks speak to his mind—a mind that searches for social values to guide its identity. In essence, they say the same thing: "The best people rule, and rule develops the best people." This is how aristocracy and idealism defend their respective positions. But is what they are saying true? When the searching mind probes into the realism of these claims and then judges them to be false, it can become either cynical or pathetically lost. These conditions stem from disappointment and disillusionment. Erikson's suggestion is most logical and of significance for parents and teachers. It suggests finding a way to convince the young person that "in the adult world, those who succeed have an obligation *to be the best.*"

Let us now concretize certain ideas in the material we have read in the lecture notes to this point. I have selected as examples a few categories that are applicable to all subjects.

Facts That May Cause Adolescent Identity Difficulties:

Examine Erikson's statement (p. 2) "Time of Breakdown."

1. "A state of acute identity confusion becomes manifest when the young individual finds himself exposed to a combination of experiences which demand his simultaneous commitment."
2. How does this condition apply to cultural, religious, and national commitments?
3. Apply this "state of confusion" to the questions, Why am I Jewish? and Why should I be Jewish?
4. Consider steps to solve the problem.
5. Consider ways of evaluating the solutions.

Facts from Which Problems Can Occur:

A Jew is different from other members of the society in which he lives.

1. How does his being different affect his Jewish identity?
2. How does his being different affect the desire of the self to know its nature?
3. Is being different peculiar only to Jews?

5.
Lecture III: Why Should I Be Jewish?

Why Am I Jewish?

From the Jewish standpoint, there is only one answer to this question, the definition of being Jewish given by the Halakhah, the religious law. Sociological or psychological definitions are not binding on Jews. The Halakhah's definition is definitive for all Jews, regardless of theological orientations.

According to the Halakhah, a child born of a Jewish mother is automatically Jewish. The mother gives the child legitimate certainty and traces his lineage to the patriarchs Abraham, Isaac, and Jacob. A convert to Judaism is by legal fiction declared a newborn and enters the Jewish people through certain rituals and considerations. The male convert enters the Jewish people through circumcision, ritual immersion, by accepting the religion of Judaism, and the appellation of Ben Avraham, son of Avraham. The female convert enters the Jewish people through ritual immersion, by accepting the religion of Judaism, and the appellation of Bat Avraham, daughter of Abraham. The child born to a mother after her conversion is automatically Jewish.

Rabbi Joseph B. Soloveitchik explains the required procedures of the *halakhah* as follows:

> The mother establishes the child's "sanctity" and (status of) his "belonging to" or identification with the Jewish people. True and proper conversion is gained only by means of circumcision and immersion for a male, and through ritual immersion for a female.

From an historical perspective, the custom of tracing a child's lineage to his mother is very ancient, going back to the Patriarchal period. The historian Roland de Vaux (*Ancient Israel,* McGraw-Hill, 1961), explains this custom:

As a type of family, matriarchate is much more common in primitive societies. The characteristic mark of this type of society is not that the mother exercises authority (this is rare), but that the child's lineage is traced through the mother. The child belongs to the mother's family...even rights of inheritance are fixed by maternal descent.

In citing the requirements the *halakhah* proscribes for one being or becoming Jewish, it is necessary in the interest of clarity to explain the form of these laws. There are two categories of laws: customary laws and enacted laws. Customary law is codified traditional law that never breaks with tradition. Enacted law does not depend entirely on tradition and at times even contradicts tradition. Sociologists have pointed out that "enacted law is not possible until reverence for ancestors has been so weakened that it is no longer thought wrong to interfere with traditional customs by positive enactment." This distinction between the two forms ought to be kept in mind whenever one confronts the different religious orientations in the Jewish community.

How does the principle enunciated by *halakhah* affect the question, What makes a person Jewish? The answer is that since neither Reform nor Conservatism rejects the basic traditional concept of tracing a Jew's lineage to the patriarchs and the Covenant, a person born to Jewish parents or converted to Judaism is a Jew for the rest of his life. It is, however, to be noted that Reform does differ with Orthodoxy and Conservatism in the requirement of certain rituals pertaining to conversion. Thus, the traditional religious answer to the question, Why am I Jewish?, is clearly and permanently defined.

In the context of our discussion, the question, Why am I Jewish?, does not pertain to the Jewish lineage but to the person's status in, and loyalty to the Jewish people. Status means social relationship and obligations to society. Loyalty means allegiance to the people. When the question, Why am I Jewish?, is posed to young adults, it should be made clear that it is not their Jewish lineage that is in question but the extent of their social relationship and allegiance to the Jewish people.

Ideas to Think About

The conditions of birth and voluntary conversion that determine a person's membership in the Jewish people are very much like the verdict of American law; children born of parents who are American citizens automatically become members of the American people. Where the two legal systems differ is in the matter of a citizen's desire to terminate membership in his respective nation. An American citizen may permanently give up his citizenship for whatever reason he wishes. A Jew, according to the *halakhah*, remains a member of the Jewish people for the duration of his life.

> In Jewish religious law, it is technically impossible for a Jew born of a Jewish mother (or properly converted to Judaism) to change his religion. Even though a Jew undergoes the rites of admission to another religious faith and formally renounces the Jewish religion, he remains—as far at the *halalkah* is concerned—a Jew, albeit a sinner (Talmud: Sanh. 44a). For the born Jew, Judaism is not a matter of choice, and for the proselyte it ceases to be once he has converted. (See *Encyclopedia Judaica*, Vol. 3, page 211.)

Mordecai M. Kaplan adds the comment: "There is no Jewish authority that can rid a Jew from his people." This view, postulated by the *halakhah*, is the accepted norm by all orientations of Judaism.

If a Jew is incapable of relinquishing membership in the Jewish people, why is the threat of assimilation so frightening to positive Jews? The term *assimilation* has several sociological meanings. It may mean "blending of divergent cultures." In that sense, assimilation is similar to acculturation, in which a culture is modified through contact with one or more cultures. In another sense, assimilation involves the complete elimination of cultural differences and unique group identifications. In the latter sense, it is a one-way process in which an individual or group takes over the culture and identity of another (usually larger) group and becomes an indiscernible part of that group. Its own culture and identity disappear.

When we speak of the assimilation of Jews into their non-Jewish environment, we generally mean the one-way or total absorption of individuals or segments of the Jewish community into the majority population. This is done either through conversion into another religion, as was the case with the German Jews in the nineteenth century, or in the disappearance from the Jewish community of individual Jews or whole families. There is another group who can be identified as assimilationists: those who still acknowledge their Jewish origins and do not actively terminate their membership with the Jewish people, yet are still assimilationists. Such Jews may support Jewish causes and needs, but relinquish the cultural, religious, and national ingredients of the Jewish civilization that account for the differentiating Jewish group identity. Although Jews in that category recognize themselves and are recognized by others as Jews, in the course of time and by the process of modulation (sometimes through a number of generations), they often disappear from the Jewish community. In other words, either they or their offspring would be the last Jews in their families. An interesting case in point is the following story that has circulated in England about Benjamin Disraeli.

Benjamin Disraeli (1804–1881), British chancellor of the exchequer and prime minister, was knighted by Queen Victoria as the Earl of Beaconsfield. At the age of thirteen he was baptized by his father, who had a quarrel with the London Sephardic community. The story is told that on one occasion, when Disraeli accompanied the queen to church, she noticed that the prime minister was not praying and put the question to him; "Disraeli, what are you, Jewish or Christian?" Disraeli replied, "Your Majesty, I am the blank page between the Old and New Testaments!"

What did Disraeli mean by describing himself as "the blank page between the Old and New Testaments"? The answer is found in the meaning of "a blank page," which is lacking the features of completion. On the one hand, it indicates emptiness and vacantness, and on the other, bewilderment and confusing. In short, the blank page expresses nothing. In a volume that contains the Old and New Testaments, the blank page has the single function of separating the two testaments while it bears no writing—it is empty space.

Disraeli's description of himself as a blank page may be applied to Jews whose identity consists only of their awareness that they are Jews because they are not non-Jews. Their Jewishness is incomplete, having no meaning and expressing nothing. They are like a check with no amount filled in.

Why Should I Be Jewish?

This is a more complex question to answer than Why am I Jewish? The main difficulty resides not so much in the nature of the question as in the person who is likely to ask it. In the context of our discussion, the question should be viewed as a springboard to arouse interest in a topic with which many students grapple, either consciously or subconsciously.

The answer or answers should provide them with several types of information. First, it is necessary to provide information about conditions in the life of the Jew who lacks sufficient personal identity to live a full and positive Jewish life. Mordecai M. Kaplan describes this Jew as "being pulled in opposite directions by longing and desires. The strain of his inner life is nearing a breaking point. Outwardly he seems to be calm, but inwardly he is worried. He is a divided being, a Hamlet forever soliloquizing to be or not to be a Jew." Second, a body of real information provided by knowledgeable persons that supplies accurate content and uses modern pedagogic techniques is an imperative. The former derives from knowledge of Jewish history (in the broadest possible sense), and the latter is by use of the motivational methods of self-discovery in which students are given the opportunity to find their own concepts, principles, and solutions.

We shall now describe in some detail three categories of Jews who require accurate knowledge of Judaism: (1) Those whom Lewin characterizes as "standing near the margin"; (2) Those whom Kaplan characterizes as "lacking a sense of peoplehood"; and (3) Those whom Prof. Abraham Kaplan characterizes as "lacking a personal identity."

If conditions of birth or conversion to Judaism make one Jewish, being or remaining Jewish is a matter of distinctive individuality. In other words, it is an action that emanates from a voluntary decision. A positive decision may be motivated by a person's family loyalty, status in the Jewish community, conviction resulting from religious commitment, or from knowledge of Jewish culture. There are other reasons that might also be cited. On the other hand, there are conditions that cause negative decisions.

In my active years at SAJS, and previously in association with Jewish youth at Young Judea and Brandeis camps, I did not encounter any young adults* who posed the question, Why should I be Jewish? But when the question was raised by a teacher or leader in group discussions, it always engendered lively interest. Many times strong doubts surfaced, even among some who evidenced religious convictions or national loyalties. On more than one occasion, a person introduced his colloquy with, "I shall be the devil's advocate," perhaps indicating that the question had touched a sensitive nerve.

---

*Except for one pertinent incident that I shall relate later in this text.

The problem I raise here is not hypothetical. Jews who stand near a margin of groups, says Kurt Lewin, are uncertain about their belonging.

> It is characteristic of individuals crossing the margin between social groups that they are not only uncertain about their belonging to the group they are ready to enter, but also about their belonging to the group they are leaving. It is, for example, one of the greatest theoretical and practical difficulties of the Jewish problem that the Jewish people are often, in a high degree, uncertain of their relation to the Jewish group. They are uncertain whether they actually belong to the Jewish group, in what respect they belong to this group, and in what degree.

Lewin's statement can easily be applied to young Jewish adults who cross the boundary between their family and community environments to the environment of a university. I shall not belabor the characteristics of the new environment (or group, which it actually is) except to reiterate what I said earlier: At the university the young adult enters into a lifestyle that is different from the one he lived at home. Because he brings to this new environment consciousness, impressions, loyalties, and habits from his former lifestyle, he does not actually cross the boundary but rather stands near the margin of the two groups, poised and waiting.

Lewin describes his encounter with Jewish students in the Middle West:

> I have heard Jewish students in the Middle West say that they feel more like non-Jewish Midwesterners than like Jews from New York. Since the religious issue has lost importance for Jews and gentiles alike, there does not exist an easily tangible difference between both groups. To preach Jewish religion or nationalism to such Jews is not likely to have any deep effect. To speak about the glorious history and culture of the Jewish people will not convince them either. They would not want to sacrifice their lives and happiness to things past. In places with a limited Jewish population, and particularly among the adolescents, one finds many who are utterly bewildered about why and in what respect they belong to the Jewish group.

How is one to deal with such young adults? Lewin offers a suggestion that has far-reaching implications for the Jewish home and school:

> One might be able to help some of them by explaining that it is not similarity or dissimilarity of individuals that constitutes a group, but interdependence of fate. Any normal group, and certainly any developed and

organized one contains and should contain individuals of very different character. Two members of one family might be less alike than two members of different families; but in spite of differences in character and interest, two individuals will belong to the same group if their fates are interdependent. Similarly, in spite of divergent opinions about religious or political ideas, two persons might still belong to the same group.

It is easy enough to see that the common fate of all Jews makes them a group in reality. One who has grasped this simple idea will not feel that he has to break away from Judaism altogether whenever he changes his attitude toward a fundamental Jewish issue, and will become more tolerant of differences of opinion among Jews. What is more, a person who has learned to see how much his own fate depends upon the fate of the entire group will be ready and even eager to take over a fair share of responsibility for its welfare. The realistic understanding of the sociological facts is very important for establishing a firm social group, especially for those who have not grown up in a Jewish environment.

Ideas to Think About

As I suggested above, Lewin's statement has several implications for Jewish education. One relates directly to the effectiveness of cognitive knowledge upon development of personality. Psychologists define personality as "the integration of all of a person's traits, abilities, and motives, as well as his temperament, attitudes, opinions, beliefs, emotional responses, cognitive styles, character, and morals." It should be obvious that a person's identity relationships with his people is an essential ingredient in his personality. By *people*, I include his family—past and present—his community, and his nation. A Jew's relationship with his people includes all Jews who belong to the category of *a people*. The Jewish students whom Lewin describes as feeling "more like non-Jewish Midwesterners than like Jews from New York" lacked an identity relationship with the Jewish people. It is also to be assumed that they lacked correct knowledge of Judaism and firsthand experience in social, religious, or cultural activities of Jewish group life to give them an "in-group" feeling.

While I take no issue with Lewin's conclusion that it is awareness by the individual Jew that his fate is dependent on other Jews that binds him to his people, I am uncomfortable with his choice of the term *fate*. *Fate* has several connotations, "unfavorable destiny" and "inevitable events predestined by force." In common usage, both meanings are employed.

For historical reasons, however, the term is frequently used in a negative sense to describe tragic conditions in Jewish life. I do not think that Lewin had this semantic reality in mind. In the context of his solution, he uses *fate* to mean belonging to the Jewish people and sharing in their activities.

Unfortunately, awareness of an individual's dependence on his group, in whatever sense, even if it leads to participation in the activities of the group, is insufficient for a Jewish person's relationship with the Jewish people. As for young adults, awareness of their need for dependence upon other Jews may bring them solace in times of discomfort in a non-Jewish environment, but it will not always give them pride in and loyalty to the Jewish people and its historic heritage. This is particularly true of talented youth and adults who need more than a positive sense of being Jewish to enable them to contribute their talents to creative Jewish life. How often have we seen Jews become active in their communities out of fear of anti-Semitism, and when the fears subsided their ties with their people weakened? Similarly, many Jews express their sense of belonging only by making monetary contributions to causes intended to mitigate Jewish suffering from poverty or social and political ills either in their own communities or in Israel. While this is a worthwhile activity in and of itself, it does not activate the permanent bond that insures Jewish continuity. Too often, such philanthropic people are willing to help other Jews to be Jewish while they and their offspring gravitate toward assimilation because they do not, or cannot, draw upon the fundamental aspects of Jewish religion, education, and culture.

Efforts to create awareness of one's interdependence with his group in adolescents should be approached with caution. Teachers of history, Israel, and the Holocaust should realize that Jewish tragedy—whether in the past or present—is less likely to instill in a young person pride in and love for his people than it is to arouse uncertainty, fear, and disappointment. In counseling teachers, I have frequently suggested that whenever they encounter a tragic event, the ordinary method of teaching be reversed by introducing whatever positive outcomes resulted from the event prior to describing the tragedy.

Lewin's remedy for convincing Jews who lack a feeling of belonging to their people that their personal fate does depend on the fate of their group is another way of saying that such people must be reeducated. The question is how can reeducation be achieved? In his essay titled, "Conduct, Knowledge, and Acceptance of New Values," Lewin writes:

The difficulties encountered in efforts to reduce prejudice or otherwise to change the social outlook of the individual have led to a realization that re-education cannot be merely a rational process. We know that lectures or other similar abstract methods of transmitting knowledge are of little avail in changing his subsequent outlook and conduct. We might be tempted, therefore, to think that what is lacking in these methods is first-hand experience. The sad truth is that even first-hand experience will not necessarily produce the desired results. . . . Re-education influences conduct only when the new system of values and beliefs dominate the individual's perception. [Perception is "any insight or intuitive judgment that implies unusual discernment of fact or truth."] The acceptance of the new system is linked with the acceptance of a specific group, a particular role, a definite source of authority as a new point of reference. It is basic for re-education that this linkage between acceptance of new facts or values and acceptance of certain groups or roles is very intimate and that the second frequently is a prerequisite for the first.

6.
Lecture IV: Concepts of Peoplehood

What meaning can Lewin's statement that acceptance of a specific group is a prerequisite for acceptance of the group's system of values (such as beliefs and conduct) have in Jewish education? I should like to propose the following.

In formulating objectives for the Jewish school, peoplehood should be assigned the primary and central ingredient among the component elements that constitute the Jewish civilization. By *civilization*, I include religion, culture, and history. Mordecai M. Kaplan defines civilization as "the cumulative heritage of knowledge, experience, and attitudes acquired by the successive generations of a people in its striving to achieve salvation." Kaplan does not employ the term *salvation* in the Christian sense, which means deliverance from sin, but in the sociological sense. For example, in his magnum opus, *Judaism as a Civilization*, he writes:

> When we study the quest for salvation and the conditions of its fulfillment, we note that salvation presupposes a community which treats the individual as so organic a part of itself that in promoting his life it is aware that it promotes its own. The chief aim of such a community is to help him attain those objectives which constitute for him his complete self-realization.

In other words, Kaplan's view of salvation is realization of potentials, whether by the individual or the group.

Emanating from the central theme of peoplehood should come the definitive ingredients of the people's civilization, which Lewin designated as "the system of values and beliefs." These ingredients are to be taught not only as subjects related to the central theme of peoplehood, but as derivatives of peoplehood. The following constituent elements in the Jewish civilization may be defined as follows:

1. Peoplehood—The entire Jewish people, past, present, and future.

2. Religion—The religion of that specific people.
3. Israel—The state of Israel as the people's national homeland.
4. Hebrew—The people's national language (Also, Yiddish and before that Aramaic have served the people as languages of oral and written communication.)
5. Literature—the people's (Jewish) literature in its national language and Jewish literature written in foreign languages.
6. Art—the people's aesthetic art forms.
7. The people's customs, folkways, and mores.
8. Communal, national, and international institutions—the people's agencies, organizations, and movements designed to meet the people's social and cultural needs, protect the people's rights, and provide justice to the Jewish people the world over.
9. The will to live—the people's will to live as a distinct people, a nation of brothers who share a common fate and a common role in making possible the better life in a better world to come.

The above nine constituent elements in Jewish civilization can influence conduct when, according to Lewin, "the system of values and beliefs dominates the individual's perception" and "is linked with the acceptance of a specific group, a particular role, a definite source of authority as a new point of reference."

Ideas to Think About

Let us return to Lewin's reasons why some people find it difficult to belong to more than one group and to Kaplan's conceptions of peoplehood. Lewin writes:

One reason that an individual finds it difficult to comprehend whether and in what respect he belongs to the Jewish group is the general fact of the manifold overlapping groups one belongs to.... This is one of the main reasons why many individuals ask themselves again and again whether it is necessary to maintain their membership in the Jewish group. They often think that they no longer belong to the group, especially if they endeavor to avoid the disagreeable facts connected with this membership.... They may hope to cross the line individually or to destroy it entirely. One speaks in this connection of a tendency for "assimilation."

In our discussion of the question, Why should I be Jewish?, Lewin's analysis should be given serious consideration. When young adults are exposed to different social groups, some may easily be affected by uncertainty of how to maintain their Jewish loyalties and establish new loyalties to other groups. Uncertainty frequently creates conflict which, in turn, creates tension and leads to troubled behavior. The argument that children brought up in more or less observant homes celebrating religious festivals, had Bar and Bat Mitzvah and/or confirmation, and had attended religious schools should have been immunized against crossing the boundary or assimilation, is fantasy logic.

Assimilation is not a physiological malady. It is a social and mental dilemma created by the individual who chooses to surrender some of the past he carries within himself in the process of acquiring some of the future. An important factor responsible for the dilemma is the past's loss of meaning and the promise of finding significant new meaning in some immediate fashion.

What Is "Meaning"?

Meaning is an interpretation of the significance of an idea, a situation, an act, or an objective. It is also a referential symbol indicating relation, intention, or purpose of an action. It is of personal significance, importance, and value. Meaning to influence conduct must make sense to the individual according to his age and level of comprehension. Thus, meaning of beliefs and practices designed for the elementary school child must be presented on primary levels that are insufficient in exerting influence on the behavior of the adolescent or young adult. In other words, on each level of growth and comprehension, meaning of an idea or practice must respond to the question, What does it mean to me? But the "me" has different implications for the person when he is at the ages of eight to thirteen, when he is in his teens, when he enters college at eighteen, and when he becomes an adult. It would, therefore, be a serious error to believe that the meaning a child acquires on the elementary level would remain meaningful to a person as he moves to each succeeding level of maturity.

In this connection, Prof. Abraham Kaplan writes:

Religious conceptions of many Jews are limited by what they learned in grade school or in preparing for bar mitzvah. Maimonides states as the aim of his *Guide for the Perplexed* "to put an end to the fantasies that come from the age of infancy" (1.26). *Someone who never went beyond nursery rhymes and fairy tales cannot be expected in his adult life to take seriously poetry and literature.*

There is a further aspect to the idea of meaning. Mordecai M. Kaplan touches on it in his discussion of folkways and mores. He points out, "Judaism is identified in the minds of some merely with a system of beliefs dealing with the idea of God and consisting of practices intended to bring the human being into conscious relationship with God."

I take no issue with the above because it is a fundamental theological belief in Judaism. The believer's conception of religion derives from his conviction that God exists and that it is man's duty to establish a conscious relationship with Him. Religious practices, he believes, establish such a relationship. This belief gave sufficient meaning to Jews of past generations as it gives meaning to strict traditionalists in our generation to practice the rituals and observe the *mitzvot*. But these beliefs are no longer accepted by all Jews and certainly not by all young adults. Religious ideas taught to the young child in elementary school on the primary level are to the young adult abstract thoughts or, in Lewin's language, "values without the authority of a definite source of authority."

Without impinging on the religious meaning of God's authority as a frame of reference, Jewish schools should seek ways of offering their students opportunities to develop a sense of peoplehood. Mordecai Kaplan explains a sense of peoplehood as "an awareness of ethnic consciousness which plays as important a role in the lives of human beings as does the awareness of one's ego, of one's family, and of one's community...." How does ethnic consciousness, or the sense of peoplehood, function? According to Kaplan, "It functions through the medium of a living civilization, which is an organic ensemble of the following cultural elements having their rootage in a specific territory, a common tradition, a common language and literature, history, laws, customs and folkways with religion as the integrating and soul-giving factor of those elements."

Kaplan's explanation is more realistic and meaningful than Lewin's suggestion that the young Jew be made to "see how his own fate depends upon the fate of his entire group."

Developing a Time Perspective

Meaning of *peoplehood* in the sense of importance or purpose is one requisite in an educational program of identity of Jewish young adults. It is a goal for the individual that gives him a conception of himself as a Jew and orders him to dedicate himself to the purpose of being Jewish. Another requisite in such a program is a time perspective. A time perspective is a "point of view of a situation which consists of assumptions that influence what the individual perceives and how he interprets his perceptions." For example, Lewin defines "hope as a similarity between the individual's 'level of expectation' and his irreality level of his wishes." He cites an interesting example from the time Hitler came to power in Germany.

> The great majority of Jews in Germany had believed for decades that the pogroms of the Czarist Russia "couldn't happen here." When Hitler came to power, therefore, the social ground on which they stood was swept from under their feet. Naturally, many became desperate and committed suicide; with nothing to stand on, they could see no future life worth living.
> The time perspective of the numerically small Zionist group, on the other hand, had been different. Although they too had not considered pogroms in Germany a probability, they had been aware of their possibility. For decades they tried to study their own sociological problems realistically, advocating and promoting a program that looked far ahead. In other words, they had a time perspective which included a psychological past of surviving adverse conditions for thousands of years and a meaningful and inspiring goal for the future. As a result of such a time perspective, this group showed high morale—despite a present which was judged by them to be no less foreboding than by others. Instead of inactivity and encystment in the face of a different situation—the Zionist with a long range and realistic time perspective showed intimate and organized planning. It is worth noticing how much the high morale of this small group contributed to sustaining the morale of a large section of the non-Zionists of Germany. Here, as in many other cases, a small group with high morale became a rallying point for larger masses.

Ideas to Think About

The expression *time perspective* is not limited to the future, as time is a continuum from the past, through the present, to the future, and *per-*

spective is a view perceived in depth. Thus, developing a time perspective may mean acquiring a point of view that includes the past, the present, and the future. Lewin writes:

> Practically everyone of consequence in the history of humanity—in religion, politics, or science—has been dominated by a time perspective which has reached out far into future generations, and which frequently was based on an awareness of an equally long past.

A time perspective in a curriculum of the Jewish schools for young adults should contain the objective of leading the learner from the present, to the past, and to the future. The philosopher Sidney Hook (*Education for Modern Man*, Dial Press, 1946) writes:

> The past world and the present are so continuous that there are few problems which can be intelligently understood without transcending the immediate context in which they are discovered.
>
> Nothing can be taught which does not at one point or another involve the use of some tradition.... Nothing can be learned which is not continuous with something already known.

He quotes the philosopher Alfred North Whitehead, who said: "The only use of a knowledge of the past is to equip us for the present." The two requisites of meaning and time perspective should be built into the content and into the pedagogic methods of instruction. Because of a literal lack of time available in the Jewish school for in-depth study of any subject, attention should be given to carefully selected content topics which, in the language of R. M. Hutchins, are "abiding and permanent and not shifting conditions." The pedagogic method employed should be able to arouse stimuli capable of creating students' curiosity, interaction with the teacher, eliciting response, and reacting to the content. In the previous lecture notes, I spoke of the problem-solving approach tied to the self-discovery method; "a method in which the students are required to find their own concepts, principles, and solutions rather than receiving them from the teacher or the textbook." I repeat this suggestion because *meaning* and *time perspective* lend themselves to exploration, interaction, and reaction.

Psychologists N. L. Gage and David C. Berliner (*Educational Psychology*, Rand McNally, 1975), explain:

Problem-solving can occur when the student needs to explore topics of emotional significance for himself.... Intellectual understanding is improved as the complexities of the topics emerge.... Topics differ in controversality. On some topics, every informed person is in agreement and the teacher's function may be to have the students arrive at the same position as that held by all informed persons.... Discussion of such topics provide the students with methods of procedure and gives them practice in weeding out bad answers and move toward good ones. This kind of discussion rarely exhausts the subject, rather it progresses with the ascertainment of complexities.

In Summary

To build into the instruction of the Jewish school for adolescents *meaning* of content and the adolescent's age and comprehension levels, *time perspective*, and the *problem-solving* method is of fundamental significance.

7.
Lecture V: Identity and Identification of Certain Jews

The Identity of Certain Jews

Prof. Abraham Kaplan comments on the identity of a third category of Jews.

> Jewish identity in the diaspora is often a vicarious identity finding content by linkage with the attainments of other Jews without regard to the question of what their Jewishness consists. The game of "you know who else?" is widely played: the unexpected Jewish identification of someone in the public eye is revealed, providing the Jewish hearers with a satisfaction to be repaid with another unexpected revelation—if possible one involving an even greater achievement or a more hidden identification. Only minorities take such comfort in the revelation that "he is one of us." A *landsman* is close to us only when we are far from home....
>
> Identity is what makes him (the person) the individual that he is. Identifications do not disclose identity; they conceal it. An identification is an external mark by which a particular person can be distinguished from others.... Identity is the locus to which is referred everything significant in the personality.... We can be insured against loss of our identifications; no one will compensate us for loss of identity....
>
> Identity is not only many sided; it has superficial and deeper layers. Part of every identity is an involuntary self, imposed on us by our social environment. There are Jews whose Jewishness is largely involuntary, either concealed or rejected, or else embraced as a gesture of defiance. There is a peripheral self, neither imposed nor chosen but implicated in doings whose meaning lies elsewhere. Peripheral Jews may appear at High Holiday services or contribute to the United Jewish Appeal, not because doing so has intrinsic significance to them, but because it is part of what it means to them to belong to the Jewish community. The autonomous self is the seat of everything freely and wholeheartedly undertaken, with integration

and self-respect. An autonomous Jew neither submits to being Jewish nor works at it; he simply is Jewish. He is at home with his Jewishness.

There are Jews today whose Jewishness is encompassed by the fact that they are not non-Jews. Said Mendel of Kotzk (Hassidic Rebbe), "If I am only I because you are you, and you are you only because I am I, then I am not I and you are not you."...

Identity is not antecedently; it is a creation, not a discovery. It is not bestowed by others; it is an achievement, not a reward. Being born a Jew marks when the process begins; it is not a manner of completion. We can remain immature in our Jewishness, as we can in more limited dimensions of personality....

Jews have been described as the passionate people; morality is not served by spending our passion on strangers.... Morality begins with caring for one's own. It is no good loving my neighbor as myself if I have turned away from myself.... We can not do justice to more distant relatives if we are uncaring about our close kin.

After Adam had sinned, he ran and hid. God called out, "Where art thou, Adam?" Martin Buber points out that God asked not because He did not know, but because Adam did not know. The answer should have been, "In exile." Adam drove himself out of the Garden of Eden. Man is in exile the moment he hides from the voice that speaks in his innermost being. The deepest alienation is to be a stranger to oneself.

The more fragile our self-respect, the more vulnerable we are to what Buber called group egotism—the ego-imperialism and chauvinism of defensive Jewishness. The enemy within is the hardest to defend against. Jews of Diaspora have more vanity than pride, more concern with how they will appear to others than with their image in their own eyes. They are forever asking themselves, "What will the goyim think?" So-called Israeli pride is the pride that has replaced the other-directed humbleness of the ghetto.

Ideas to Think About

I began the discussion with a definition of *identity* from the point of view of crisis in the lives of young adults who "stand on the margin between social groups and are uncertain about their belonging to either group." I should like to conclude this part of the discussion with Prof. Abraham Kaplan's analysis of the identity crisis as it affects large segments of adult Jews in the community. I shall divide his views into several categories.

Kaplan's Definition of Identity

Genuine identity of a person is the configuration of all the significant elements that constitute his personality. This definition, in a broader sense, is akin to the explanation by William James: "It is the mental and moral attitude in which a person feels most deeply and intensely active and alive.... A voice inside speaks to him and says: 'This is the real me.'"

Kaplan draws a distinction between *identification* and *identity*. Identification is one's recognition; that which provides evidence of one's identity. Identity is the collective aspect of the person's distinctive characteristics. A person or group, according to Kaplan, may lose or change identification but not its identity. This is because "identity is the result of what has been taken into the self." Some aspects taken into the self are through heredity and some through habit transmitted by one generation to the next.

Identity, says Kaplan, has "superficial layers." He cites as examples some people deriving vicarious identity by associating themselves with Jews who have achieved fame for attainments, such as Einstein or other Nobel Prize winners, by saying, "He is one of us!" A second type is what Kaplan describes as "peripheral Jews." These are Jews who might attend High Holiday services. They come not because they are inherently religious, which would mean that their religious beliefs extended to all or at least some phases of life. These same persons frequently contribute to the United Jewish Appeal not because they strongly believe in the Zionist objective of "revival and survival of the Jewish people and its national homeland," but rather because such actions are "part of belonging to the Jewish community." The Jews just described are assigned to the category of *peripheral* since their identity is "superficial" or, better still, not identity at all, but rather identification.

There are also those who are Jews by name or birth or because they are recognized by others as Jews. Their own conception of being Jewish is limited to the realization that they are "not non-Jews." The *halakhic* doctrine that a Jew born of a Jewish mother is automatically Jewish is not disputed by Kaplan; it is interpreted by him. He points out that to be born

Jewish is "only a beginning, not its completion." One can be born Jewish but remain immature in his Jewishness the rest of his life. Identity, he says, is the result of what we have taken into the self. In other words, "We are what we have become and what we make of ourselves."

Kaplan's concept of Jewish identity calls for Jews feeling themselves as members of one family and caring for each other. "Morality begins with caring for one's own. It is no good loving my neighbor as myself if I have turned away from myself."

8.
Lecture VI: Summary of Ideas and Sources Responding to the Question, Why Should I Be Jewish?

The implications in the question, Why should I be Jewish?, may be interpreted to mean: (1) considering the rejection of one's Jewishness; (2) uncertainty as to whether being Jewish permits one also to be something else, such as Jewish and American; and (3) a vagueness concerning what being Jewish should encompass for the individual.

Information explaining the three questions is available in the sources and commentaries of this unit from which teachers and students can draw appropriate answers. The questions as they are presented in the classrooms should be treated as noncontroversial. They should be seen as inquiries whose aim is acquisition of knowledge and comprehension of ideas on which there is general agreement. The discussion method that relies on pro and con expressions of a topic ought not to be used. Instead, the meanings of the topics should be explored through the social process of discussion. Let us take as an example the treatment of implication, What should being Jewish mean to me?

Demonstration of a Lesson

TEACHER: Now that we discussed the question "Why am I Jewish?" and the verdict of the religious law, the *halakhah*, clarifying what makes a person Jewish, I should like to explore the idea behind the law. I shall begin with the question What should being Jewish mean to me?

This question came to my attention in a magazine article about an American Jewish writer. In an interview by a reporter, the writer was asked, "You have been writing about all sorts of people but not about Jews. Is it because you have no interest in Jewish life or in the Jewish people?" The author replied, "In reality, I have a live interest in both, but I never had a clear answer to the question, What being Jewish should mean to me? In other words, I fail to see a purpose in being Jewish." I would like to hear your reactions to the writer's confession. How would you characterize this Jew?

Following a discussion by the students, the teacher continues.

TEACHER: I compliment your thoughtful thinking and now wish to add some comments of my own. The writer's last sentence troubles me. He said that he "fails to see a purpose in being Jewish." The statement suggests that he regards being Jewish as though he had obtained a commodity from a source outside himself, a commodity that could be either kept or discarded at will. This is not the case. As we already know, a person born of a Jewish mother is automatically Jewish and remains Jewish for the rest of his life. The same applies to a convert to Judaism. Once he accepts Judaism, he cannot leave it. This is the verdict of the religious law, the *halakhah*, which is accepted by all Jews—Orthodox, Conservative, and Reform.

At this point, the teacher reviews the source material in this unit that deals with the question Why am I Jewish?

TEACHER: Now that the verdict of the *halakhah* on the matter of being Jewish has been clarified, I should like to explore the idea from which the verdict derives.

Jewish tradition traces this all the way back to the beginning of history, to the time of creation of the universe. According to this tradition, at that time (whenever it was), mankind was created from a single couple. This gives all people, regardless of race, religious beliefs, and nationality, a common origin and inclusive unity. In the course of time, mankind separated into distinct tribes and nations. The division into different entities did not change God's relationship to mankind. His concern with man embraced all tribes and nations. But to one people, Israel, He showed special consideration. Why did He choose Israel?

According to the biblical tradition, early mankind became corrupt. "The earth was corrupt before God; the earth was filled with injustice" (Gen. 6:11). God destroyed mankind by flood, but He spared Noah and his family because "Noah was a righteous man." At a later time, the Torah tells us, "The Lord said the outrage of Sodom and Gomorrah is so great and their sin so grave...." In that generation, He also found one man who lived a righteous life and "the Lord said, I have singled him [Abraham] out that he may instruct his children and his posterity to keep the way of the Lord by doing what is just and right" (Gen. 18:19). God made a covenant with Abraham and with his posterity to be their God and they His people.

Following the Exodus from Egypt, Abraham's offspring, the Israelites, still a collection of individual tribes, arrived at Sinai in the desert. It was there that Moses gave them the Torah, which, according to the biblical tradition, he received from God. The tribes were then united into one people. At this point, God's covenant with Abraham, his son Isaac, and grandson Jacob was renewed with the entire people of Israel.

The people was given the designation, "God's treasured people" and commanded to become "a holy nation." In the Torah, this people is addressed as Am, a term derived from the root "to connect" and "to unite," meaning that they, together with their descendants of all future generations, had been united into one social group. The concept of a "holy nation" is not meant as a title or name but as a task. The commandment reads: "The Lord spoke to Moses, saying: Speak to the whole Israelite community and say to them: You shall be holy, for I the Lord your God am holy" (Lev. 19:1–2). The idea of holiness, say the rabbis, refers to God's attributes of mercy and graciousness. His commandment to the people Israel means that they are to imitate God's actions of mercy and graciousness. In other words, the Torah reveals the ethical nature of God and enjoins the Israelite people to imitate His attributes in their personal lives.

The Talmud, in a passage discussing the command, "You shall be holy, for I the Lord your God am holy," asks: "How can man be like God?" It answers: "As He is merciful so you be merciful; as He clothes the naked, so you clothe the naked; as He visits the sick, so you visit the sick; as He comforts mourners, so you comfort mourners; as He is righteous, so you strive to be righteous; as God is holy so you strive to be holy." Jewish ethics are derived from the concept of holiness. Holiness has been explained as things most important, as perfection containing every kind of perfection.

The rabbis also interpret the commandment cited above in another way. "As God is separate (from the world) so shall Israel be separate," meaning unique or distinctive among the nations of the world. The uniqueness includes ethical distinctiveness, which is purity in thought and in conduct. Holiness in the sense of moral perfection and uniqueness is the idea behind the concept of God having chosen Israel as His "treasured people." The idea of God's "covenant" with the patriarchs and with the entire nation means that holiness is a task imposed on God's "treasured people."

From the beginning of their history, the Jewish people regarded the ideas behind the covenant and their election as a sacred mission—bestowed upon them and upon all future generations of their offspring. This includes every Jew born into a Jewish family or converted to Judaism. This conclusion derives from the following statement made by Moses, which is recorded in the Torah:

> You stand this day, all of you, before the Lord your God—your tribal heads, your elders and your officials, all the men of Israel, your children, your wives, even the stranger within your camp, from the woodchopper to waterdrawer—to enter into the covenant of the Lord your God, which the Lord your God is concluding with you this day, with its sanctions; to the end that He may establish you this day as His people and be your God, as He promised you and as He swore to your fathers, Abraham, Isaac, and Jacob. I make this covenant, with its sanctions, not with you alone, but both with those who are standing here with us this day before the Lord your God and with those who are not with us here today (Deut. 29:9–14).

The rabbis have interpreted the last verse to mean "the covenant is one which must be held to bind not only the living who were present that day, but their distant posterity as well."

The writers claim that because he "fails to understand what Judaism should mean to him," he feels no responsibility to the Jewish people actually mean two things: (1) That he lacks the will to be Jewish. Had he possessed the will, he would have sought and found the correct answer to his question; (2) He feels no sense of duty for the continuation of the Jewish people. Both attitudes are unreasonable. The first, as we have seen above, being Jewish by a person who was born Jewish, is not a matter of personal choice. At his birth, it is the Jewish people who makes him Jewish, and again it is the Jewish people who holds on to him as a member of its social group for the rest of his life. Second, the Jewish people has existed close to four thousand years, and there is no indication that the majority of Jews in the world are prepared to assimilate and disappear.

The minority who lack a desire for the Jews to continue as a distinct people stand "near the margin," unable to shed their Jewishness and become non-Jews.

As Mordecai M. Kaplan writes:

> Such Jews stay forever in the No-Man's Land of the spiritually homeless, and live through agonizing experiences. The individual Jew is a Jew by virtue of the existence of the Jewish people, just as a soldier is such only by virtue of the existence of an army. But a people is not like an army; it cannot be disbanded at will. That should be proof enough that there cannot be Judaism without the continued existence of the Jewish people as an international corporate entity.

Questions Raised in Actual Class Sessions and the Explanations to These Questions

The following questions and answers provide supplementary material that expands on ideas introduced in the text.

Question 1. What is the meaning of Judaism?

STUDENT: I have always been under the impression that *Judaism* means the religion of the Jewish people while *culture* refers to secular or nonreligious things. In your discussion, I have noticed that sometimes you speak of Judaism as religion, but at other times you use the term to describe the culture and civilization of the Jews. What is the real meaning of *Judaism*?

A.K.: Your observation is correct. The dictionary gives the following definitions of Judaism: "Religion; conformity to Jewish rites and practices; the cultural, social and religious beliefs and practices; the whole body of Jews." This practice, according to Mordecai M. Kaplan, can be confusing, inconsistent, and misleading. Kaplan suggests that the term *Judaism* should have the shared meaning of "total Jewish civilization." He writes:

> We ought not speak of the Jewish religion and Judaism as they were synonymous terms. Judaism refers to the whole Jewish civilization, just as Hellenism refers to the whole of Hellenic civilization. Jewish religion, on the other hand, signifies those beliefs and practices centering on the idea of

God, with which the Jewish people assess all elements of its civilization and seeks to implement them. It does interpret all elements of the Jewish civilization as Judaism, as a man's personal idea affects all his conscious behavior.... Jewish religion is that aspect of Jewish civilization which gives it purpose, direction and a definite orientation to the life of nature and of mankind.

Question 2. What is meant by the National Character of the Jews?

In a course titled, "The History, Culture, and Religion of the Jews," which I taught at the University of Pittsburgh, a Protestant minister (who had studied in Israel) posed the following question: "As a student of comparative religions, I have always understood the distinctive Jewish character to be the religion. In Israel, I was introduced to another aspect of 'the national element or character.' At first, I thought that the term *national* refers to the political conditions of the state itself, but I was assured that this was not the case. *National*, I was told, refers to an element in the Jewish character which remains separate from religion but is an integral part of the Jewish collective identity. Could you clarify this conception?"

A.K.: When Jews speak of their *national character*, they mean certain features in the personality of the Jewish people that have shaped their history and are also products of their history. *National character* is akin to the German expression *nationalgeiste*, "the national spirit," meaning a quality or qualities by which a people differentiates itself from all others.

The historian Hans Kohn quotes an explanation of the *national character* by the Swedish count Karl August Ehrensward: "Each nation has a beauty peculiar to it; none deviate from its nature nor from the temperament peculiar to it." Actually, the elements that enter into a people's national character are the aggregate of all the peculiar qualities of its peoplehood. For example, the conception the people has of itself as an entity, its language, culture, the uniqueness of its historical moments, and numerous other qualities.

Mordecai M. Kaplan substitutes the term *peoplehood* for *nationhood* or *national group*. He explains *peoplehood* as follows:

> A people is a chain of generations united by a common history and culture the origin of which can be traced to life in a particular land. To the extent that the various groups with which the individual French-Canadian identifies himself conform to this definition, they may be considered peoples.

The idea that the same person can belong to more than one people is a new one that has emerged with the development of social and cultural democracy. It is a natural outgrowth of the inalienable right to "the pursuit of happiness." This distinguishes the concept of peoplehood from that of political nationhood, since it is obvious that at present one cannot owe political allegiance to more than one national government. But a person may, and in democracies most persons do, identity themselves with more than one spiritual or cultural people....

What makes a group into a people?

Ethnic consciousness makes a group into a people. Ethnic consciousness is not some mysterious entity that hovers over a people. It is the experience which every individual has when he senses and becomes aware of the existence of the people he belongs to as an individual corporate entity. That experience expresses itself as a consciousness of kind or "we-feeling."

The Kabbalists described the unity of the elements that are intertwined in the character of the Jewish people as Israel, God, and Torah. The latter two refer to religion, while the former indicates nationalism or peoplehood.

In sociological language, when we speak of a people's national character, the term *ethos* is employed. *Ethos* is a Greek word meaning custom which, in modern language, is defined as "character, disposition, or basic values peculiar to a specific people, culture, or movement." Religion is part of the ethos, but so are other elements in the people's character. When Jews in Israel speak of the Jewish character, they actually mean the Jewish ethos. To be more specific, the Jewish ethos has two essential elements: One is peoplehood, and the other the Covenant. The first is national existence, and the second is the special role that the nation has to play in history. Religion in Judaism is different from religion in Christianity. Christianity is a faith that does not depend for its existence upon a special people or nation. All it requires is belief in Christ. Judaism is a religion of a distinct people. Without this particular and distinct people, the religion has no meaning and is incapable of existing. The national elements that you found in Israel are elements of the Jewish people's ethos: Am, peoplehood, and Brith, covenant.

The historian Abraham A. Neuman writes:

Judaism appears under two aspects: the universal and the national. As a system of religious thought it is transcendent and universal. As a religious cult, it is characterized by historic association and even geographic coloring. Its ethical principles embrace all mankind; its religious discipline binds only its adherents.... Judaism views theology through the eyes of history in contrast to Christianity, for instance, in which theology is primary and history is secondary.... The indissoluble bond between the people and religion is a basic part of Judaism. Judaism was not given full grown to the Jewish people as was Christianity to the pagan nations. To its adherents, the Jewish religion in essence is not the distillation of the tears and sorrows of others, freely given them by an act of divine grace or acquired through the mysteries of faith. Slowly and painfully over the course of many centuries it was beaten out of the historic experiences of the nation, illumined by the vision of its prophets and sages.... ("Judaism," in *The Great Religions of the Modern World*, Ed. E. J. Jurgi, Princeton University Press, 1967)

When Jews speak of their national character, they have in mind the people Israel as a distinct national entity, their religion, which is "a people's religion," and the land that was promised them for eternal possession. I realize that these concepts might not be easy to comprehend by one who is not Jewish, or even by Jews who are unfamiliar with their people's history.

Question 3. Why should the Jewish people exist?

I was teaching a tenth-grade class at SAJS when a visitor joined us. The person introduced himself as an avid reader of contemporary Jewish literature. The topic being discussed at that session was "Lessons of the Holocaust for American Jews." I read to the class a quotation from the writings of Prof. Emil Fackenheim:

The voice of Auschwitz commands: Jews are forbidden to hand Hitler posthumous victories. They are commanded to survive as Jews, lest their Jewish people perish.... A Jew may not respond to Hitler's attempt to destroy Judaism by himself by cooperating in its destruction. In ancient times, the unthinkable Jewish sin was idolatry. Today, this is the response to Hitler by doing his work.

The visitor asked permission to speak to the students. Permission granted, he posed the following question: "Professor Fackenheim suggests that the most important lesson which the Holocaust teaches us is for the

Jews to rebuild themselves into a nation after Hitler decimated six million of them; otherwise, we will complete Hitler's efforts to destroy the Jewish people. My question is, Why is it important for Jews to exist as a nation? Aren't there enough nations in the world?"

STUDENT: Your question was once asked by one of my teachers in the day school that I attended. He gave the following answer: "It is God's will that the Jewish people shall exist forever. He made this information known to Abraham, which is written in the Torah."

VISITOR: If God ordained that the Jewish people should exist forever, wouldn't God preserve them? Why should it be man's responsibility to do God's work?

At this point, I decided to intervene in the discussion.

A.K.: The answer which the day school teacher gave is the traditional religious reason. I do not dispute it but rather wish to elaborate on it also from a religious point of view. First, let me say that both the question and answer have to do with theology, which is the science that treats religious ideas. Jewish theology is found in the Bible and is expounded by the sages in the Talmudim and Midrashim and by Jewish philosophers like Moses Maimonides and other rabbinic commentators. In their explanations of the Torah, the sages and commentators discuss God's attributes (qualities of character) and His relationship to the universe, to mankind, and to the Jewish people. The following ideas should be helpful in comprehending the question and answer we have just heard.

The sages tell us that "the Torah speaks according to the language of men." By this, they mean that the Torah uses concise and simple language for all kinds of people to understand. But beyond the simple meanings are deep thoughts and hidden ideas that require interpretation. This applies also to God's promises in the Covenant.

One obtuse idea, according to the rabbinic sages, is man's cooperation with God in the acts of creation. At the time of creation, they said, God bestowed on man the ability to participate in His work. "God said to Adam, hitherto I alone was engaged in the work of creation; henceforth, you also must work." In the Midrash, we find the following explanation of this thought. "God did not create at the outset loaves of bread. Rather, He created wheat and man makes them into loaves." In other passages the sages say, "From the very beginning, God desired that man become His partner in creation."

Consider another thought: "Man in the image of God, is possessed of unique attributes that are Divine—reason, freedom, creativeness, and moral goodness. These attributes were not bestowed on man in vain but in order to enable him to participate in the work of God." Thus, Judaism conceives man's relationship to God as that of a partner (a coworker) cooperating with Him in the fulfillment of His purpose.

How do we explain these thoughts? In brief, God inspires man with wisdom, knowledge, and the will to create and maintain a just and righteous society on Earth. Man's share in God's plan depends on his will to choose between obeying and disobeying God's inspiration of knowledge and wisdom. If man obeys, he prospers and survives; if he disobeys, he perishes. This is also the meaning of the promises in the Covenant that God made with the patriarchs and at Sinai with the entire people.

The religion reason for the existence of the Jewish people has been accepted by past generations of Jews as it is accepted by religious believers in our time. Historians and sociologists, however, neither dispute nor affirm the religious explanation but employ a different method for analyzing the reasons that inspire people to exist as social groups. Their method is known as the scientific method of cause and effect. *Cause* refers to forces in the lives of social groups and *effect* to the results that the causes produce. For example, "Gravitation is the cause of a stone falling; malice is the cause of crime." In other words, every change or new existence requires a cause. When historians search for reasons to explain a nation's survival or disintegration, they apply the scientific method to their studies. They examine the roles that the nation's social, political, cultural, economic, or religious conditions played as causes and effects in the nation's existence. Jewish historians follow the same scientific approach.

VISITOR: Would you explain the views of the historians and sociologists as to why the Jews always had and still have the will to exist as a separate nation?

A.K.: I shall try to give two explanations. One is that social groups are not inherently different from individuals. The will to live is a normal instinct of life that the individual person shares with his social group, whether it be a tribe, sect, or nation. It is present even in nations, which, having existed for a time, were subdued by other nations and lost their independence. At their first opportunity to gain independence, they come to life again. For example, Lithuania, a small nation that borders on the Baltic Sea and has a population estimated at 2,800,000 people, traces its existence to the 2nd century C.E. In medieval times, Lithuania was one of the largest states in Europe. In the 18th century, it passed to Russia. Following World War I (1918), it regained independence, established itself as a republic, and revived its ancient language and culture.

The Jewish people received the original impulse to exist as a nation at Mount Sinai when Moses consolidated the twelve tribes into one people. It existed during their conquest of the Promised Land, during the periods of the Kingdom, in Babylonian exile, in the Second Commonwealth (in the Greco-Roman period), in the second Babylonian exile after the fall of the Judean state, and during the two thousand years in Diaspora. Jews have expressed this will in daily prayer and dreamed of the day when God would send the Messiah, redeemer, to return them to their homeland and nationhood. This is the first reason.

The second reason is more complex. Each nation, having received its original impulse from the past, regards its cultural and/or religious heritage as a unique mission or task of universal significance. For example, when Alexander the Great crossed to Asia, he "decided upon a new aim: to unite the men of the earth in a new, peaceful order based not upon ties of blood but upon a community of spirit and civilization." Christianity, which came into being during the Roman period, converted the pagans into Christian nations and imposed on them the doctrines of Christendom. The church acted as a state, and the state assumed the mission of preserving and spreading the Christian faith. A new kind of civilization, termed *modern*, evolved in the eighteenth century. Nations began to think of humanism, which encompassed man's right to think, the sanctity of life, and the conception of history "as a dynamic process towards a more perfect world." The church-state eventually gave way to the national or political-state, and finally the democratic state emerged. This was the start of the modern period of history.

In the United States, religion has been separated from the political state, and democracy is the ideal mission of this nation. In our day, democracy is the mission of all enlightened nations, but there is also another mission in the offing, communism. The communist mission is fostered and spread by totalitarian nations, such as the Soviet Union and its satellites. Thus, when we speak of a mission or role espoused by Judaism, we must not regard it as unusual but rather as a normal phenomenon in the history of mankind.

VISITOR: You spoke of a Jewish mission. How did the Jews understand their mission?

A.K.: *Mission* is an act of sending or being given a duty to perform or a service to be done. In theological language, it means destined, or chosen to spread religious teaching. In some instances, *mission* is replaced by *vocation*, which means a calling signifying "any occupation or pursuit for which one qualifies oneself or to which one devotes one's time or life." When Jews use the term *mission* as an essential element in their purpose of existence, they mean their special role in history, which is embodied in the covenant between God and the people Israel. As seen above, first God chose a family (the patriarchs) to whom He designated a special role in history. The role contained two elements. When the family enlarged to become a people, it would become an ideal or model nation, then God's blessings or privileges to that nation would extend through that nation to all humanity. When in the course of time the family enlarged and qualified as a nation, God freed them from Egyptian bondage, led them into the wilderness, and at Sinai renewed the covenant with the entire people. The renewed covenant contained more than promises. It included a complete social, legal, and religious system as a way of life for the Israelite nation and a social or moral system for all other nations. Israel, by accepting the renewed covenant at Sinai, also accepted the mission of bringing the divine instructions to other nations. The prophet Isaiah describes Israel's mission as follows:

> For He [God] said: It is too little that you should be My servant.... I will also make you a light of the nations, that My salvation may reach the ends of the earth (49:6).

To what extent have the Jews fulfilled their divine mission? With regard to themselves, they fulfilled the first requirement by preserving their peoplehood. From the time of Abraham to the present, each generation of Jews cherished the will to exist not only as a distinct national entity, but also as the people that was charged with the role of bringing the divine instruction to mankind. From a traditional religious standpoint, the purpose of this mission was "to establish God's Kingdom on earth." In non-theological language, this means, as modern thinkers explain, to improve the quality of human life and transform and perfect the society of mankind. Irrespective of their loss of the homeland, which led to their dispersion among the nations of the world where they lived as immigrants and minorities under the most unbearable conditions of hate and persecution, their will to exist overcame all obstacles and kept them alive as a nation among nations.

I might add that to a great extent the Jews fulfilled also the second function of their mission to serve as "a light of the nations." To repeat a statement in Prof. A. A. Neuman's essay:

> Christianity and Islam are the Jews' daughter religions. Jewish teachings recognized Israel's spiritual kinship with them. It has regarded these dynamic conquering faiths as carriers of Divine truths to the nations of the world.... They were unconsciously—but by God's design—Israel's apostles to the heathen nations. They were the active agents spreading the basic truths which God revealed to Israel in forms which were more readily assimilable to the nations because of their pagan background....

Source Material for Lesson Planning

Explanations to Questions Raised in Seminars

Topic: Jewish Self-Hatred

QUESTION: I have recently come across the phrase *Jewish self-hatred*. How authentic is this accusation among Jews, and what does it really mean?

A.K.: Let me begin with a definition of the expression. The anthropoligist Raphael Patai explains:

> Studies carried out among such groups—e.g. blacks, Irish, French Canadians, and Jews—have shown that each of them tends to develop negative self-stereotypes. The negative features in this self-stereotype can be so strong that they assume the character of self-hatred. Kurt Lewin's explanation of the phenomenon was that in low-status minority groups, the desire arises for the respect and rewards enjoyed by the higher-status majority. This supplies the impetus to leave the low-status group and become part of the higher-status majority. When the way to accomplish this is found

barred, frustration is generated which, in turn, gives rise to aggression. The aggressions cannot be directed against its logical target, the high-status majority, because it is powerful and still remains the ideal, albeit unattainable. Therefore it is directed instead against one's own low-status minority group which one is prevented from leaving, and ultimately, against oneself. Thus hatred of one's own group, and of oneself as a member of it, is developed.

Kurt Lewin devotes a chapter in a book of essays to "Self-Hatred among Jews." To quote a few of his comments:

> Jewish self-hatred is both a group phenomenon and an individual phenomenon.... The self-hatred of a Jew may be directed against the Jews as a group, against a particular fraction of the Jews, against his own family, or against himself. It may be directed against Jewish institutions, Jewish mannerisms, Jewish language, or Jewish ideals. There is an almost endless variety of forms which Jewish self-hatred can take.

Mordecai M. Kaplan categorizes such Jews as "marginal."

> Marginal Jews regard Judaism as a liability and a misfortune. Since they cannot advocate its forcible suppression, they would like to devise for it some kind of euthanasia or death-kiss. "If only Jews were not so stubborn, and permitted themselves to be quietly and blissfully absorbed by the rest of mankind!" they reason. "That would put an end once and for all to the Jewish problem which bedevils the world and upsets everybody's peace of mind."
>
> They are known as Jews, least by what they themselves are or do, more by the company they keep, and most by their antecedents. Some belong to temples; their membership, however, is motivated not by religious convictions but by loyalty to the memory of parents, or by the desire to conform to social expectation. As a rule, to which there are few exceptions, these Jews are abysmally ignorant of the Jewish past and of its cultural treasures. They may be highly literate otherwise, but as Jews they are not even embarrassed at being illiterate. Everything connected with Judaism is for them an exotic orientalism which is entirely out of place in, and out of step with, the occidental way of life....

QUESTION: What can be done to prevent self-hatred in teenagers?

A.K.: Kurt Lewin gives an interesting answer:

To counteract fear and make the individual strong to face whatever the future holds, there is nothing so important as a clear and fully accepted belonging to a group whose faith has a positive meaning. A long-range view which includes the past and the future of Jewish life and links the solution of the minority problem with the problem of the welfare of all human beings, is one of the possible sources of strength. A strong feeling of being part and parcel of the group and having a positive attitude toward it is, for children and adults alike, the sufficient condition for avoidance of attitudes based on self-hatred. To build up such feeling of group belongingness on the basis of active responsibility for the fellow Jews should be one of the outstanding policies in Jewish education.... Our children should be brought up in contact with Jewish life in such a way that phrases like "the person looks Jewish" or "acts Jewish" take on a positive tone.

Topic: The Jewish Image of the Jewish People

QUESTION: Jews are well aware of the image that non-Jews have of the Jewish people. However, one rarely hears of the image that Jews have of themselves. Have Jewish intellectuals ever considered the question, What is the Jewish image of the Jews?

A.K.: I don't know what you mean by *intellectuals* nor in what period of history you place the intellectuals. As to the topic, I assure you it is dealt with in every phase of Jewish literature beginning with the Bible, through the Talmudim, Midrashim, commentaries on the two, philosophical treatises, literary and historical writings to the present in a variety of languages in endless time and space. It is therefore obvious that I could not answer this question as a general statement. However, I shall confine myself to an explanation of several basic ideas that came down from the past and are still the correct answers to your question.

The Jewish image of themselves has always been from a perspective of values consisting of attitudes toward the world of nature and humankind. In more specific terms, it came from a strong faith in God, faith in Israel's destiny, that is, the role it was ordained to play in history as a model people, and faith in themselves as a distinct and unique people.

Faith in God

Faith in God meant reliance upon God and trust in Him. He had chosen them as His people through His deeds in history and promised to preserve them as His people through His deeds in history. Trust in God stems from His moral attributes and holiness. In the Torah, God reveals His attributes as merciful, gracious, slow to anger, abundant in kindness and truth, keeping loving kindness to a thousand generations, forgiving iniquity and sin who will not clear the guilty (Exod. 34:6–7).

Another quality of God's character that kept their faith firm in Him has been the belief in His transcendence and immanence. *Transcendence* means otherness and independence of the world of nature. The world is dependent upon God, but God is not dependent upon the world. *Immanence* means "that there is no element or phase of existence that does not reflect His presence and activity." The prophet Jeremiah explains this connection between God and mankind: "Am I only a God near at hand—says the Lord—and not a God far away? If a man enters a hiding place, do I not see him? For I fill both heaven and earth—declares the Lord" (23:23–24).

The idea of Israel's faith in God is explicated by Rabbi Isidore Epstein (*The Faith of Judaism*, Soncino Press, 1954):

> The unfolding of divine purpose in history, which Judaism bids us to discern, is nowhere made so manifest as in the history of the Jewish people, the people whom God has chosen as the special instrument for the fulfillment of His purpose. The whole history of Israel is shot through with the presence of the divine. "Here," in the words of Professor Peake, "God who is never absent from history strikes into its stream with an intense energy." Hoe else are we to account for the unique place this small nation has come to occupy in the history of mankind, and for the all-pervasive influence of its religious thought and moral teaching? Among what other people do we find that intimacy with God, that knowledge of His character and insight into His purpose, which Israel derived from the succession of those peerless prophets who made known and justified the ways of God to man? And what of the peculiar historical destiny of the Jewish people? Where in the annals of mankind are we to find a parallel to that amazing survival and miraculous emergence of the Jewish people into Statehood after two thousand years of exile, dispersion, martyrdom, and suffering? How can we account for all this except by the fact that God has chosen Israel as the people to serve His eternal purpose, and that, in some unique sense, He is ever present in their wonderful history?

Faith in the Role Which Destiny Bestowed on Them

As seen above, the essence of this idea is in the covenant. For individual Jews, as for the nation, the message of the covenant has always been the purpose of their existence. They saw themselves as instruments to spiritualize the world through a covenant relationship that God had established with their ancestors. In biblical language, this ideal is expressed as a vocation or task "to establish God's Kingdom on earth." In other words, God and Israel have entered into a partnership to make the world of men what God had intended it to be at the time of creation. Because mankind either lacked knowledge of the idea that the Creator had for the world or failed to understand His intent, it corrupted its ways and "the earth was filled with lawlessness." Punishment by destruction of a flood did not bring mankind to its senses. So, the course of time, God decided to spiritualize man's world. He chose one man whom He sent on "a quest for spiritual truths." He chose this man's offspring as His people and revealed His plan for mankind. He gave them instructions, laws, injunctions, and a land of their own in which to establish a social order to comply with His requirements of mankind.

The election of Israel and the revelation of the divine instructions (Torah) signified two tasks imposed upon them: One, that they remain a distinct nation possessing God's spiritual truths; and two, that they share these truths with the rest of mankind. The first task was clearly spelled out to the Israelite people at Sinai and thereafter on their journey of forty years from Egypt to the Promised Land. The second task was clarified by Israel's prophets:

> Thus said God the Lord,
> Who created the heavens and stretched them out,
> Who spread out the earth and what it brings forth,
> Who gave breath to the people upon it
> And life to those who walk thereon:
> I the Lord, in My grace, have summoned you,
> And I have grasped you by the hand.
> I created you, and appointed you
> A covenant-people, a light of nations—
> Opening eyes deprived of light,
> Rescuing prisoners from confinement,
> From the dungeons those who sit in darkness.
> I am the Lord, that is My name; . . . (Isa. 42:5–8).

This has been the image that Jews have of their mission or role bestowed on them by destiny.

Faith in Their Distinctiveness and Uniqueness

The Torah confers upon Israel the qualities of distinctiveness and uniqueness. Martin Buber describes these qualities in his essays "Nationalism" and "The Two Foci of the Jewish Soul." In the first essay, he writes:

> Judaism is not merely being a nation. It is being a nation, but because of its own peculiar connection with the quality of being a community of faith, it is more than that. Since Jewry has a character of its own, and a life of its own, just as any other nation, it is entitled to claim the rights and privileges of a nation. But we must never forget that it is, nevertheless, a *res sui generis* (unique), which, in one very vital respect, goes beyond the classification it is supposed to fit into.
>
> A great event in their history molded the Jews into a people. It was when the Jewish tribes were freed from the bondage of Egypt. But it required a great inner transformation to make them into a nation. In the course of this inner change, the concept of government of God took on a political form, final for the time being, that of the "anointed" kingdom, that is, the kingdom as the representative of God....
>
> We Jews are a community based on memory. A common memory has kept us together and enabled us to survive. This does not mean that we based our life on one particular past, even on the loftiest of pasts; it simply means that one generation passed on to the next a memory which gained in scope—for new destiny and new emotional life were constantly accruing to it—and which realized itself in a way we call organic. The expanding memory was more than a spiritual motif; it was a power which sustained, fed, and quickened Jewish existence itself. I might even say that these memories realized themselves biologically, for in their strength the Jewish substance was renewed. (Ibid. *Israel and the World*, Schocken Books, 1948)

To comprehend the above quotations is to realize that Buber does not preach a religious philosophy but analyzes, interprets, and speaks as one man to all men.

N. N. Glatzer, in his introduction to his collection of Buber's essays (*The Way of Response*, Schocken Books, 1966), writes:

To whom does Buber speak? Naturally, to everyone who cares to listen. But actually to whom? Not to the philosophers as philosophers, not to theologians as theologians, but to the human person in both and in everyone. Not to those who argue well and master the art of intellectual debate, but to those who in speech and answer are able to establish communion.

In the second essay, Buber begins with a definition of the word *faith*. He makes a distinction between "cult, ritual, and moral—religious standards, and faith which means trust and loyalty." He explains, "I do not start from a Jewish theology, but from the actual attitude of faithful Jews from the earliest days down to our own time." In other words, Buber admits that what he is trying to formulate is an analysis of those whose faith in God affected their personal lives and is visible in popular religion. "The truth of the history of religion is the growth of the image of God, the way of faith."

Buber continues by pointing out that "the question has often been raised whether a Jewish dogmatic does or does not exist." He suggests that the question should rather be about "the relative power of dogma in Judaism." Citing Maimonides's thirteen articles of faith, which have been included in the liturgy, he concludes that there are dogmas in Judaism. "But dogma remains of secondary importance. In the religious life of Judaism, primary importance is not given to dogma, but to the remembrance and the expectation of a concrete situation: the encounter of God and man." He describes this encounter as "the dialogical situation.... The fealty (loyalty) of the Jew is the substance of his soul. The living God to whom he has pledged himself appears in infinite manifestations in the infinite variety of things and events; and this acts as an incentive and as a steadying influence upon those who owe him allegiance. In the abundance of his manifestations, they can ever again recognize the One to whom they have entrusted themselves and pledged their faith...."

How does Buber describe the dialogical situation between God and man?

> In this dialogue, God speaks to every man through the life which he gives him again and again. Therefore man can only answer God with the whole of life—with the way in which he lives his given life. The Jewish teaching of the wholeness of life is the other side of the Jewish teaching of the unity of God. Because God bestows not only spirit on man, but the whole of his existence, from its "lowest" to its "highest" levels, man can fulfill the obligations of his partnership with God by no spiritual attitude, by no worship,

on no sacred upper story; the whole of life is required every one of its areas and everyone of its circumstances. There is no true human share of holiness without the hollowing of the everyday. . . .

Another idea in Buber's essay about man's partnership with God begins with the following statement:

> The second focus of the Jewish soul is the basic consciousness that God's redeeming power is at work everywhere and at all times, but that a state of redemption exists nowhere and at no time. The Jew experiences as a person what every openhearted human being experiences as a person: the experience, in the hour when he is most utterly shaken, of a breath of above, the nearness, the touch, the mysterious intimacy of light out of darkness; and the Jew, as part of the world, experiences, perhaps more than any other part, the world's lack of redemption. He feels this lack of redemption against his skin, he tastes it on his tongue, the burden of the unredeemed world lies on him. . . . The Rabbi of Koznitz used to pray, "If you do not yet wish to redeem Israel, at any rate redeem the goyim."

The apocalyptics (prophets who taught that a future disaster would destroy the world) wished to predict an unalterable, immovable future event; they were following Iranian conceptions in this point. According to the Iranians, history is divided into equal cycles of thousands of years, and the end of the world, the final victory of good over evil, can be determined with mathematical accuracy. Not so the prophets of Israel. They prophesy "for the sake of those who return" (Bab. Talmud 34b). That is, they do not warn of something that will happen in any case but that will happen if those who called upon to turn do not turn.

The Book of Jonah is a clear example of what is meant by prophecy. After Jonah tries in vain to flee from the task God had given him, he is sent back to Nineveh to prophesy its downfall. But Nineveh turns and God changes its destiny. Jonah is vexed that the word for whose sake the Lord has broken his resistance had been rendered void; if one is forced to prophesy, one's prophecy ought to stand. But God is of a different opinion; He will employ no soothsayer but messengers to the souls of men—the souls that are able to decide which way to go and whose decision is allowed to contribute to the forging of the world's fate. Those who turn cooperate in the redemption of the world.

Man's partnership (with God) in the great dialogue finds its highest form of reality at this point. It is not as though any definite act of man could draw grace down from heaven; yet, grace answers deed in unpredictable ways, grace unattainable, yet not self-withholding. It is not as though man has to do this or that to hasten the redemption of the world—"He that believeth shall not make haste" (Isa. 28:16); yet those who turn, cooperate in the redemption of the world. The extent and nature of the participation assigned to the creature remain secret. "Does that mean that God cannot redeem His world without the help of His creatures? It means that God does not will to be able to do it. Has God need of man for His work? He wills to have need for man...."

The Dream of Messianism

Buber's idea of the prophetic conception of *"redemption"* leads to a third ideal (the former two being "the election of Israel" and "the covenant") known as Messianism, which became an essential doctrine of Judaism. As an ideal in which Jews believed, it is a product of the Second Commonwealth, but in its original form it appears in the Bible in the word *Meshiah*, "anointed," and refers to the King and High Priest who were anointed with oil. At the time of King David, the idea arose that the House of David would reign over Israel forever. In the Persian period, the doctrine that the House of David would again rule over Israel became the symbol of the redeemer-Messiah who would bring justice and peace to the world.

Prior to the destruction of the First Temple, the prophet Isaiah envisioned a time in "the End of Days" when God "will judge among the nations and arbitrate for many peoples, and they shall beat their swords into plowshares and their spears into pruning hooks; nation shall not take up sword against nation; they shall never again know war" (Isa. 2:4).

In the Second Commonwealth, this vision assumed eschatological and messianic meaning:

> In Jewish eschatology, at the end of the Second Temple era, national hopes mingled with more universal vision. The End of Days was not only the time when Israel would be purified and its enemies punished, but also the day when all men and all nations would be judged. Even in the physical sphere there would be a great change; this would pass away and a new, wonderful one would arise in its place. Concurrent with the universalism there was also a development in the direction of individualism; the vision of the End of Days was not only an answer to the hope for national redemption but

also to the sufferings of the individual. The fullest expression of this was a belief in the resurrection of the dead. (A *History of the Jews*, edited by H. H. Ben-Sasson, Harvard University Press, 1976)

In that period the hope arose that a Davidic Messiah would redeem the Jews from Roman occupation. This led to the rise of Messianic movements and numerous pretenders to that office.

In the course of the centuries, belief in a Messiah grew and developed into a variety of complex religious, philosophical, mystical, and political visions and interpretations. The overall traditional conception upon which the idea of Messianism was nurtured is formulated as follows: "The Messiah was expected to attain for Israel the idyllic blessings of the prophets; he was to defeat the enemies of Israel, restore the people to the land, reconcile them with God, and introduce a period of spiritual and physical bliss. He was to be a prophet, warrior, judge, king, and teacher of Torah" (*Encyclopedia Judaica*, Vol. 11, pages 1407–1427).

The underlying idea of redemption in the doctrine of the Messiah has prevailed in a variety of forms and concepts. In modern times, one view replaced the personal Messiah with a Messianic Age in which the prophetic vision of a perfect world will come into being. Another view has been suggested by Mordecai M. Kaplan. He writes:

We can no longer believe that any person, or semidivine being, is Divinely destined to rule as the Messiah and usher in the millennium. Nevertheless, the idea of the Messiah can still figure symbolically to express the valid belief in the coming of a higher type of man than this world has yet known. This is how the prophet Isaiah conceived of the type of man the Messiah would have to be.

> The spirit of the Lord shall alight upon him:
> A spirit of wisdom and might,
> A spirit of counsel and valor,
> A spirit of devotion and reverence for the Lord:
> He shall not judge by what his eyes behold,
> Nor decide by what his ears perceive.
> Thus he shall judge the poor with equity
> And decide with justice for the lowly of the land.
> He shall strike down a land [ruthless] with the rod of his mouth,
> And slay the wicked with the breath of his lips.
> Justice shall be the girdle of his loins,
> And faithfulness the girdle of his waist (11:1–5).

Due to the tendency of the human mind to personify its hopes and embody them in concrete images, Judaism projected the ideal man of the future into the image of the Messiah.... It is appropriate to project our hopes for mankind on a future society, or era, than on any individual past or future. That is why non-Orthodox prayerbooks contain prayers for the Messianic era, but not for the advent of a personal Messiah.

Not all modern thinkers accept Kaplan's interpretation. Some are of the opinion that history cannot be trusted to improve mankind without the intervention of God. Several religious Zionist movements believe that the establishment of the state of Israel and the ingathering of the exiles are signs of *athaltah ha-geulah*, "a beginning of the redemption."

The anthropologist Emanuel Patai (*The Jewish Mind*, Charles Scribner and Sons, 1977) writes:

> Deferred gratification is the psychological mechanism which made it possible, inevitable, for the Jew to hold on to the hope of the coming of the Messiah through two millennia of painful Diaspora life. Jewish Messianism was but the enlargement to national dimensions of the individually internalized conviction that one must bear hardships in the present so as to reap rewards in the future. For the individual, the time of future rewards was either later in life, or in afterlife, or vicariously in the achievements of one's children. For the people as a whole, it was the Days of the Messiah, the great futurity, which although it never arrived, was always just around the corner. In this eschatological view of deferred gratification, the suffering of the present, of the Exile, was a necessary precondition to the triumph of the future. And just as the certainty of the individual reward would come kept the individual Jew working at his unavoidable and self-imposed tasks, so the conviction that redemption was a fact of the future made Jewish survival in every doleful present a matter of preordained destiny.

Epilogue
Teaching Biblical Personalities as History Questions Raised in a Seminar on Methods of Teaching Bible as History

After a series of lectures in the Enrichment Seminars, teachers requested explication of meaning and suggestions for methodological application of the following statements I had made in the lectures:

"In teaching biblical history, don't bring the past to the learner; lead the learner to the past."

"History informs directly and moralizes indirectly; the Bible moralizes directly and informs indirectly."

A.K. The past is distance, the present is nearness. The learner in nearness. Whatever he knows of the past is retained in his memory, and whatever new information he acquires of the past resides in his imagination. When Abraham, for example, is brought out of the past, he emerges from a distance with which the learner has had little, if any, contact. He appears as an imaginary figure in an unfamiliar and imaginary environment. Since the purpose of discovering Abraham, who lived long ago, is to establish a personal relationship between the learner and the patriarch, it might be advisable to reverse the teaching process and lead the learner to Abraham. In a broad sense, this should mean leading the learner in search of his family's antecedents who were his own original grandparents.

Concepts and Methods

A person is neither born nor lives out his life as a clean slate. Human nature is what heredity transmits and the environment manipulates. To quote psychologists, "Studies in selective breeding show that human beings do not enter the world as *tabula rasa*, a blank tablet. Instead, they are born with certain abilities and propensities that are further accentuated by the environment.... Through increased awareness of the fact that individual differences exist, that they are of great magnitude, to a fair degree, they are of hereditary nature."

I should like to connect the idea of hereditary abilities and propensities with two other ideas. First, the idea that the "human self wishes to know its own nature and understand what constitutes our individual identity" (Nozick). I should like to connect this idea with the idea that the self wants to know its antecedents, who share qualities of themselves with the self of the inquirer. Second is the idea of interrelationship between the individual and his family. I am referring to the institutional family in which the family's wishes and hopes influence the member's feelings and behavior. In such a family, interest in and loyalty to members of the kinship unit extend beyond those who are presently alive, but also to those who lived long ago. The Jewish family has always been a consanguineous organization in which blood relatives occupy the central position. Thus, if we accept these assumptions, a person's curiosity of his family who is alive or dead is a natural impulse in human nature. Leading the learner to his antecedents the patriarchs should be a direct way of establishing motivation for his study of his antecedents.

By identifying the Jewish people as the learner's consanguineous family, I follow an ancient Jewish tradition. In Jewish parlance, Abraham is not described as "the first Jew," nor as the first prophet, not even the first man who discovered the One God. He has been given the title of Abraham Avinu, our father. The three patriarchs are called Avot, and their wives, Imo'oth, mothers. The first blessing in the Amidah begins, "O Lord Our God and God of our fathers, God of Avraham, God of Isaac, and God of Jacob." In the Torah, the origins of the Jewish people are traced to a family with parents and children. In Deuteronomy we read, "Yet it was to your fathers that the Lord was drawn in His love for them, so that He chose you, their lineal descendants, from among all the peoples" (Deut. 10:15). The characterization of Israel as a family-nation is maintained all through the biblical literature. Even the designation of Am, translated as people, attests to this. Am derives from a root "to assemble," "to unite." In the Torah, it has the meaning of uniting the tribes and families into a people. The same holds true of the term Goi as applied to Israel, meaning combining and uniting as an assembly.

How Is the Learner Led to the Past?

I cannot postulate a definitive method. At best, I can recall two approaches that I found effective in my experience of teaching a course in the early history of the Jewish people on the secondary and college levels.

The Secondary Level

In "Lecture Notes, Talks to Teachers," I have recorded the following experience:

Upon visiting a class of teenagers, I noticed a description on the blackboard that read, "Today's lesson is about Abraham, the first Jew." I asked the teacher's permission to speak to the class. Permission granted, I explained to the students that in our school, it is customary to team teach. Therefore, today I shall team teach with their teacher.

I began by asking, "Who in this class remembers his great-great-great-grandfather?"

STUDENT: Do you mean who has seen his great-grandfather or heard about him?

A.K.: Either seen or heard.

No response.

A.K.: Since no one has seen or heard about his great-great-great-grandfather, I shall describe him to you. Your great-great-great-grandfather lived a very long time ago, let us say in the Middle Ages. He lived in a beautiful castle surrounded by meadows, fields, and forests. He was clean shaven but wore a thick mustache. Instead of a cloth coat, he wore a coat of armor. One sunny morning, he left his castle, mounted a beautiful stallion, and with spear in hand proceeded on a journey of several hundred miles to rescue a fair lady. How many of you agree that this man could have been your great-great-great-grandfather?

STUDENT: You're talking about a knight.

A.K.: You are right. Couldn't your grandfather have been a knight?

SEVERAL VOICES: No, he couldn't, because he was a Jew, and Jews weren't knights.

STUDENT: But he could have traveled to save a lady if she had fallen into the hands of the Christians who tried to convert her.

A.K.: You, too, are right. Now I shall describe another image of your grandfather. He was born and raised in a small town, and like his parents was very poor. He had a beard and *pe'oth* (earlocks). His head was always covered by a hat or skullcap. Since the age of five, he had attended school and each morning, afternoon, and evening went with his father to the synagogue to pray. He had three sons, and after their Bar Mitzvahs he said to his wife, "Sarah, our sons are bright and eager to study Torah, but they have outgrown the schools in our town. We shall, therefore, have to move to a bigger city where there are better schools for them to attend."

His wife replied, "But, Reuben, how could we earn a living in the big city? We don't know any people there and nobody knows us. I think we ought to remain in this town."

Reuben answered his wife, "Sarah, we must not permit the problem of making a living to interfere with our sons' study of Torah. God will provide a livelihood for us. When people hear that we gave up our livelihood for our children's education, they will help us."

A few months later, Reuben, Sarah, and their children climbed into a covered wagon and traveled a long distance to the big city, where they found several good schools for their children and settled there.

STUDENT: Did the people in the big city help them?

A.K.: Of course, they did. Do you think Jews would neglect a Jew who wanted his children to become learned in Torah? Now, I ask you, could you imagine this man being your great-great-great-grandfather?

CLASS: Yes!

This parable offers many possibilities for discussion, but my purpose in telling it to the class was to lead the children to the past and make their grandfathers living persons to them.

A Visit to Abraham in the Torah

Step One

The second approach I used on the college level was a course of study titled "The Religion and Culture of the Jews," at the University of Pittsburgh. I have also demonstrated this method to teachers at SAJS and recommended it without reservation for eighth- and ninth-grade teenagers. To assist teachers who lack a knowledge of ancient history and archaeology, I have prepared numerous monographs containing adequate information on both subjects to be used in preparing their lesson plans. I also provided up-to-date bibliographies of books that are available at the SAJS library.

Preview

Students can be led to the origins of their Jewish people by establishing a live connection with Abraham as their personal grandfather. One way of accomplishing this objective is by posing and answering the question, What makes one Jewish? The answer is, "Every Jewish child traces his lineage through his mother to the patriarch Abraham." A male convert to Judaism accepts the name Ben Avraham, "son of Avraham," and a female convert, Bath Avraham, "daughter of Avraham." This is the verdict of Jewish religious law, the Halakhah. Jewish law goes even further. It ordains that one who is born a Jew, or a Gentile who converts to Judaism, cannot terminate his or her connections with the Jewish people. In the eyes of the Halakhah, they remain Jewish for the rest of their lives, even though they may have been converted to another religion. In sociological terminology, this type of kinship unit is known to exist in a consanguine family, i.e., a family in which the emphasis is upon blood relationship rather than upon marital relationship. This is the only positive explanation that is both reasonable and meaningful for young and old alike. It also answers such questions frequently asked by children: "I am not religious. Am I still Jewish?"; "My father doesn't believe in God. Is he still Jewish?"; "My sister intermarried. Is she still Jewish?"

On the child's and young adult's levels, the idea beyond the religious verdict is that the Jewish people never gives up on any person who belongs to that people. As in Judaism each person is precious to the human race, so is a Jew precious to the Jewish people. This applies even to the Jew who converts to another religion. He is an apostate, a sinner, but in the eyes of the Jewish people and the religion, he remains a Jew forever.

Step Two

The second step is a journey to Abraham, which we follow on the road of the biblical tradition according to the Book of Genesis.

From one standpoint, the purpose of the first biblical book, Genesis, is to portray the origins of the Jewish people. But it does not begin with the first Jew, Abraham. The first eleven chapters are devoted to primeval history, which is introduced with the creation of the cosmos and of man and woman in forty-six verses. With the exception of the institution of the Sabbath (God resting on the seventh day from which derives the commandment "to observe the Sabbath day") and God's instruction to the human pair, "Be fruitful and increase," the text does not moralize. But as soon as the information about creation of the cosmos is completed, the story of God and man couched in primeval history begins and continues to the time God chose Abraham.

What did the biblical tradition with to teach through primeval history? For our purpose, the following explanation is appropriate: To prepare the ground for a kind of new relationship between God and man that began with Abraham.

God created man in His image, which, according to rabbinic interpretation, means that He gave him the divine qualities of comprehension, discernment, and free will. He put him in charge of the world (Earth) that he inhabited, hoping that he would use his divine attributes to good advantage. But Adam and Eve sinned against God. As time continued, other people sinned even to a greater extent. Cain slew his brother, Abel; Lamech killed a man; divine beings took human wives; and, by the time of Noah, "the earth was corrupt," and "the Lord regretted that He had made man on earth." In each case, God's response to sinning man was that of punishment and forgiveness. He punished Adam and Eve but kept them alive; He protected Cain against those who would take vengeance on him. He destroyed the generation in which Noah lived by a flood but swore never again to wipe out mankind.

But neither punishment nor forgiveness brought men to their senses. A new generation decided to build a city and a tower to reach the sky, which alludes to "man's folly" in building the religious temple in Babylon. "God dispersed the people from there over the whole earth." In primeval history, man's relationship with God was rebellious. But God's relationship to man took a turn away from punishment and even from dealing with humanity as a whole. Mankind can be saved, determined God, by a single man who would "instruct his children and posterity to keep the way of the Lord by doing what is right and just." The man chosen by God for that mission was Abraham.

Step Three

Who was Abraham? Where did he come from? What kind of person was he? These are important questions. First, the biblical tradition establishes him as the first grandfather of all future generations of Jews. Second, no other ancient nation has preserved such detailed historical records of its early beginnings as the Jews. This means that the biblical traditions in Genesis give full details of the first four generations of the Hebrews who were also known as Israelites. Historians and archaeologists consider the traditions historically true, and a large part of them actually go all the way back to the time of the patriarchs. Therefore, the above questions can be answered with a good deal of accuracy.

Who was our grandfather Abraham, and where did he come from? In chapter eleven, tradition traces Abram (this was his original name, which was later changed to Abraham) to Noah's son Shem (from Shem derives the term Semites). From Shem, a straight line is drawn consisting of nine names that indicate nations who once existed and were related to each other. The last in that table of names is Nahor, the father of Terah, who was the father of Abram. When Abram was born, Terah's family lived in the Sumarian city of Ur of the Chaldeans. From Ur, Terah moved to the city of Haran, a distance of about six hundred miles in northwestern Mesopotamia. It was in Haran that the biblical tradition begins the story of God bidding Abraham to leave his native land for an undisclosed destination.

Step Four

Having established Abraham as a real person and the learner's personal ancestor, it is now necessary to place him in his environment. The biblical tradition is very conscious of this need. It does not begin with God's decision to find a qualified person to realize His purpose. It says nothing about God or His heavenly abode. God speaks to Abraham in the latter's abode on earth. No mention is made of Abraham perceiving a vision or an angel appearing to him. All God's promises are to be fulfilled on earth. The above conditions should be kept in mind by the teacher of this lesson.

In the first monographs that I published under the title *Lecture Notes*, I dwell at length on Abraham's environments in Sumeria and Canaan, on the purpose of his migration, on his experiences with members of his own family and with neighbors, and his relationship with God. In the context of our present discussion, I wish to emphasize two approaches to teaching a historical personality such as Abraham. The approaches are proposed by Prof. Jerome Bruner and consist of pedagogic techniques:

1. *"Problem solving,* which leads the learner through a sequence of statements and restatements of a problem or a body of knowledge that increase his ability to grasp, transform, and transfer what he is learning."
2. *Teaching through contrast. Contrast* is "a vehicle by which the obvious that is too obvious to be appreciated can be made noticeable again."

The Contrasting Environments in Abraham's World

Although his travels took Abraham to neighboring countries (e.g., Egypt and the Philistine city of Gerar), the two contrasting environments to which the learner is to be led are Sumeria and Canaan. Our journey to Ur and Haran should explain the reason for Abraham's separation from his family and taking the long road to Canaan. In the "Lecture Notes—Talks to Teachers," the reason is given in a description of Sumeria's cultural and religious civilization by the leading historians Samuel S. Kramer and Sir Leonard Wooley. Two conclusions are derived from these descriptions.

First, at that time Sumeria was the center of the moon god worship. The divine pantheon functioned like a city-state, and little distinction was drawn between moral and ritual offenses. In such an atmosphere, deviation from the religious cult of the state was impossible. It is interesting to note that although the biblical text avoids any reference to Sumerian culture, the Midrash does dwell on this subject in relation to Abraham's condition in that land. It tells how Abraham destroyed his father's idols and how Nimrod, the king of the city, condemned him to death. The Midrash does not claim historical accuracy in the modern sense. It has preserved ancient traditions of a homiletical nature as commentaries on biblical personalities and narratives. In the stories about Abraham, the Midrash depicts his rejection of pagan idolatry and the response by Sumerian authorities to his deviation from the state religion. The following comments by Professor Speiser are not based on the Midrash, rather on implications of the biblical text. He writes:

> Abraham's journey to the Promised Land was thus no routine expedition of several hundred miles. Instead, it was the start of an epic voyage in search of spiritual truths, a quest that was to constitute the central theme of all biblical history.
>
> Against the background of the Sumerian pagan civilization (see the

previous unit), the teacher presents Abraham as a proponent of monotheism. To clarify the contrasts between paganism and the Israelite religion that was built on the principles of monotheism, I suggest that teachers become familiar with two chapters, "Pagan Religion" and "Israelite Religion," in Yehezkel Kaufmann's work *The Religion of Israel* (see bibliography).

Another opportunity for contrasting Abraham's environments is the choice of Canaan to which he migrated. I am quoting Sir Leonard Wooley's description of Canaan:

> The people who at the beginning of the Third Millennium inhabited what we may call Syria, forebears of those described in the Old Testament as Moabites, Edomites, Canaanites, Phoenicians, and the rest, were all of Semitic stock and shared what were essentially the same religious beliefs, but very different conditions of life inevitably introduced variations in local cults which almost obscured the underlying unity. It was not to be expected that the nomads of the eastern deserts should be moved by the same ideas as were natural for the dwellers in the fertile coastland, nor would the southern tribes have those political contacts which in the north added such a god as Hadad to the pantheon. [Hadad or Hadder was the Canaanite storm god and king of the gods.] The Phoenicians, according to their own tradition, were immigrants whose original home had been far to the east, somewhere on the Persian Gulf, and the faith that they brought with them as in all likelihood was the relatively simple one which in much later times persisted in the east....

Living among a population of mixed origins and different cultic practices, Abraham's religion of monotheism would not be resented, as was the case in Sumeria. The biblical text bears out this expectation. The encounters by Abraham and his offspring with the people of Canaan were socially, politically, and religiously harmonious, although fundamental cultural differences separated them.

Step Five

The teacher should introduce a biblical reference that sheds light on the contrasting environments discussed above. The reference I have chosen is from the Passover Haggadah, which took it from the Book of Joshua. The Haggadah uses the statement as it occurs in the Talmud (Pes. 116a). The first two sentences were added by the Talmudic sages:

In the beginning, our Fathers were worshippers of strange gods: But now, the All-Present [God] has brought us to His service, as it said: "Then said Joshua to all the people: Thus said the Lord, the God of Israel: In olden times your forefathers—Terah father of Abraham and father of Nahor—lived beyond the Euphrates and worshipped other gods. But I took your father Abraham from beyond the Euphrates and led him through the whole land of Canaan and multiplied his offspring. I gave him Isaac, and to Isaac I gave Jacob and Esau. I gave Esau the hill country of Seir as his possession while Jacob and his children went down to Egypt. (Josh. 24:2–4).

I wish to pause for a moment to explain the reasons that motivated me to include this quotation as it appears in the Haggadah. The sole purpose of the Seder is ritual, and literary composition in the Haggadah is instruction. The historical and religious events that are commemorated on Passover are symbolically acted out in rituals and their meanings are taught through literary recitations. Thus, the Jew practices as he studies and studies as he practices. This aspect is too frequently overlooked at the Seder. Calling attention to this quotation in a course of history will give meaning to the learner when he reads the same passage in the Haggadah at the Seder.

Teachers in Jewish schools are aware of the paucity of time available to them to acquaint their students with the literary treasures of our people. To the average learner, the Bible remains a closed book and the Talmud only the name of a series of books. The Siddur and Haggadah are read by many Jews without comprehension. With this view in mind, I utilize every opportunity that presents itself in any course I teach on the secondary and college levels to call attention to biblical, Talmudic, and philosophical sources. In our discussion of the contrasting environments that confronted Abraham, we have an excellent opportunity to introduce the Torah, the Book of Joshua in the Former Prophets, the Talmud, and the Haggadah.

Step Six: The Image of Abraham in Genesis

When we return to Abraham, we find him settled in the Promised Land. The biblical tradition now devotes thirteen chapters to the events and experiences of his life in the new environment. When I reached this place in the lesson I had taught on the secondary level, I distributed copies of the Torah (*A New Translation* by the Jewish Publication Society) and assigned the class a research project. The instructions were as follows:

"We have met Abraham, the grandfather of the Jewish people who is also our personal grandfather. We have ascertained that the biblical tradition has transmitted to us many events and experiences in his life that give a detailed image of the kind of person he was and of the religion he practiced. I wonder what kind of information about Abraham you would want to find in the Book of Genesis?"

The students were given sheets of paper and requested to write their comments. When the assignment was completed, the students, with my help, organized their questions in five categories under the following headings: (1) Abraham's religion; (2) Abraham's God concepts; (3) Abraham's family life; (4) Abraham's ethical behavior; and (5) Abraham as progenitor of the Jewish people.

Step Seven: The Research Project Continued

At the next session, the students were asked to explore the biblical text of Genesis for information that would answer their questions. I distributed a document that contained questions selected at the previous session and the sources in Genesis to explore. I directed the mechanics of the project and offered comments as commentary. The following are a few illustrations of how the students and I cooperated on the project.

Topic: Abraham's Religion
Selected Question: Did Abraham discover a new religion in Canaan? What was his religion like?
Directed Sources in Genesis: 12:6–8; 13:18; 21:33

In these passages we are told that upon his arrival in Canaan, Abraham settled for a time in the vicinity of Shechem, at the terebinth of Moreh, where he built an altar. Then he moved to Beth-el (ten miles north of Jerusalem) and built there another altar and "invoked the Lord by name." From there, he moved to Hebron and built an altar. In Beer-sheba, he planted a tree "and invoked the name of the Lord, the eternal God." The students were directed to verify the references in the biblical text.
Some of you have understood the questions to mean whether Abraham discovered new God concepts in Canaan, which were different from the Canaanites' god concepts. I take this to mean whether Abraham dis-

covered the belief of monotheism. If that is what you meant, then the answer is that the Torah does not attribute the discovery of monotheism to Abraham or to any other person. According to the biblical tradition, during Abraham's time almost all people believed in polytheism, and only Abraham and his descendants were monotheists. However, monotheism was not a new belief; it was the first God belief of ancient man, going all the way back to Adam. Abraham was a link in a long chain of believers in the One God.

Some of you interpreted the question to mean whether Abraham introduced new forms of worship. To answer this question accurately, *worship* has to be defined. If by *worship* is meant rituals or religious ceremonies, the answer could be perhaps. If worship includes "man's relationship to God and God's relationship to man," the answer is yes.

Why did I use the word *perhaps* in relation to rituals? Because the biblical text does not tell of rituals or ceremonies performed by Abraham on the altars which he built, it only says that "he evoked the name of the Lord." In connection with the altars, the text relates that the Lord appeared or spoke to Abraham, and Abraham responded by evoking the Lord, who appeared to him. How did God appear to Abraham? In one instance the text tells: "The word of the Lord came to Abraham in a vision" (15:1). Maimonides explains the term *vision* as "intellectual perception" and "prophetic inspiration."

Evoking God's name was a form of worship that was not associated with the cult of offering sacrifices practiced in pagan worship. It was a sort of dialogue between the divine and man. Abraham heard God speak to him and responded by speaking his thoughts to God. The Talmud explains the expression, "Abraham evoked the name of the Lord," to mean that "Abraham proclaimed the knowledge of the true God." In other words, Abraham's concept of worship was to reveal his ideas of God, which were in contrast to the ideas of the pagans worshippers. This might be considered a new conception in man's relationship to God.

Did Abraham discover a new religion? If we understand *religion* as man's belief that God is concerned with the way he lives out his life on Earth and man responds to God by living the kind of life God requires of him, then Abraham discovered a new religion.

I shall cite another question posed by a student.

Topic: Abraham's God Concepts
Question: How does the Bible describe Abraham's God concepts?

The pedagogic method I suggest to be used in finding an answer to this question is more sophisticated than the one used to answer the first question. For younger teenagers, it should be modified and summarized. For older students, certain ideas, such as Maimonides's conception of "vision and insiration," "Abraham's intercession for Sodom," and the "Akedah, the ordeal of Isaac," should include rabbinic interpretation. This method is more suitable in a course of Bible study than in history. I have also used this interpretation in a history course for teenagers in a modified format.

In Genesis the biblical traditions do not speak of divine attributes as such. The beliefs and ideas that the early Israelites conceived of God are expressed in divine revelations to the patriarchs. These were of two kinds—oral communications of instructions, blessings, promises, and divine deeds, such as protecting Abraham and Sarah from harm in the royal courts of Egypt and the Philistines, and the destruction of Sodom and Gomorrah. In the dialogues between God and Abraham are revealed Abraham's conceptions of God's attributes, which were transmitted to his descendants.

Yehezkel Kaufmann describes the God conceptions of the early Israelites and contrasts them to the pagan conceptions of polytheism.

> Monotheism asserts that there is only One God who is creator and ruler of the universe. God is supreme over all. He is utterly distinct from, and other than, the world; He is subject to no laws, no compulsions, or powers that transcend him. He is, in short, non-mythological. This is the essence of the Israelite religion and that which sets it apart from forms of paganism.

The Pagan God Concepts:

The pagan conceives of the gods as powers embodied in nature, or as separate beings connected with nature in some fashion.... There are gods of sky and earth, of life, love, and fertility, of death and destruction. The gods have specific roles. There are gods of light and darkness, of thunder and lightning, of wind and rain, of fire and water. Mountains, springs, rivers, and forests have their gods. The gods have sexual qualities, the existence of male and female deities being essential to pagan thought.... Theogonies tell of their birth and lineage. Myths tell of their wars, loves, hatred, and dealings with men. The cult is closely connected within myths, which are the vital care of priestly and, in a measure, of popular religion.

Following Kaufmann's explanations of monotheism and polytheism, I felt that the answer to the question about Abraham's God concepts ought to be expanded. On the college level, and in a simpler language on the secondary level, I introduced the following thoughts.

It is not easy for a modern person living in a Christian or Moslem society, whose religion is based on the belief of monotheism, to comprehend the immensity of intellectual and spiritual revolutions made by biblical monotheism to human civilization. Rabbi Jacob Agus (*The Evolution of Jewish Thought*, Abelard-Schuman, 1959) writes:

> It is certain the introduction of monotheism upon the stage of history represents a tremendous advance over the ways of thinking and living that are native to humanity.... Monotheism is a deep and mighty spiritual revolution that begins with a series of affirmations concerning God and ends by transforming the entire structure of human society. This marvelous reorientation of the human soul achieved its first triumph among the children of Israel some time during the biblical period, roughly from the fifteenth to the fourth century B.C.E. In later centuries, a similar metamorphosis was to transmute the spirit of the Greco-Roman world, the emergence of Christianity, and still later, the lands of Western Asia and Northern Africa were similarly affected by the rise of Islam. The first and original revolution took place within the heart of Israel.

What does Rabbi Agus mean by "monotheism transformed the entire structure of human society"? How could a belief in one God change human society? The answer is that the one God concept is not the only fundamental ideal in monotheism. Upon the belief in one God are built structures of spiritual, intellectual, and behavioral concepts that embrace God's management of the universe, His relationship to mankind, and mankind's relationship to Him. Rabbi Agus points out:

> In Judaism, God is conceived as the ideal personality, who is judge and active ruler of the universe. Thus Abraham exclaims, "Shall not the judge of all the earth do justly?" In contrast to the Greek ideal, which rejects personality as a being utterly self-sufficient and unconcerned with any person or thing, the Israelites conceived perfection in the active terms of practical sainthood. Thus Aristotle portrayed the Deity as being aloof from all earthly matters, busying Himself with the most perfect of all conceivable occupations, namely, the contemplation of His own perfection. In Scriptures, on the contrary, the Lord is portrayed as the "judge of the entire earth," descending to examine the corruption of Sodom and beholding with pro-

found sympathy "the poor, and him who is of a contrite spirit, and who trembleth at my word" (Isaiah 66:2). Free from the limitations of the human judge, He looks to man's inward self, and His judgments are "righteous altogether."

In brief, the Israelite conception of monotheism is not limited to God's own perfection; rather, it is a kind of perfection that emerges from God and penetrates man's world where it commands man to imitate that perfection in his relationship with all of God's creatures. The rabbinic sages explain this idea as follows: "As God is merciful, so you be merciful; as God is called righteous, so you be righteous; as God is holy, so do you strive to be holy." By pursuing righteousness, man "imitates" God. It is when man makes God's perfection the ideal of his own behavior that the structure of human society is transformed.

Abraham's God Concepts

Abraham's God concepts share common elements with the God concepts of Moses, except that in their experiences and manner of revelation they are different. To Abraham, God did not reveal His nature nor communicate standards of behavior that emanated from His divine attributes. God provided Abraham with experiences in which His divine attributes become explicit. For example: In His promise, "And all the families of the earth shall bless themselves by you," God reveals His universality, i.e., that He is the God of the entire universe. In his intercession on behalf of Sodom, Abraham perceives God to be bound by the norms of justice that He requires of man.

To Moses, however, God reveals His attributes. Moses asks God to disclose His nature and the fullness of His name. God responds:

> The Lord! [is] a God compassionate and gracious, slow to anger, rich in steadfast kindness, extending kindness to the thousandth generation, forgiving iniquity, transgression, and sin; yet He does not remit all punishment.... (Exod. 34:6–7).

Although a concept cannot adequately express the experience to which it refers, experience provides fertile ground for a concept to develop and grow. In the biblical traditions, Abraham's experiences incorporate the earliest and basic concepts of monotheism as the people Israel understood them. In the first eleven chapters of Genesis, God is established as the universal deity. Beginning with chapter twelve, the universal God brings into world history a single family that will grow into a full nation, and through that nation new things will happen in the world. That nation will accept the universal God as their own God, and God will accept them as His special people.

Summary of Abraham's God Concepts Explicit in His Experiences

1. God is Creator of Heaven and Earth (14:22).

    Following his victory over the Eastern Kings, Abraham declares to the king of Salem: "I swear to the Lord, God most high, Creator of heaven and earth."

2. The entire earth is God's possession; He gives a portion of it to Abraham and his descendants (13:15–16).

    God says: "I give all the land that you see to you and your offspring forever. I will make your offspring as the dust of the earth, then your offspring too can be counted."

3. Abraham traverses throughout the land. He settles in various places, builds altars, digs wells, and purchases a burial plot in Hebron (13:17).

    His movements are attributed to God's instructions: "Up, walk about the land, through its length and its breadth, for I give it to you."

4. Abraham's faith in God is complete, but it has its rational moments. On several occasions, he raises serious issues with God (15:1–18).

    Up to this point, Abraham envisions (Maimonides, *va-yera*, "appeared," refers to intellectual perception) God promising him an offspring while he and Sarah remain childless. Then he hears God speaking to him in a vision: "Fear not Abram, I am a shield to you; your reward shall be very great." Without questioning God's intentions, he demurs, "O Lord God, what can You give me, seeing that I shall die childless, and the one in charge of my household is Dammesek Eliezer! . . . Since you have granted me no offspring, my steward will be my heir." The vision continues. God is not offended by Abraham's question. He assumes a position of intimate relationship with him as one person speaks to another and tells him, "One shall not be your heir; none but your very own issue shall be your heir." Abraham, says the text, "put his trust in God," and God rewards him for his faith in Him. "He reckoned it to his merit" (12:1–6).

In the same prophetic vision, Abraham sees himself brought outside (Maimonides, ibid), where first God assures him that his offspring will be as numerous as the stars, then He tells him that the purpose for having brought him out from Ur of the Chaldeans was to bequeath this land to him. But Abraham is still apprehensive and demurs, "O Lord God, how shall I know that I am to possess it?" In his reply, God orders Abraham to perform a ritual that in ancient times was symbolic of concluding a covenant between two parties. The ritual performed, Abraham falls into a deep trance and hears God unfolding for him the fate of his descendants a long time later in history: "You should know that your offspring shall be strangers in a land not theirs, to be enslaved and oppressed for four hundred years. But I will bring judgment on the nation they must serve, and in the end they shall leave with great wealth." That day the Lord concluded a covenant with Abram saying, 'To your offspring I give this land, from the river of Egypt [the Nile] to the great river, the Euphrates' " (Ibid 7–19).

5. The Covenant and Circumcision (17:1–14)

In his visions and deep trance, Abraham is the recipient of God's blessings and promises. In the covenant, it is again God who pledges Himself to fulfill His promises to Abraham's offspring. Nothing is said either by God or by Abraham about the latter's share in their relationship, except that Abraham trusted God's promises. In a new vision, God identifies Himself as El Shaddai, "Almighty" (meaning "self-sufficient") and instructs Abraham to "follow My ways and be blameless." God's ways are not defined here, but in a later revelation He explains, "I have singled him out in order that he may instruct his sons and his future family to *keep the way of the Lord* by doing what is just and right." In other words, God's promises in the covenant are conditioned on Abraham teaching his descendants to obey God's instructions of ethical conduct.

Then God defines the covenant in greater detail and informs

Abraham of his human obligations: "For your part, you must keep My covenant, you and your offspring to follow, through the ages." As a sign that the second party to the covenant (Abraham's offspring) keeps the agreement, "You shall circumcise the flesh of your foreskin, and that shall be the mark of the covenant between Me and you." Thus, circumcision is the sign of the acceptance of God's revealed will. Whoever refuses to accept God's revealed will breaks the covenant "and shall be cut off from his kin." Professor Speiser points out, "Eventually the rite became a distinctive group characteristic, and hence also a cultural and spiritual symbol" (18:1–14).

6. Abraham Intercedes for Sodom (18:1–32)

The narrative begins with a vision in which Abraham experiences God's presence. "The Lord appeared to him by the terebinths of Mamre..." and remained there until after He terminated His dialogue with Abraham about Sodom and Gomorrah. Then, "as soon as the Lord finished speaking with Abraham, He departed."

God Concepts in the Dialogue about Sodom and Gomorrah

The biblical tradition introduces this incident with the explanation that God reflected on whether to share with Abraham His intentions to punish the sinful people of Sodom and Gomorrah. The Lord reflected, "Shall I hide from Abraham what I am about to do?" Then "the Lord said, 'The outrage of Sodom [meaning the whole area of Sodom and Gomorrah] is so great, and their sin so grave! I will go down to see whether they have acted altogether according to the outcry that has come to me; if not, I will know.'" These verses convey significant moral attitudes in God's dealing with sinful people and shed light on the God conceptions of the biblical tradition.

The outcry that reached God indicates "a cry for help from one who suffers a great injustice. With this cry for help, he appeals for protection of the legal community. What it does not hear or grant, however, comes directly before the Lord as guardian of all right. God is, therefore, not concerned with punishing Sodom but rather with an investigation of the case, which is serious, to be sure." What were the sins of Sodom and Gomorrah?

Jewish commentators follow closely the interpretation of the sins that is given in the Talmud. These were sins of injustice, violence, keeping strangers out from their cities in order to keep all the wealth for themselves.

The expression, "I will go down and see," does not mean that God did not know whether the complaints were true; rather, it indicates God's personal concern for the sufferers. The implication is that God, who transcends the world, is also immanent in the lives of mankind. In other words, while He is other than the world, there is no element of the world's existence that does not reflect His presence. When man appeals to Him, He responds in a personal manner.

Abraham understood God's investigation of conditions in Sodom and Gomorrah as unwillingness on His part arbitrarily to pronounce punishment on the guilty. He and Abraham knew the results of the investigation and their consequences. This is obvious from Abraham's question, "Will you sweep away the innocent along with the guilty?" In other words, what will happen if the investigation reveals that in addition to the majority of guilty men exists a minority of fifty innocent men, "Will you wipe out the place and not forgive for the sake of the innocent fifty who are in it? Far be it for You to do such a thing, to bring death upon the innocent as well of the guilty, so that the innocent and guilty fare alike. Far be it from You! Shall not the Judge of all the earth deal justly?"

Erich Fromm characterizes Abraham's dialogue with God as "the most dramatic expression of radical consequences of the covenant.... Precisely because God is bound by the norms of justice and love, man can challenge God—as God can challenge man—because above both are principles and norms." In a passage of the Talmud, Abraham is characterized as the defender in God's investigation of Sodom and Gomorrah.

Summary:

The God concepts explicit in the above narrative are:

God is not only creator and ruler of the universe but also the personal deity of each human being. He is concerned with how man lives out his life on earth.

The man of faith is conscious of God's presence everywhere. He appears to him and speaks to him. Having endowed man with comprehension, discernment, and freedom, He allows man to challenge Him as He challenges man.

God holds man accountable for transgressing the "way of the Lord." "The way of the Lord" is just and righteous behavior. Faith or trust in the Lord is rewarded, but no mention is made of punishment for lack of trust. When man demurs at God's failure to fulfill His promises, He reasons with him and assures him again and again that in due time they will be realized.

In His covenant relationship with man, God binds Himself to the same principles and norms that He requires of man.

In the expression, "I will go down and see whether they have acted altogether according to the outcry that has come to me...," God reveals the attributes which He later proclaimed to Moses: "The Lord [is] a God compassionate and gracious, slow to anger, rich in steadfast kindness, extending kindness to the thousandth generation, forgiving iniquity, and sin" (Exod.. 34:66–7).

The Akedah—Ordeal of Isaac (Gen. 22:1–19)

The most dramatic episode in Abraham's life was when he received God's call to sacrifice his son Isaac. The biblical tradition tells of this occurrence in concise and poignant language. It does not introduce it as a vision nor does it give the time in the patriarch's life when it took place. The story opens with an explanatory verse: "Sometime afterward, God put Abraham to test." In this terse statement, God's purpose for His command is made clear. But what does the word *test* mean? Didn't God know the outcome of the test or that Abraham would obey His command? Another question is, For what purpose has this event been included in the biblical text? I shall answer the questions seriatim.

Medieval Jewish commentators suggest several meanings of the term *test*. Some read the Hebrew word *nisah* to mean demonstration. God provided Abraham with an experience to strengthen his character and demonstrated His righteousness for others to follow. There is almost general agreement among Jewish commentators that God ordered the test to intensify Abraham's love of God. Joseph Albo (Spain, fifteenth century) writes, "The deed will intensify love of God since every action leaves its indelible mark on the performer." This practice of good action is termed *nisayon*.

Modern commentators suggest a variety of explanations. For example: The object of the test was to register God's protest against the pagan practice of human sacrifice in general and child sacrifice in particular.

Another explanation is:

> The aim of the story is to extol obedience to God.... The process that Abraham set in motion [to possess the land as God's promise and the patriarch's offspring to become a great and numerous people] was not to be accomplished in a single generation. It sprang from a vision that would have to be tested and validated over an incalculable span of time, a vision that could be pursued only by single-mindedness of purpose and absolute faith—an ideal that could not be perpetuated unless one was ready to die for it or had the strength to see it snuffed out. The object of the ordeal [test] was to discover how firm was the patriarch's faith in the ultimate divine purpose. It was one thing to start out resolutely for the Promised Land, but it was a very different thing to maintain confidence in the promise when all appeared lost. The fact is that short of such unswerving faith, the biblical process could not have survived the many trials that lay ahead (Speiser).

The second question is partly answered in the explanations of the word *test*, but it calls for an analytical study of the structure of the narrative. There is more to the story than God testing Abraham. "This narrative is the most perfectly formed and polished of all the patriarchal stories" (Von Rad). The rabbinic sages and commentators explore here not only God's demand, but also Abraham's and Isaac's frames of mind. They read into the text religious and psychological meanings and embellish them with homiletical thought. Let us review some of the important comments on the text by Jewish commentators:

"He said to him, 'Abraham' and he answered, 'Here I am.' " *Comment:* "So do the righteous answer; the phrase denoting humility and readiness" (Rashi).

God: "Take your son, your favored one, Isaac, whom you love." *Comment:* Abraham replied: "But I have two sons." God: "Thine only one." Abraham: "But each is the only one of his mother!" God: "Whom you love." Abraham: "But I love both!" God: "Isaac." "Why did not God name Isaac at once? Lest Abraham's mind reeled under the sudden shock" (Rashi). God: "Offer him." (The Hebrew text does not use the term to offer or sacrifice, rather "take him up"). *Comment:* "God did not tell him to sacrifice Isaac, but only to take him up...because it was not His intention to have him sacrificed" (Rashi).

In the above explanations, the rabbinic commentators reveal a concern that the story of the Akedah should not detract from the conceptions of God's ethical attributes of kindness, righteousness, and mercy. They call attention to the fact that although the command God was about to give Abraham was harsh, even cruel, in His description of Isaac, He showed consideration for the father's tender feelings for his son, and in Abraham's response of, "Here I am," they detected the faithful man's readiness to obey God at all cost. They found God's attribute of mercy in His avoidance of the expression "sacrifice him," but instead, "take him up." The Midrash Rabbah (Genesis, Vayera) gives this interpretation. It quotes the sage R. Aha who said: "[Abraham wondered and complained to God.] Surely Thou indulgest in prevarication! Yesterday thou sayest: 'For through Isaac that offspring shall be continued for you' (Gen. 21:12); Thou didst then retract and say, 'take your son.' God replied: 'Did I tell you slaughter him? No! but take him up. Thou hast taken him up. Now take him down.'"

Another implication the commentators found in Isaac's inquiry to his father as they were proceeding to the mountain where Abraham was to erect an altar was:

ISAAC: Father!
ABRAHAM: Yes, my son.
ISAAC: There is the wood and the firestone, but where is the sheep for the burnt offering?
ABRAHAM: God will see to the sheep for the burnt offering, my son. And the two of them walked on together.

Rabbinic commentators interpret the expression, "They walked on together," to mean Isaac understood that he was to be the sacrifice, yet father and son walked with equal mind.

Whatever reason the editors had for including the Akedah among the traditions that came down to them of Abraham's life, the important fact is that in his narrative we have a clear view of the religious and moral aspects of monotheism as the Jews have understood it.

To summarize:

God's intimate relationship with man. The God of the universe does not appear as a dictator who, without consideration for His human subject, orders decrees. He reveals Himself as an intimate of man, understanding of his sensitive nature and concerned with his needs. Although His ways are not always obvious to man, in the end man realizes that they were intended for his benefit. It is this thought that moved the rabbinic commentators to interpret the word *test* as an act of experience for Abraham and demonstration for all who follow.

Since God requires obedience of the person who believes in Him, the ideal believer makes obedience to God's instructions his solemn duty, even to the extent of giving his most precious thing in life to God.

Does God really demand of man unlimited sacrifice? Only as it relates to man's behavior, which is "to keep the way of the Lord by doing what is just and right." This is contrary to the pagan conception that the gods required human sacrifice as a form of worship. This thought is emphasized in the reward that the Angel announced to Abraham: "Because you have acted thus...I will bestow My blessing upon you." He defines the action as, "You did not withhold your beloved son from Me." This refers to Abraham's obedience as Isaac was not sacrificed. In other words, God rewards the faithful man for obeying Him.

9.
Exploring One's Jewish Identity: Summary of Ideas

I am pleased to include a teacher's guide prepared by Dr. Eunice R. Baradon. Dr. Baradon's selection of ideas, questions, explanations, and interpretations have been designed for two purposes. The first purpose is to guide the teacher in selecting ideas upon which to structure lesson plans for a teaching unit. The questions are intended to make the obvious ideas more obvious by isolating, concretizing, and, where necessary, simplifying them for the busy teacher. The second purpose is to provide a framework for a series of instructional units, a sort of modified textbook to be developed for use by students.

The material contained in the *Lecture Notes* and in Dr. Baradon's "Summary of Ideas" served as one unit in a course of study titled "The Contemporary Society," for senior students at SAJS in the Fall of 1986.

I have often been asked by people who lack practical knowledge of education and particularly of Jewish education, "Why aren't the old textbooks from which we studied good enough for our children?" The answer I generally give is, "For the same reason that airplanes built in the 1940s aren't good enough in 1996." In other words, it is not only because the airplane has changed, it is also because people have changed. The more people become modern, the more they realize that they must not permit progress to bypass them.

In previous generations, we taught textbooks; today, we must teach children. This conclusion should be obvious to every intelligent person. But there is also another reason which is obvious only to Jewish educators "who love children and Judaism." Judaism is an intellectual religion and culture. Jewish history, says the historian Simon Dubnow, is the story "of the historical people of all times and is a microcosm of world history." Therefore, the student must not be bent to the book; rather, the book must be bent to the student. The competent Jewish educator who understands this truism realizes that he is duty bound to tailor the knowledge of Judaism to the student's physical and mental patterns of growth and development, to his emotional needs and interests, and to the influences which the environment exerts on the respective stages of his life.

Educators who bend the child to the book love books, not children. They are zealots. "A zealot," says the philosopher George Santana, "is one who lost his purpose but redoubled his efforts."

I am grateful to Dr. Baradon for bending the book to our children.

—Aharon Kessler

Lecture I: Exploring One's Jewish Identity

Summary by Dr. Eunice Baradon

1. What is identity?

    "Identity points to an individual's link with the unique values fostered by a unique history of his people." (Erik Erikson)

2. Why must a Jewish school be concerned with the "personal identity" of its students?

    a. Living in two cultures, American Jewish youth are faced with challenges to their personal identity.
    b. These challenges become intense when the adolescent leaves the protective environment of home and community to enter university life or the world of work.
    c. It is the responsibility of the school to prepare the students to meet the challenges of living in a bicultural environment.
    d. This preparation consists of two interrelated areas: transmission of a knowledge and appreciation of the Jewish cultural heritage and conscious efforts to assist the students in acquiring links of identification to the values of this heritage.

3. What is culture shock?

    Culture shock is "physical and social maladjustment when individuals experience mental conflict as a result of living between two cultures and failing to establish organic unity between the two cultures."

4. Why do many Jewish adolescents experience a culture shock upon entering college?

    These adolescents are "marginal" in their Jewishness. They did not acquire an understanding and appreciation of their heritage in their respective religious schools, nor did they acquire feelings of commitment to the values and standards of Judaism. These marginal Jewish adolescents thus experience a state of mental conflict, being exposed to two worlds that they cannot reconcile.

5. What are the frequent results of culture shock?

    Interdating, mixed marriages, joining of cults and missionary groups.

6. In helping adolescents explore their Jewish identity, what are the first questions we must help them answer?

    What am I?
    How am I different from others?

7. What is the answer we give to these questions?

    I am a human being. I am a Jew.

8. How does each human being differ from every other human being?

    Each human being has a "distinct" personality.

9. What are the sources for the uniqueness of personality?

    a. The distinctive human nature of the individual.
    b. The cultural environment and social interactions within that environment.

10. Of what significance is the question, "How does a Jew differ from other members in society?"

    The significance of the question is in the fact that a Jew differs from other members of the society because:

    a. He lives in two cultures: the dominant majority culture and the Jewish minority culture.
    b. By living in two cultures, the Jewish individual acquires specific cultural traits, which others in society do not have. These traits are products of his heritage, home, and community life.

11. How is living in a bicultural environment consistent with American democracy?

    America was founded and is populated by many ethnic groups and American democracy is based on the principle of unity in diversity.

12. Why did Horace Kallen, the father of the theory of cultural pluralism, compare ethnic groups to instruments in a symphony?

    Although each is a single instrument in the orchestra and plays is own part, it contributes to a harmonious whole of the entire orchestra. In brief, each instrument contributes something unique to the symphony.

13. How do sociologists explain the exceptional ability of Jews to live in two cultures:

    Jews have a long history of living as a minority in a majority culture—dating back to 70 C.E. with the destruction of the Second Commonwealth.

    Diaspora Jews, who were forced for centuries to live in two worlds and in two cultures, acquired a very special ability to adjust—to acculturate to the majority cultures and yet not to assimilate.

14. How did Bezalel Sherman, a Jewish sociologist, describe the Jew-

ish immigrant who came to a foreign country?

The Jew always wore two garments. His inner garment consisted of his own particular culture. The outer garment reflected the culture of the country in which he lived. Each time the Jew came to a new country, he put on a new outer garment, all the while retaining and never discarding his inner garment.

15. What ideas should be stressed in helping the adolescent understand the uniqueness of living Jewishly in a bicultural environment?

   a. History has conditioned the Jewish people to live creatively in two cultures—in the majority culture and in their own minority culture.
   b. The ability to live creatively in two cultures can help to explain the miracle of Jewish continuity throughout the ages.
   c. We are fortunate to live in America, which is based on the foundation of cultural pluralism—wherein all ethnic groups are encouraged to maintain their ethnicity and at the same time contribute to the American culture and society as a whole.
   d. The Jew who is committed to the values of Judaism is unlikely to experience psychological or social problems of maladjustment in his bicultural environment. He is able to live and contribute to the enhancement of both cultures.
   e. The Jew who feels a sense of belonging to his people's historical continuity is able to hear a voice inside of him saying, "This is the real me." He does not then suffer from a culture shock or does not experience identity confusion. He is proud of the two garments he wears, his inner and outer garments.

Lecture II: Stages of Growth and Development

1. In structuring a curriculum in the Jewish school for the teenager, what aspects of adolescence must be kept in mind?

   a. The adolescent period is the second decade of life, the transitional and very critical period between childhood and adulthood.

    b. It is not only a time of significant physical and emotional growth and development, but also a time of potential intellectual expansion and development of values.
    c. Adolescent views of life and death, of God, religion, and *ethics* are undergoing varying stages of growth and development during this period. The growth is subject, and dependent on the particular environmental forces of home, school, and community.
    d. Adolescents who belong to peer groups tend to merge into the group and to assume the attitudes and views held by the group.
    e. All of these above factors are crucial challenges to those involved in structuring a curriculum for the Jewish teenager.

2. What basic principle of John Dewey is pertinent in a curriculum geared to promoting strong Jewish identity?

    a. Knowledge must lead to action and interaction. When it remains dormant, it dissipates.
    b. Knowledge or learning should lead to change of behavior.
    c. Teaching must be performed on three levels:
        (1) Teaching of facts
        (2) Teaching of concepts
        (3) Teaching of values
    d. Unless a young person acquires values, one cannot expect commitment and modification of behavior in accordance with these values.

3. What role should the Jewish teacher assume in helping adolescents discover their religio-cultural identity?

    a. The teacher must view the knowledge of Jewish history and religion acquired on the *elementary* level as mere beginner building blocks.
    b. On the secondary level, a more sophisticated approach of teaching advanced subject matter should be taken.
    c. All subject matter dealing with the religion and culture of Judaism must be taught on the three levels of facts, concepts, and values.

d. Special emphasis must be placed on helping the learner perceive the values inherent in Judaism and the individual's connection to these values.
e. With this intellectual and psychological background, the teacher must be prepared to help Jewish youth understand why they are Jewish and why they should remain Jewish.
f. These subjects must be structured and taught in consideration of the intellectual and social development of teenagers, as well as consideration of their particular interests.

Lecture III: Why Should I Be Jewish?

1. Who is a Jew according to Halakhah, Jewish law?

   A child born of a Jewish mother is automatically Jewish. The mother gives the child legitimate certainty and traces the child's lineage to the patriarchs Abraham, Isaac, and Jacob.

2. How does a female convert enter the Jewish people?

   Through ritual immersion, by accepting the religion of Judaism and accepting the designation of Bat Avraham, daughter of Abraham.

3. How does a male convert enter the Jewish people?

   Through circumcision, ritual immersion, by accepting the religion of Judaism and the designation of Ben Avraham, son of Abraham.

4. What is the status of a child born to a mother after her conversion to Judaism?

   The child is automatically Jewish.

5. When posing the question, "Why am I Jewish?" to young people, what classifications should be made?

6. In what way does Jewish religious law and American civil law operate on similar principles in the determination of the status of a newborn?

   a. Children born of parents who are American citizens automatically become members of the American people.
   b. Children born of Jewish parents are automatically Jewish and members of the Jewish people.

7. In what way do the two legal systems differ in the case when an individual desires to terminate membership in his respective nation?

   a. An American citizen may give up his citizenship permanently, if desired.
   b. According to Jewish law, a Jew remains a member of the Jewish people for life.

8. What is the accepted norm on the status of being Jewish?

   "There is no Jewish authority that can rid a Jew from his people." (Mordecai M. Kaplan)

9. What are the characteristics of the various groups of Jews who are assimilationists?

   a. One group is made up of those Jews who completely eliminate their Jewish cultural differences and take over the culture and identity of another group, usually that of the larger group.
   b. Through conversion of individual Jews, or whole families into another religious group, this group endeavors to disappear completely from the Jewish community.
   c. A third group acknowledges its Jewish origins and may support Jewish causes and needs. Yet it relinquishes the cultural, religious, and national elements that make up a positive Jewish identity.

10. Why are we so concerned with threats of assimilation if the Jew is incapable of relinquishing membership in the Jewish people?

In the course of time, as history has shown, extreme assimilationists disappear completely from the Jewish community and are lost to the Jewish people.

11. How did Benjamin Disraeli (1804–1881), the prime minister of England, answer Queen Victoria's question, "Disraeli, what are you, Jewish or Christian?"

    a. Disraeli was baptized by his father at the age of thirteen.
    b. The question was put to Disraeli when he was in the church with the queen and was seen not praying.
    c. He answered that he was the blank page between the Old and the New Testaments — indicating a sense of emptiness, vacantless, as well as bewilderment and confusion.

12. How does the sociologist Kurt Lewin characterize Jews who stand near a margin of groups?

    a. Individuals who are uncertain about their belonging to both the group they are leaving and the group they are ready to enter are in this category.
    b. They do not actually cross the boundary but stand near the margin of the two groups, poised and waiting.

13. What suggestion does Lewin offer to those dealing with marginal young people?

    He suggests that these young people be made to realize how interdependent each Jew is to another, and that a common fate or sense of belonging ties each Jew to the entire Jewish people.

14. Why must this approach of creating awareness of group interdependence be approached with caution?

    Jewish tragedies are a major part of Jewish history. Too often, this perception can arouse uncertainty, fear, and disappointment in marginal young people.

    Unless the teacher introduces the positive outcome that evolved from the event, the student may never acquire a sense of pride and love for his people.

15. How can the outlook of the marginal Jewish adolescent be changed?

A complete process of reeducation is needed. This should include the task of helping students acquire a new system of values and beliefs, while at the same time linking these values and beliefs with the Jewish people and the role of the Jewish people in today's society. The overall objective in this reeducation is to have the new system of values and beliefs dominate the individual's perception and behavior. These students would no longer feel marginal but would acquire a sense of in-group feeling and readiness to live as responsible members of the Jewish people.

Lecture IV: Concept of Peoplehood

1. Why should the concept of peoplehood be viewed as the primary component constituting Jewish civilization?

   According to Kurt Lewin, acceptance of one's group, or peoplehood, is a prerequisite for the acceptance of one's group value system.

2. What is meant by the term *Jewish civilization*?

   "Civilization is the cumulative heritage of knowledge, experience and attitudes acquired by successive generations of a people in its striving to achieve salvation." (Mordecai M. Kaplan)

3. How does Mordecai M. Kaplan define the term *salvation*?

   He does not use this term in the Christian sense of deliverance from sin, but from the point of view of the realization of individual or group potentials.

4. What are the basic components within the concept of Jewish civilization?

a. Peoplehood—past, present, and future
   b. Religion
   c. Israel—the people's national homeland
   d. Hebrew language
   e. Literature
   f. Art
   g. Customs, folkways, and mores
   h. Communal, national, and international institutions established and maintained to care for Jews the world over.
   i. The will to live as a distinct people—sharing a common fate and working together in building a better world.

5. Why does Lewin place great importance on the system of values?

   a. The system of values and beliefs that dominate an individual's perception of Judaism is derived from the elements making up the Jewish civilization.
   b. These values are linked with the individual's feelings of belongingness to the Jewish people.
   c. Therefore, the nine elements mentioned above are basic to one's value system and one's acceptance of belongingness to the Jewish people.
   d. In turn, one's conduct is a product of these influences.

6. Why do some people find it difficult to belong to more than one group?

   a. Groups tend to overlap in their commitments, options, time, and interest.
   b. When exposed to different social groups, some young people are uncertain as to how to maintain their Jewish loyalties while at the same time establishing new loyalties to other groups.
   c. Assimilation is the option accepted by those who choose to surrender some of their past in the process of acquiring a new future.
   d. This social and intellectual dilemma occurs when an individual does not perceive meaning in the past of his group and looks to a new group for the promise it holds of yielding significant new meaning.

7. Why must an educator be aware of the many implications of the "you" question, i.e., when asking teenage students, "What does this mean to you?"

   a. A specific meaning a student perceives on the elementary level is not adequate and cannot satisfy the same student when he reaches adolescence or when he enters college.
   b. It is erroneous to believe that the meaning a child acquires on the elementary level would remain meaningful as that individual moves on to succeeding levels of maturity.
   c. This principle demands that facts and concepts be presented on each grade level in accordance with the specific intellectual and social maturity level of the learner.
   d. It is only then that the question "What does this mean to you?" can be educationally sound.

8. In helping young people discover their Jewish identity, why is it important that they find meaning in the concept of Jewish peoplehood?

9. What is meant by the term *time perspective?*

   A time perspective refers to one's point of view, which includes the past, the present, and the future.

10. Why is it important for the Jewish school to develop a time perspective in its students?

    a. A time perspective leads the learner from the present to the past and to the future.
    b. The present cannot be understood without an awareness of the past conditions leading up to the present.
    c. The present must also be viewed in light of the influences it holds for the future.

11. Why, then, should a Jewish school be concerned with structuring a curriculum that gives the learner meaning and a time perspective?

Unless a student finds meaning in the history, religion, and culture of the Jewish people and perceives a relationship of his people's past to his present and future, we cannot expect that the individual will develop a sense of Jewish identification and commitment.

12. Why is the problem-solving approach advocated as a means of helping the adolescent explore his Jewish identity?

   a. The adolescent is, at this stage of his life, suspicious of indoctrination on the part of adults.
   b. The problem-solving technique encourages the process of self-discovery.
   c. The method of problem solving that encourages self-discovery thus stimulates student curiosity, interest, and desire to evaluate data and make value judgments. It also results in greater interaction between students and teachers.
   d. Through this process, the learner will acquire a time perspective and meaning to his Jewish identity.

Lecture V: Identity and Identification of Certain Jews

1. What distinction does Prof. Abraham Kaplan make between *identification* and *identity*?

   a. *Identification* is recognition or evidence of one's identity. It is only the beginning. The individual recognizes that he is not a *non-Jew*. This awareness comes by birth, by name, and because others see him as a Jew.
   b. *Identity* is the collective aspects—the distinctive characteristics of the individual. It is the configuration of all the significant elements constituting one's personality. It is the inside voice saying, "This is the real me." It is what we have become and what we have made of ourselves.

2. Identity has been perceived as consisting of various superficial and deep layers. Explain the three layers of identity as it is reflected in the *involuntary self*, the *peripheral self*, and the *autonomous self*.

A. *Involuntary Self*
   (1) Part of every identity is an involuntary self imposed by the social environment.
   (2) Jews who possess only this superficial layer of identity with no deeper layers are in this category.
   (3) The Jewishness of these Jews is largely involuntary. Some conceal their Jewishness. Others reject it, and still others embrace their Jewishness as a gesture of defiance.

B. *Peripheral Self*
   (1) These Jews possess superficial layers of identity. These layers are not quite as superficial as the layers characteristic of the involuntary self.
   (2) This type participates in some Jewish communal activities as attending High Holiday services, contributing to UJA, etc. They are not motivated by a deep sense of religious commitment, but rather they express some need for belonging to the Jewish community.

C. *Autonomous Self*
   (1) This is a deep-layered type of Jewish identity.
   (2) These type of self is at home with his Jewishness. He feels himself a member of a large family, the Jewish people.
   (3) As a member of a family, he feels it his moral duty to "care" for his family.

3. Prof. Abraham Kaplan writes that Jewish identity in the Diaspora is often a "vicarious" type. Explain.

There are certain Jews who find their identity by linkage with the attainment of other Jews, such as Nobel Prize winners and the like. This linkage is made without regard to the nature of the Jewishness of these people. Minorities are said to take comfort in the revelation that "he is one of us."

4. What is the deepest kind of alienation a person may experience?

To be a stranger to oneself; to hide from the voice within which is speaking and saying that this is the real me.

5. How does Martin Buber illustrate this point with the biblical figure of Adam?

When God called out to Adam and said, "Where art thou, Adam," He asked not because He did not know, rather because Adam did not know where he was. Adam drove himself out in the Garden of Eden because he hid from the voice that spoke in his innermost being.

6. According to Martin Buber, what certain Diaspora Jews display group egotism?

These are Jews living in the Diaspora who are more concerned with how they appear to the non-Jew than with their image in their own eyes.

7. What type of Jew did Buber believe was most vulnerable to group egotism?

The ego imperialist and the defensive Jew. These certain Jews are obsessed with what the goyim will think and evidence more vanity than pride.

8. What must be our emphasis in the teaching of Jewish identification and Jewish identity?

Our objective is to help students avoid an identity crisis by acquiring deep layers of Jewish identity, making them possess a self at home with his or her Jewishness, and function as caring members of the Jewish family, the Jewish people.

Lecture VI: Why Should I Be Jewish?

1. What are the three possible implications to the question, Why should I be Jewish?

    a. The individual asking the question has negative feelings about being Jewish and is considering the rejection of his Jewishness.

b. The individual is concerned with the possible conflict of dual loyalism and wonders whether one can be both a Jew and an American.
   c. The individual has a vague understanding of what it means to be a Jew.

2. What approach should a teacher take when dealing with the question, Why should I be Jewish?

   The teacher should take this opportunity to present knowledge and ideas that will help the student understand what it means to be a Jew. Debates and pro and con discussions should be avoided.

3. What are the sequential ideas presented in the model lesson of this lesson?

   a. Teacher presents a case history of an individual who asks the question, Why should I be Jewish?
   b. Students analyze and characterize the individual as one who has only a vague understanding of what it means to be Jewish and thus sees no purpose in his Jewishness.
   c. Teacher reviews the Jewish Halakhah as it applies to the individual in the case history.
      (1) One's Jewishness cannot be viewed as a commodity to be kept or discarded at will.
      (2) A person born of a Jewish mother is thus a Jew by birth and remains a Jew for the rest of his life.
   d. Teacher presents a review of how our ancestor Abraham made a covenant with God, and how it was renewed at Sinai with the people and with future generations.
      (1) All people have a common origin—Adam and Eve. Eventually, mankind separated into tribes and nations.
      (2) Biblical tradition tells of man's corruption, the punishment by the Flood, and the sparing of Noah and his family because Noah was righteous.
      (3) God made a covenant with Abraham and with Abraham's posterity to be their God and they His people.

(4) At Sinai, God renewed His covenant with the entire nation. Israel now becomes God's "treasured people."
(5) Israel is commanded to be holy because God is holy. They are to imitate God's ethical attributes of mercy and righteousness.
(6) To be God's treasured people and to fulfill the covenant with God, Israel must strive to be holy and maintain an ethical distinctiveness in thought and in conduct.
(7) From the beginning of their history, the Jewish people regarded their election as a treasured people and their covenant with God as a sacred mission bestowed on them and on all future generations of their offspring.

e. Teacher refers to the case history. The American Jewish writer cited had no will to be Jewish; therefore, he never tried to find out what it meant to be Jewish. He also felt no duty or responsibility for the continuation of the Jewish people.

f. Teacher summarizes the conclusions to be drawn from this lesson.

(1) A Jew is a Jew by birth.
(2) It is the Jewish people who make one Jewish and holds on to the individual as a member of the social group for the rest of his life.
(3) Individual Jews who do not possess a desire for Jews to continue as a distinct people are marginal Jews. They are unable to shed their Jewishness and cannot become non-Jews either. They are in a no-man's land of the spiritually homeless.
(4) A Jew is a Jew by virtue of the existence of the Jewish people. There cannot be Judaism without the continued existence of the Jewish people.

Bibliography

Agus, Jacob. *The Evolution of Jewish Thought*. Abelard-Schuman, 1959.
Beauchamp, E.A. *Elementary Method*. Abby & Bacon, 1959.
Ben-Sasson, H. H., Ed. *A History of the Jews*. Cambridge: Harvard University Press, 1976.
Brandeis, Louis D.. *Brandeis on Zionism*, Foreword by Justice Felix. Frankfurter, ZOA, 1942.
Bruner, Jerome S. *Toward a Theory of Instruction*. Cambridge: Harvard University Press, 1966.
Buber, Martin. "Nationalism" and "The Two Foci of the Jewish Soul." *Israel and the World*. Schocken Books, 1949.
_____. *The Writings of Martin Buber*. Ed. Will Herberg. Meridian Books, World Publishing Co., 1958.
De Vaux, Roland. *Ancient Israel*. New York: McGraw-Hill, 1961.
Dubnow, Simon. *Nationalism and History*. Ed. K. S. Pinson. Jewish Publication Society, 1958.
Encyclopedia Judaica, Vol. 3, page 211. Vol. 11, pages 1407–1427.
Epstein, Isidore. *The Faith of Judaism*. Soncino Press, 1954.
Erikson, Erik H. *Childhood And Society*, W. W. Norton & Co., 1963.
_____. *Identity and the Life Cycle*. New York: W. W. Norton & Co., 1980.
Gage, N. L., and Berliner, David C. *Educational Psychology*. Rand-McNally, 1975.
Gesel, A., ILG, F. L., Ames, L. B. *Youth, the Years from Ten to Sixteen*. New York: Harper & Bros., 1956.
Glatzer, N. N. *The Way of Response*. Schocken Books, 1966.
Hertzberg, Arthur. "The Lessons of Emancipation." *Diaspora, Exile and the Jewish Condition*. Ed. Etan Levine. Jason Aronson, 1983.
Hook, Sidney. *Education for Modern Man*. Dial Press, 1946.
Kaplan, Abraham. "Identity and Alienation," *Diaspora, Exile and the Jewish Condition*. Ed. Etan Levine. Jason Aronson, 1989.
Kaplan, Mordecai M. *The Future of the American Jew*. Reconstructionist Press, 1967.
_____. *Questions Jews Ask*. Reconstructionist Press, 1959.
_____. *Judaism as a Civilization*. Reconstructionist Press, 1957.
Kaufmann, Yehezkel. *The Religion of Israel*. Translated and abridged by Moshe

Greenberg. Chicago: University of Chicago Press, 1960.
Kohn, Hans. *The Idea of Nationalism.* New York: Collier Books, 1960.
Lewin, Kurt. "Psycho-Sociological Problems of a Minority Group," "Self-Hatred among Jews." *Resolving Social Conflicts.* New York: Harper & Bros., 1948.
Neuman, Abraham A. "Judaism." *The Great Religions of the Modern World.* Ed. E. J. Jurgi. Princeton: Princeton University Press, 1967.
Nozick, Robert. *Philosophical Explanations.* Cambridge: Harvard University Press, 1981.
Patai, Raphael. *The Jewish Mind.* Charles Scribner & Sons, 1977.
Salengut, Charles. "Cults and Jewish Identity." *Midstream,* January 1986.
Sherman, C. Bezalel. *The Jew within American Society.* Wayne University Press, 1961.
Speiser, E.A. *At the Dawn of Civilization: The World History of the Jewish People.* New Brunswick: Rutgers University Press, 1964.
_____. *Genesis.* The Anchor Bible, Doubleday & Co., 1964.
Wooley, Sir Leonard and Hawkes, Jacquetta. *History of Mankind,* Vol. I, New York: Harper & Row, 1963.

IV

Voices from Our Past: Moral Implications of Holocaust Literature

by Penina Kessler Lieber

Dedicated to my father, Aharon Kessler,
for whose depth of knowledge, strong
Jewish principles, and personal inspiration
I am forever indebted.

Foreword

The College of Jewish Studies was among the first of secondary Jewish schools to introduce a course in Holocaust education for adolescents. It was agreed by the faculty that Jews have a moral obligation to remember the Holocaust and to teach it to their children.

An awareness of the catastrophic events that occurred in Europe between 1933 and 1945 in an attempt to destroy much of European Jewry has resulted in educators feeling a commitment to the importance and relevance of the subject of the Holocaust in the classroom.

The monograph *Voices from Our Past: Moral Implications of Holocaust Literature* was published in November 1978 and taught to the senior class in the School of Advanced Jewish Studies. It concludes with the following statements:

> The Holocaust exists as a microcosm of human history. It testifies to the greatest evil that man has perpetuated against his fellowman and in the survival of the Jewish People. Its lessons present both Jew and non-Jew alike with an indisputable moral imperative if we are to survive as Jews and as human beings.

Preface

During the winter months of 1977, I was asked to deliver a series of lectures on the moral implications of the Holocaust. The lectures were to be given to the senior classes of the School of Advanced Jewish Studies, to the parent body of the school, and to the board of directors of the Women's Division, United Jewish Federation of Greater Pittsburgh. In order to best concretize the subject at hand, I chose to employ the vehicle of the literature of the Holocaust.

Personal writings such as these contain the ability to open new vistas of understanding and identification in a remarkably immediate way. The stories, dramas, and autobiographical accounts would enable my listeners to crawl inside the consciousness of this otherwise unimaginable moment and to participate in it as if they were actually there. Once the impact of the Holocaust had been personally experienced, I hoped that the vast moral and philosophical implications of the tragedy would be brutally illuminated in light of our present Jewish existence. At that point, the moral imperative to remember and to survive could be drawn, linking our own days with the nights of the Holocaust.

These lectures were not intended to cover the entire spectrum of Holocaust literature. Selections were made to limit the scope of our discussion and to arouse an immediate emotional involvement.

My deep thanks go to my students who were touched by the chosen materials, and who urged me to transpose these lectures into published form, to the staff of the School of Advanced Jewish Studies who assisted me in all ways, and especially to my family who served as an encouraging sounding board for the development of my ideas.

Penina Kessler Lieber

Pittsburgh, Pennsylvania
September, 1978

1.
Memory and the Holocaust

The Holocaust casts an ominous shadow upon our historic horizons. Its black presence threatens to obscure our view and limit our perceptions. We do not understand it today any better than we did a generation ago, and its frightening character leaves us vulnerable in an insecure age. Nevertheless, the moral implications of the tragedy take on brighter form if we look beyond the cloud and farther back into a more distant past.

We Jews have learned early in our history the importance of memory. The effectiveness of reliving an experience, even a painful one, in order to establish it firmly in our community consciousness dates far back in our teachings. Only by remembering the past can the present insure a better future.

The Passover Seder testifies to the emphasis on memory in our tradition. The Haggadah is specific in its injunction: "In each generation, every Jew is duty-bound to regard himself as if he had gone out of Egypt. God did not only save our forefathers, but us along with them."

The Haggadah further declares: "It was not only Pharaoh who sought to destroy us; in every generation there are those who rise up to destroy us, but the Holy One, blessed be He, saves us from their hand." In order to implement this directive, some Eastern Jewish communities still enact dramatizations of the Exodus at their Seder. Such a custom physically stimulates interest in the past event, just as the Western Seder intellectually provokes questions and answers applicable to the present.

A similar call to remember the past appears in the prophetic book of Joel. In the fifth century B.C.E., the prophet urged his community:

> Listen to this, you elders:
> All inhabitants of the country, attend.
> Has anything like this ever happened in
> your day, or in your father's days?
> Tell it to your sons,

Let your sons tell it to their sons,
And their sons to a generation after them. (Joel 1:3)

This obligation to learn from past experience has gained significant meaning in our society. We who live in a world tainted by the Holocaust find it necessary to understand what befell the European Jewish community in order to insure our own survival in a most precarious moment.

Several questions concerning our personal relationship with the Holocaust must be answered before we can draw pertinent moral implications. We find ourselves tormented by an often unexpressed dilemma: Why is it necessary that we who live today confront the Holocaust? We do not like to think about it and much less choose to discuss it either in public or in the intimacy of our own families. We are all familiar with the facts of the nightmare. Why dwell any longer on the disquieting and horrible details? Surely, it is a depressing subject of fire and ashes, anger, despair, guilt, and suffering. It evokes the most hidden fears buried deep within our hearts. Should we not turn our cheeks and let it rest in peace?

Certainly, it would be simpler not to confront the Holocaust. There are no easy answers to it. The more that we remember, read, and study of the tragedy, the more it eludes all reason.

The chronicler of the Holocaust Elie Wiesel, has commented on this problem:

> The Holocaust still transcends all dimensions of consciousness. We still cannot grasp how it all happened and why. The mystery remains intact. Just as we will never be able to penetrate the harrowing memory of the victim, so we cannot peer into the twisted mind of the assassin. Everything to do with Auschwitz must, in the end, lead into darkness.[1]

Even if reason fails us, do we have the right to shy away from the reality of the Holocaust? Yehuda Amichai, an Israeli poet, suggests that "most people in our time have the face of Lot's wife, turned toward the Holocaust and yet always escaping."[2] This characterization aptly describes our generation. We must constantly remember that despite our squeamishness, we are turned toward the Holocaust. It has affected our lives as Jews both personally and collectively. Its lessons have crucial meanings for Jews in particular and the world in general.

What lessons do we Jews learn from the Holocaust? At once we realize that anti-Semitism must be taken seriously. The hatred of the Jew because he is a Jew has been on the world scene for a very long time. It existed in antiquity when the Jews were first regarded with suspicion and distrust because they were out of step with their time. While the other peoples of the world worshipped idols, the Jews were shaping the lofty concept of ethical monotheism. In order to retain their uniqueness, they chose to remain separate from the pagan world. At a time when religion and political life were intertwined, when kings were worshipped as deities, the Jews remained a distinct people striving to fashion a civilization based on righteousness and holiness.

Anti-Semitism continued into the Second Jewish Commonwealth, the time of the Persians, Greeks, and Romans. During this period, so highly revered as the Classical Age of Greek and Roman thought, the infamous blood libel originated. The historian Josephus Flavius relates a ritual murder accusation in his book *Against Apion*. This libel alleged a secret Jewish law commanding Jews to kidnap a Greek every seven years, fatten him for slaughter, cut him into pieces, and finally eat his entrails. Thus, the Jews were supposedly pledging themselves by oath to hate the Greeks. Paganism and Judaism clashed not only as distinct religions but as diametrically opposed cultures. To quote the Swedish historian Hugo Valentin:

> In the ancient world antisemitism was more a literary than a popular phenomenon, whereas in the Middle Ages the masses of the people were imbued with hatred of the Jews in proportion as the Church through rites and education inspired them with her view of Jews as a race accursed of God. Until this came about the European peoples had left the Jews in peace.... In classical antiquity the Jews initiated the non-Jewish world by denying all gods but God and by voluntarily severing themselves from the pagans. During the Middle Ages the cause of antisemitism was Christian intolerance of the Jews, who were regarded as the murderers of the Saviour.[3]

In medieval Europe the carefully cultivated hatred of the Jews spilled over into social antipathy and violent persecution. We have only to recall the countless instances of anti-Semitic outrage throughout European history to understand how it could finally have culminated in the Holocaust of the twentieth century. The Crusades of the eleventh and twelfth centuries, too often romantically depicted as noble ventures, in reality killed tens of thousands of Jews and burned one community after another. The fourteenth century Black Death of Europe was blamed on the Jews who were accused of poisoning the wells; in actuality, it was caused by infected rats who spread the Bubonic Plague through every town and hamlet of Europe. Mass expulsions of Jews from Spain and Portugal, the Inquisition, pogroms in Eastern Europe, enforced ghettos, obligatory dress distinctions, abject poverty, social ostracism—all were brutal manifestations of European anti-Semitism. Was it then such a shocking phenomenon what occurred in Nazi Germany? Has anti-Semitism disappeared? Are we finally free from this same fear that has haunted our past?

A second lesson that we Jews must learn from the Holocaust is that the world remained apathetic toward the plight of the Jew. Today, we understand that the world felt that Jewish lives were expendable. Though they could have helped, the nations of the world watched as spectators while the Jewish people was humiliated, dehumanized, deprived of basic human rights, and finally mass murdered. Has any of this changed? Are we any more fairly regarded by the hypocrisy of world opinion? Is our present existence any more secure?

A third lesson to be learned by Jews is that the fate of the Jewish people is universally linked. During the Holocaust, *one out of every three Jews* was murdered. We are painfully aware that were it not for the geographical accident of our birth, we, too, would have been destroyed by the Nazis. We remain responsible for ourselves and for our own survival. By remembering the Holocaust, we hope to be vigilant enough to prevent the sacrifice of more Jews.

In 1967, a symposium was held by writers and critics, in which Elie Wiesel posed the question: "Why should we tell the story of the Holocaust?" The answer given by the literary critic George Steiner relates directly to us who live today in a highly assimilated society:

> We must tell it to be on our guard, so that our children know when it may happen the next time. You know better than I, Élie, that in France there were two modes of horror when one was in the trains. One was to be with your child and to know why you were going—because you are a Jew. Worse, was to have to explain to your children, as countless assimilationists did: "Qu'est-ce que c'est qu'un Juif? Pourquoi moi?"[4] (What is a Jew? Why me?)

The lessons of the Holocaust are not limited only to Jews. All humankind must reap the painful benefits of the recent past. Humankind in general must be on guard against an evergrowing tendency to devalue human life.

The Holocaust occurred because the Jew was dehumanized, taken out of the society of mankind. By making the Jew the antithesis of all human values, the Nazis were able to carry out their program of extermination: to make their country and the world *Judenrein*, free of Jews. The Holocaust desensitized man to the value of human life. The question has been asked: Without Auschwitz could there have been a Hiroshima? Can there any longer be any instance in which we find ourselves insensitive to the plight of human beings whenever they are? We of this generation find that we have a historic and moral obligation to remember the Holocaust. We also have a moral imperative to teach it to our children if they are to live in a humane world. Carved on the wall of Yad Vashem is a poem by Abraham Schlonsky entitled "Neder," "The Vow."

> My eyes have seen desolation and grief
> And heaped anguish upon my heart;
> My goodness begged and urged to forgive
> But the infinite horror forbade a new start.
>
> I vow to remember as long as I live;
> Forgiveness to me is lost as an art.
> To the tenth generation not to forget,
> Until the offense has abated and also the vow.
>
> And my wrath has faded and finally set.
> I promise to carry in me all I know.
> I promise not to unlearn and later regret
> But to inscribe and remember all that I saw.

These poetic words embody for us the essence of our moral imperative to remember the Holocaust. The understandings and sensitivities that derive from such hallowed memory offer us hope for a more noble world in future days.

2.
The Literature of the Holocaust

If we wished to go backwards in time, perhaps thirty-five or forty years, cross an ocean, and crawl into the bodies and minds of our brothers and sisters of the European Holocaust, how would we do it? How would we gain entry into hell? What kind of a passport would we use?

The Holocaust cannot be taught; it must be experienced. We must peer into the dark days and the burning nights. We must feel the terror that immobilized even the strongest, and we must sense the unshakable love of life that strengthened those who should have had no hope left. In short, we must reach what Joseph Conrad called the *Heart of Darkness*.

The writing of the Holocaust is both powerful and challenging. It encompasses numerous points of view and a variety of experiences. It finds form in varying literary genres. In viewing the literature of the Holocaust, we see before us diaries, poems, short stories, novels, plays, essays, eyewitness accounts, and even court testimonies. Some are angry. Some are sad. Some are philosophical. Some are deeply personal. Despite all their differences, however, they share a common sense of urgency. This urgent need to repeat, to remember, and to teach unites the literature of the Holocaust.

Eugene Heimler was a young man in his twenties when he was taken to Auschwitz. He survived to tell his story in *Night of the Mist*. His desperate determination after being liberated from the death camp finds expression in these unforgettable words:

> There were messages I had to deliver to the living from the dead. There were things I had to do, words I had to speak, moments which I had to dissect in order to show the world what I had seen and lived through, on behalf of the millions who had seen it also—but could no longer speak of their dead, burnt bodies—I would be the voice.[5]

Like Heimler, the writers of the Holocaust serve as the voice of the dead; yet they must be regarded as more than writers of "instant catharsis." They do not write as sensationalists, for it is of their blood and the blood of their loved ones which they write. We must take care not to concentrate solely upon their hatred, justified as it may be, or upon the revenge that surges through their words. Rather, let us accept these writers as moral teachers: witnesses remembering for a purpose to improve the world, to insure that it might never happen again. It is to us that they speak. They remind us that in the twentieth century man created hell here on earth, and that just as society became murderous, we, too, must always be alert to our own murderous instincts. Primo Levi, author of *If This Is Man* and a survivor of Auschwitz, warns:

> If from inside the Lager, a message could have seeped out to free men, it would have been this: take care not to suffer in your own home what is inflicted on us here.[6]

In other words, take care to always cherish freedom, value human life, and never negate it of its nobility.

As we approach the literature of the Holocaust and examine the fabric and texture of those days, we find it to be brittle, dusty, covered with ashes, But where we would expect it to crumble beneath our touch and to disappear into nothingness, we are surprised. We find that it clings to our fingers and enters into our very pores until it becomes an indisputable part of us. We learn that while the Nazis did everything possible to totally dehumanize the Jew, to force him into the role of an *Untermensch*, a being less than human, they could not destroy his free spirit and human soul. In work after work, we encounter the same paradox. On the one hand, the Jew is humiliated, deprived of the barest physical needs, tormented, and tortured; on the other hand, he retains his spiritual nobility. Anne Frank, the little teenager in the *achterhuis* (attic) in Amsterdam, confronts brutal reality with her question: "Who has inflicted this upon us? Who has made us Jews different from all other people?" Instead of rejecting her God or despising mankind, Anne replies, "It is God who has made us as we are, but it will be God, too, who will raise us up again.... If God lets me live... I shall not remain insignificant; I shall work in the world and for mankind!"[7]

Anne Frank was young, and, as many adolescents, she was imbued with an unwavering sense of idealism, yet her strength and conviction reverberate in many other stories of the Holocaust. The heroism of *Terezin*

Requiem by Josef Bor startles us in its iron-clad refusal to compromise its human dignity. Bor relates how the musicians of the Terezin camp, summoned to prepare a concert for the leaders of the SS including Eichmann, found within their innermost selves the courage to defy. The German high command had chosen Verdi's Requiem Mass for the performance. This mass expresses man's plea to Christ for eternal deliverance. It builds to a climax as the singers chant in timid voices of supplication: "Libera me." ("Deliver me...redeem me.") The Germans ironically intended publicly to force words of pleading into the mouths of the doomed Jews. A strange spirit, however, infects the Jewish symphony. A seed of rebellion takes hold as the voices and instruments crescendo into a defiant trumpeting of "Libera me!" as if to deny the temporal authority of those gathered in the audience. Their bold stance affirms the prisoners' belief in a higher morality and imparts to them a courageous dignity despite the tragic brevity of their rebellion.[8]

From the early moments of the Nazi threat, the Jew refused to be spiritually destroyed. We have only to recall the essay entitled "Wear the Yellow Badge with Pride" by Robert Weltsch, which appeared in the prestigious Zionist periodical *Jüdische Rundschau* in April 1933, or the famous Kol Nidre Prayer offered by Leo Baeck, the leader of German Jewry in 1935, and echoed in numerous synagogues despite strong prohibitions in order to feel the depth of their resistance. This spirit endured despite the hardships and defeating odds of the death camps. Two strong voices speak to us out of the darkness of Auschwitz: Primo Levi, an Italian Jew, and Viktor Frankl, a former professor of psychiatry and neurology at the University of Vienna.

> Even in this place, one can survive, and therefore one must want to survive, to tell the story, to bear witness.... We are slaves, condemned of every right, exposed to every insult, condemned to certain death, but we still possess one power, and we must defend it with all our strength for it is the last—the power to refuse our consent....[9]

Frankl was asked by his fellow prisoners to counsel those in his barracks. He himself was ailing, cold, hungry, despondent, and yet he found the strength within himself to say: "Was Du erlebst, kann keine Macht der Welt Dir Rauben."

> What you have experienced, no power on earth can take from you. I told my comrades that human life, under any circumstances, never ceases to

have a meaning, and that this meaning of life includes suffering, and dying, privation and death. I asked the poor creatures who listened to me attentively in the darkness of the hut to face up to the seriousness of our position. They must not lose hope but should keep their courage in the certainty that the hopelessness of our struggle did not detract from its dignity and meaning.[10]

The literature of the Holocaust provides us with a graphic picture of what life was actually like for those who were trapped in its web. Through the words of the many authors, we come to feel the insurmountable pressures and choices that were heaped upon them in every instance of their effort to survive. One of the most realistic representations of the moral crises faced by the Jews in Nazi Europe appears in a play published in November 1977 by Shlomo Katz, the former editor of the Jewish periodical *Midstream*. This drama, entitled *Verdicts*, takes place in 1944 in a small town deep in Nazi-occupied Holland. The author prefaces his play with a quotation from *Crime and Punishment* that effectively sets the mood of the piece and states his theme.

> Where is it, though Raskolnikov, where is it I've read that someone condemned to death says or thinks, an hour before his death that if he had to live on some high rock, on a narrow ledge that he had only room to stand, and the ocean everlasting darkness, everlasting solitude, everlasting tempest around him, if he had to remain standing on a square yard of space all his life, a thousand years, eternity, it were better to live so than to die at once! Only to live, to live, and live! Life, whatever it may be![11]

And life, with its indignities and its hardships, was still of the essence for the captured Jew. Imagine this scene: A Jew, chairman of the local Jewish council, is called into the office of the Nazi Gauleiter and is offered a choice. He may choose immediate deportation and death for himself and the community he represents, or he may strike a bargain. A phenomenal amount of money may be exchanged for the freedom of five Jewish families. What is he to do? Is the offer sincere? Will these families actually gain freedom, or will they be duped for their money? What right has he to choose who is to live and who is to die? The proposed ransom is outlined in this scene between Gauleiter Todt and Isaac Levi:

> TODT: *(Sits down.)* So, here's the proposition. For fifty thousand dollars in gold we will release five Jewish families from this town. . . . Don't interrupt

me. This is a bargain, isn't it? *(Pokes his stick into Levi's chest and grins.)* Isn't it? Ten thousand dollars for a family of Jews. What's more, I don't care how big the family is. But it must be parents and children only. No grandparents, no brothers or sisters. Just father and mother and such children as they have. No adopted children. Or every Itzik and Moishe would be adopted by the family chosen to escape. I know you people and your tricks. But, Izzie, you can pick the biggest true families you have in this town. I don't care. Didn't I tell you I'll make a generous offer? *(Laughs).* And as soon as you deliver the gold, or other valuables such as diamonds, of equal value, together with the list of five families, we will load your Chosen People onto trucks and take them to the coast and let them hire boats, and . . . bye-bye Izzie. You can go to Sweden, or to America, or even to your—what do you call it—E-r-e-z I-s-r-o-e-l. It's all the same to us. We Nazis are good sports. We will give you a running start. *(Laughs).* Well, Herr Levi, *(pokes him in the chest with his stick)* isn't it a good deal?[12]

What choice should be made? Who can judge? As the play unfolds, we agonize with Levi in his soul searching. He is caught in a web of torment and guilt as it falls upon him to dispense the power of life and death.

Most Jews, however, had no choices to make. Caught within an inescapable network of brutality, they could only survive from one day to the next. With each reprieve came increased hardship, until finally there existed nothing more than black night and total darkness. One of the leading figures of the Holocaust calls to us from the depths of the Warsaw Ghetto. Chaim Kaplan had served as the principal of the Warsaw Hebrew Day School for forty years. A Hebrew scholar and educator, he commanded respect in the community as a leading intellectual. His *Scroll of Agony*, a diary written in Hebrew and dating from the arrival of the Nazis in 1939 until Kaplan's own deportation to Treblinka in 1942, illuminates the Warsaw community's desperate struggle to survive. Hidden in 1942 and not found until 1965 when it was discovered by Pres. Abraham Katsch of Dropsie University, this journal brings to life once more the tragic days of the ghetto. In it we see how the Jews of Warsaw preserved their will to live despite the shrinking boundaries, poverty, and raging typhus. On November 30, 1939, only three months after the occupation of Poland, Kaplan wrote:

We live broken and shattered lives; lives of shame and dishonor; lives of suffering and grief. But the power of adaptability within us is miraculous. Conditions change—the mode of work changes too. We have drawn together within ourselves; we have shriveled and shrunk; we follow the advice of the prophet: "Come, my people, enter thou into thy chambers, and shut the doors about thee: hide thyself for a little moment, until the indignation be overpast."[13]

But the indignation did not pass. Murder followed murder, until the deportations and block selections became a routine way of life—or death. On August 4, 1942, Kaplan prepared for his own deportation the following day. As he looked ahead into a future that held no surprise for him, he concluded:

Sometimes, from among tends of thousands of the ravaged, your eyes are drawn to a face which haunts you no matter where you turn, does not leave you alone, follows you like a shadow and disturbs your rest.[14]

We follow his face and we hear his voice, yet Kaplan speaks to us from among a multitude of other faces and other voices.

One of the most touching and inspiring personalities in our literature is that of a little girl, Raja Englanderova. Thirteen years old at the time of her deportation from Prague to Terezin, Raja survived. What was Terezin? It was a strange place. Sixty kilometers from Prague, built two hundred years ago by Emperor Joseph II of Austria and named after his mother, Maria Theresa, Terezin existed as a walled fortress in the shape of a star surrounded by green meadows, fruit trees, and tall poplars. During the war, Terezin was a place of fear and famine. It was a stopover on the road to death. Actually, Terezin had been designed by the Nazis as a model camp which foreigners, especially those from the International Red Cross, could be shown. At first, Jews from Bohemia and Moravia were brought to Terezin, but finally they came from all over Europe and from there were shipped further east to the gas chambers and ovens of Poland. Everything in this camp was false, invented. Every one of its inhabitants was condemned in advance to die. It was only a matter of time. Some were resigned; some were deceived. The children who were brought here, though, knew nothing of what awaited them. Confronted by the evil reality around them, they still maintained their childish outlook of truth, hope, and trust. And, so they lived, locked within the walls, apart from their parents and with only each other. Out of fifteen thousand children, only one hundred came back. As we remember their haunted faces and hear their tremulous voices, we stand in awe of the adults who took charge of these bereft children and gave them love in a loveless world. Older children cared for the littler ones, and two teachers taught them to draw, write, play, and sing. Their drawings reflect cruel fairy tales filled with evil witches, wizards, and cannibals. Their poems speak painfully of "the little girl who got lost" or dream of a place where there are "kinder people." They recall homes they would never see again, homes once secure with fluttering white curtains and cups of steaming hot chocolate. Still, despite the earthshaking trauma, these children frantically attempted to grasp the beauty of life.[15] "I Never Saw Another Butterfly," a poem written by a young boy named Pavel Friedman who died in Auschwitz on September 29, 1944, lends its name to both a collection of poems and drawings by the children of Terezin as well as to a dramatic presentation by Celeste Raspanti. This play imaginatively recreates the story of little Raja from the various documentary materials available: poems, diaries, letters, journals, drawings, and pictures. In moving language, Raja and her friends enable us to experience their struggle to retain the essence of human dignity:

> My name ... is Raja. I was born in Prague. Father, Mother, Pavel, Irca — Irena, Honza — they are all gone, and I am alone. But that is not important. Only one thing is important — that I am a Jew, and I survived. . . . [16]

Through the use of emotional flashbacks, we grasp the personal tragedy that befell young Raja. We see her formerly happy home destroyed by the Nazi onslaught, and we share the fearful loneliness that engulfs her. The desperate strength of her friend and teacher, Irena Synkova, beckons to us a light of courage in an otherwise dark vacuum. This valiant woman, obsessed with the necessity of survival, took charge of the little victims. Her makeshift school and her quiet determination provided them with the basics of security and love they had lost. As the transports become more frequent and the children are taken away in larger numbers, Irena's voice becomes more filled with bitterness. Yet, her purpose is not dulled, even as she faces her own death. Her courage inspires Raja and enables her spiritually to resist destruction:

> IRENA: Raja, listen to me. You are no longer a child — this minute, you are no longer a child — and so I tell you . . . *(She gently forces Raja to sit down and, holding her hands, continues.)* I have a child — she is nine years old — she was torn away from my arms and thrown from the train by an angered guard. I tried to throw myself after her — but I was dragged back into the car. I wanted to die until I came to Terezin and found thousands of chil-

dren waiting for me—and I knew I must not die... Do you understand? *(Raja has listened, stunned but calmed. She turns away.)* You are no longer a child—and so I tell you. I have a child and she lives wherever I comfort another child or dry her tears. *(Raja turns away in despair. Irena stands waiting helplessly but tenderly. Irena opens her arms and Raja, in a gesture that recalls their first meeting, puts her head on Irena's shoulder and weeps. She rises with a new-found strength and walks downstage as the lights go down on the scene.)*

REJA: Fear—this is half the story of Terezin—its beginning, but not its end. I was a child there, I knew that word. I became a woman there because I learned another word from Irca and Pavel, from Father and Mother, from Irena Synkova. I learned the word "courage" and found the determination to live—to believe in life....[17]

Such unforgettable words draw us into the midst of the SIX MILLION. Their faces and their voices are no longer distant. They have become part of our lives. Their bravery underlines in an immediate way the determination of the Jew not to be dehumanized despite insurmountable force. But the force *was* there, and for most there were no witnesses to the evil perpetrated upon them. They were martyred in mass and dispatched into vast reaches of silence. We must continue to remember those writers who have chosen to bear witness. Like Émile Zola, the nineteenth-century French novelist, they, too, shout "J' accuse" at the conscience of the world. At times, this accusation takes the form of an autobiographical novel like *Night* by Elie Wiesel. We can never forget the brutal scene in which the son, transformed into a depraved human beast, attacks his own father:

> Felled to the ground, stunned with blows, the old man cried. "Meir, my boy! Don't you recognize me? I'm your father.... You're hurting me.... You're killing your father! I've got some bread... for you to.... for you too."
>
> He collapsed. His fist was still clenched around a small piece. He tried to carry it to his mouth. But the other one threw himself upon him and snatched it. The old man again whispered something, let out a rattle, and died amid the general indifference. His son searched him, took the bread, and began to devour it. He was not able to get very far. Two men had seen and hurled themselves upon him. Others joined in. When they withdrew, next to me were two corpses, side by side, the father and the son.[18]

Literary accusation also appears in much of the court testimony given at the various war crime trials. These were actual eyewitness reports by plain people, neither authors nor poets, whose words possess the same power. Rivka Yoselewska was born in Zagrodski, a town containing some five hundred Jewish families in the Pinsk district. Her father owned a leather goods shop and was considered a local notable. Mrs. Yoselewska was married in 1934, and when the Germans arrived, she had one child, a daughter. The events she describes in her testimony at the Eichmann Trial took place in mid-August 1941, when the Jewish community was rounded up and transported to a huge ravine outside of town. Gideon Hausner, the prosecutor for the state of Israel, recalls her testimony which shattered the courtroom as she spoke for an hour and a half in a tone that was both quiet and restrained:

> 'Even when I saw the naked people who had arrived before us, I still did not believe they would kill us, I hoped it would be just torture,' she said. Taking off her clothes, she stood there clinging to her six-year-old daughter. Her mother, her grandmother and her sister were all nearby. Her hopes were in vain. The SS men started shooting the Jews one by one, firing point-blank into the back of each victim's head, then kicking the body into the open pit. Yoselewska saw her father and mother disappear into the ditch. Then the Germans approached her grandmother, who was holding two little girls in her arms, comforting them and pointing to heaven, where they would soon meet all their beloved ones. In a moment all three were shot. 'Then I saw my sister embrace a girl friend; the two of them tried to cover their nakedness with each other's bodies, pleading with a uniformed SS man to spare their young lives. In reply they were both shot and went down.
>
> 'As I stood there paralyzed with horror,' continued Mrs. Yoselewska, 'my little daughter, Malka, was wrung from my arms and killed.' At that particular moment, she said, she felt nothing more. The German who shot her missed his aim, and the bullet merely grazed her head. She only felt a booted leg kicking her into the ditch to bleed to death or die of suffocation.
>
> Later she regained consciousness. 'I felt I was choking and desperately needed air,' she said, 'and so I lifted myself from among the bodies, many of which were still alive and were biting at me and pulling me down. By then the shooting was over and the Germans were gone.' She had only leaden skis above her head and an endless grave under her feet.
>
> 'I fell down, scratching my nails into the thin layer of earth covering the bodies, begging to be admitted back to my family. Blood was oozing from the grave; whenever I pass a spring now I remember the red fountain.'
>
> She sat there in a daze for three days, waiting for death to come. People passing by thought she was a ghost or a madwoman, and hurried on. Finally a farmer, more courageous than the others, approached her, gave

her clothing and food, and led her away into the forest. There she was looked after by partisan fighters, whom she joined. Her wounds healed; she managed to survive the war. She is married now in Israel and has two children.[19]

Her dramatic testimony brings to us that same urgency that we find throughout the literature of the Holocaust. Rivka Yoselewska lived, and in her survival she gives life to those who perished. Her words need neither literary frills nor contrived plots to express the depths of the Nazi terror; her words, simple and direct, speak for themselves.

On February 21, 1961, the state of Israel convened the famous Eichmann Trial. Its intent was larger than merely to punish a single perpetrator of war crimes. The prosecution understood that it was too late in history to avenge the death of six million by the death of one man. The intent of the trial aimed at a greater necessity — to keep the Holocaust alive before the conscience of the world. It hoped to insure that people would not forget the recent past and to guarantee that future generations of young people would learn what had occurred in the middle years of this century. The Eichmann Trial underscored the rallying cry of Israel's survival: "Never again!"

This concern of the Israeli government was certainly to the point. I, personally, shall never forget that in the early 1960s a friend of mine, exceptionally well educated and otherwise sophisticated, believed that the Nazis had only persecuted those Jews guilty of political crimes. We visited Europe together. When we arrived in Dachau, this young woman suffered a shocking revelation. She abruptly learned that Jews were killed merely because they were Jews. Unable to cope with this brutal reality, she became physically ill. This story indicates the uneasy withdrawal from the subject the American Jewish community experienced in the postwar years. An entire generation of Jews and Christians alike chose not directly to confront the enormity of the Holocaust. Israel conceived its role to be as the principal educator of world conscience.

In his opening speech at the trial, the attorney general Gideon Hausner delivered the indictment against Adolph Eichmann in words powerful enough to rank among the best literature of the Holocaust:

> When I stand before you here, Judges of Israel, to lead the Prosecution of Adolph Eichmann, I am not standing alone. With me are six million accusers. But they cannot rise to their feet and point an accusing finger towards him who sits in the dock and cry: "I accuse." For their ashes are piled

up on the hills of Auschwitz and the fields of Treblinka, and are strewn in the forests of Poland. Their graves are scattered throughout the length and breadth of Europe. Their blood cries out, but their voice is not heard. Therefore I will be their spokesman and in their name I will unfold the awesome indictment.[20]

In language both biblical and epic in tone, Hausner relates the catastrophe of the Holocaust. He traces the history of the Jewish people from earliest time and describes the Nazi crime of genocide in all its magnitude. Hausner reminds us in majestic language of the denial of human rights, the apathy of the German majority, the passion of hatred with its slogans of "Deutschland erwache—Juda verrecke!" ("Germany awaken— Jewry die!") and the theme song of "Wenn Judenblut von Messer spritz— Dann geht's nochmal so gut!" ("When Jewish blood spurts from the knife—Then all goes doubly well.") His conclusions to the court are both specific in regard to Eichmann's personal guilt and far reaching concerning the guilt of Nazi Germany:

> ...It is beyond our power to give a complete description of this terrible disaster in all its depth. I am afraid that even after submitting all the evidence and material which is in our possession, we shall not be able to do more than give a pale reflection of the enormous human and national tragedy which beset Jewry in this generation.
>
> Adolph Eichmann will enjoy a privilege which he did not accord to even a single one of his victims. He will be able to defend himself before the Court. His fate will be decided according to law and according to the evidence, with the burden of proof resting upon the prosecution.
>
> And the judges of Israel will pronounce true and righteous judgment.[21]

Thus we encounter the literature of the Holocaust. It speaks to us in numerous voices and from various moments. Some words burn with the passionate heat of the moment; others have benefited from the luxury of passing time and echo a more peaceful climate of reflection and hindsight. It expresses many moods: from anger to despair to hope and to the ultimate transcendence of the terror. While the authors range a full gamut of ages and languages, a common humanity unites them. Their writings all express a shared reverence for life. They point to the Nazi as if to say, "You hold life cheap; we do not." For the Jew has never negated the beauty and the purpose of life. Throughout the thousands of years of our existence, we have imbued human life with meaning, direction, and, above all, sanctity. It is this reverential belief in the human spirit that has enabled us to rise above the self-destructiveness of mankind and to survive in a world that has not yet achieved the same level of morality.

The martyrs of the Holocaust did not die unmourned. Their martyrdom, in a long chain of Kiddush HaShem (Sanctification of God's Name), has meaning for us as we look to the future. Their memory may help us to shape our own lives around moral principles and cause us always to remember the dignity and holiness of human life.

3.
The Moral Imperative of the Holocaust

The Holocaust contains moral implications for contemporary life. Where was God during the Holocaust? Why didn't He intervene? Questions such as these concerning the Divine presence have been posed by philosophers and theologians. Many varied interpretations have been advanced. Some have denied God's existence. This theory claims that God died at Auschwitz. Others have preached that suffering as punishment for human sin serves to teach man to be more virtuous in the future. This medieval concept teaches that pain deters man from evil. Still others have conceived of God as a limited God, one who has imperfect control over human beings. Thus, God is a God of nature, not of history. The explanation given by those of great faith has traditionally stated that we simply cannot fathom God's purpose.

The question, nevertheless, remains of legitimate concern to our generation. For, on the one hand, we hope to instill within our young people a belief in the moral nature of a divine universe; on the other hand, they regard the shadow of the Holocaust as the epitome of immorality and evil.

What can we propose as an answer? Where can we turn for a point of view consistent with traditional Jewish thought and relevant to our modern frame of reference?

I suggest that we refer back to the primary source of the Bible itself. The Book of Genesis serves as the foundation stone upon which the entire Torah is erected. Within its pages, a traditionally Jewish approach to this question can be found.

The Torah depicts God as bestowing upon man the qualities of comprehension, perception, and free will. Genesis never portrays God as preventing man from committing immoral actions. Were He to intervene in human affairs before man actually committed them, then He would be denying those very qualities of self-determination upon which Judaism is anchored. Instead of preempting human actions, the biblical God reveals Himself as the redeemer and punisher of man's deeds after they have occurred. Man is not prevented from sinning. God does not stop Adam from tasting fruit from the Tree of Knowledge, nor does He deflect Cain from killing his brother, Abel. The generation of the Flood is not arrested from sinning, just as Sodom and Gomorrah are allowed to continue on their evil course. God refuses to exercise His omnipotence to deter man's evil, even at the time of the Exodus from Egypt. The desert generation, though God's Chosen People, must experience the results of their own actions, for the living of life falls completely into man's own hands. As he possesses free will, man must choose his own way, good or bad, noble or wicked. As the Book of Deuteronomy points out:

> See, I have set before you this day life and
>   prosperity,
> death and adversity . . . I call heaven and
>   earth to witness against this day;
> I have put before you life and death,
>   blessing and curse.
> Choose life—if you and your offsprings would live.[22]

The prophets conceived of a universal God whose kingdom encompassed all peoples; therefore, one must conclude that man's innate free will applies to both Jew and non-Jew alike. As God's rule envelops all nations and races, so his teachings apply to humanity as a whole. Evil will disappear only when mankind learns from within itself how to create a moral and ethical universe. Judaism does not preclude the ability to benefit from past error. The hope for ultimate salvation shines throughout biblical thought. As the prophet Isaiah so beautifully sings in his vision of the end of days, God will guide man to great heights of fulfillment, but the resources to arrive at the pinnacle must be drawn from within humanity itself.

The evil perpetrated during the Holocaust by man on his fellow man forces us to take stock of our own lives and of our future directions. Today we must commit ourselves to the betterment of the world around us. Just as the Bible teaches that man possesses the ability to benefit from the past, so do the lessons we learn from the Holocaust apply to contemporary society. Stephen Schwarzchild has proposed that we incorporate an additional set of commandments into our lives:[23]

1. *Thou shalt not be the executioner:* Murder is evil in any guise, be it here or abroad, for any immoral purpose.
2. *Thou shalt not be silent:* One can no longer separate himself from the problems and responsibilities of his society, for a just society depends on the conscientious participation of every man.
3. *Thou shalt not be the spectator:* Indifference and apathy are as destructive in a society as overt evil. Man must be concerned with the quality of life around him, for in the words of John Donne, "No man is an island entire of itself; every man is a piece of the continent, a part of the main."[24] Jean Paul Sartre, the French existentialist, claims that the ultimate evil is that of making abstract that which is concrete, of removing one's self from a personal involvement in the world about him.
4. *Thou shalt not be the dog:* One must not compromise his humanity. Man was created in the image of God; he ranks above the animals. When we negate our humanity, we sink into the depths of bestiality, thus permitting the destruction of human society.
5. *Thou shalt not look too long into the fire:* Man should not become blinded by the brightness of the fire. Instead of losing our direction, we need to recall the lessons of the past so that they may be applied to the future.
6. *Thou shalt continue to interrogate:* Man alone has been given the gift of reason, as the French philosopher Descartes stated in the eighteenth century, "Je pense, donc je suis"; "I think, therefore I am." The ability to think, question, evaluate, necessitates constant introspection. We are obligated to pose difficult questions and to search for reluctant answers. Man must rise above the beasts and hold the lantern up against the darkness, illuminating the universe about him.

The Holocaust exists as a microcosm of human history. It testifies to the greatest evil that man has perpetrated against his fellow man, and in the survival of the Jewish people, it expresses the greatest strength that man contains within his soul. Its lessons present both Jew and non-Jew alike with an indisputable moral imperative if we are to survive as Jews and as human beings.

In the eighteenth century, Voltaire concluded his famous satire *Candide* with the following statement: "Il faut cultiver notre jardin" ("We must cultivate our garden"). He intended this to mean that man should concern himself with bettering his own world, even at the exclusion of the greater world beyond. The Holocaust teaches us that we can no longer cast our gaze inward. Our garden, as safe, beautiful, and peaceful as it may be, is no longer sufficient; for beyond our garden lies an even larger world that is daily coming closer and more immediate. It can be an extension of the beauty of our own lives, or it can be a jungle rapidly encroaching upon everything we have so carefully cultivated. Today, our garden must encompass the entire world. We must at all times nurture the totality of our existence, so that we never give Hitler a posthumous victory—and that another Holocaust may never again occur.

Notes

1. Irving Halperin, *Messengers from the Dead: Literature of the Holocaust* (Philadelphia: Westminster Press, 1970) 12.
2. Ibid., 14.
3. Hugo Valentine, *Anti-Semitism, Historically and Critically Examined* New York: (Viking Press, 1936) 27.
4. Ibid., 18.
5. Ibid., 13.
6. Ibid., 16.
7. Albert Friedlander, *Out of the Whirlwind: A Reader of Holocaust Literature* (New York: Union of American Hebrew Congregations, 1968) 34.
8. Ibid., 68–78.
9. Halperin, 133.
10. Ibid., 26.
11. Shlomo Katz, *Verdicts: A Play in Three Acts, Midstream*, November 1977, 3.
12. Ibid., 6.
13. Halperin, 51.
14. Ibid., 63.
15. *I Never Saw Another Butterfly: Children's Drawings and Poems from Terezin Concentration Camp 1942–1944* (New York: McGraw Hill, 1962) 59–62.
16. Celeste Raspanti, *I Never Saw Another Butterfly*, 7–8.
17. Ibid., 29–30.
18. Halperin, 23.
19. Gideon Hausner, *Justice in Jerusalem* (New York: Harper and Row, 1966) 73.
20. Ibid., 323–324.
21. Ibid., 325.
22. Aharon Kessler, *God and the Holocaust* (Pittsburgh, 1978).
23. Halperin, 123–124.
24. John Donne, "Devotions Upon Emergent Occasions, XVII," *Major British Writers* (New York: Harcourt, Brace and Company, 1954) 392.

Bibliography

Donne, John. "Devotions Upon Emergent Occasions, XVII." *Major British Writers*. New York: Harcourt, Brace and Company, 1954.

Friedlander, Albert. *Out of the Whirlwind: A Reader of Holocaust Literature*. New York: Union of American Hebrew Congregations, 1968.

Halperin, Irving. *Messengers from the Dead: Literature of the Holocaust*. Philadelphia: Westminster Press, 1970.

Hausner, Gideon. *Justice in Jerusalem*. New York: Harper and Row, 1966.

I Never Saw Another Butterfly: Children's Drawings and Poems from Terezin Concentration Camp 1942–1944. New York: McGraw-Hill, 1962.

Katz, Shlomo. *Verdicts: A Play in Three Acts. Midstream,* November, 1977.

Kessler, Aharon. *God and the Holocaust*. Pittsburgh, Pa., 1978.

Raspanti, Celeste. *I Never Saw Another Butterfly*. Chicago, 1971.

Valentin, Hugo. *Anti-Semitism Historically and Critically Examined*. New York: Viking Press, 1936.

Summary

In "Challenges and Confrontations in Jewish Education" Aharon Kessler presents Professor Meir Ben Horin's seven categories of questions which the learner at the conclusion of his Jewish education in the secondary school should be able to answer.

1. Questions that relate to self:
   a. What kind of person am I as a Jew?
   b. How did I come to be what I am?
   c. Where, as a Jew, do I go from here?

2. Questions that relate to the Jewish people:
   a. What kind of people are we Jews?
   b. How did we come to be what we are?
   c. Where, as a people, do we want to go?

3. Questions that relate to the world we live in:
   a. In what kind of world do we live?
   b. How must we relate ourselves to this world?
   c. What may this world expect of us?
   d. Where do we want to go as we move into the future?

4. Questions that relate to the universe we live in:
   a. What kind of universe do we live in?
   b. How shall we relate ourselves to man's expanding horizons, and do so as members of the Jewish people?

5. Questions that relate to the Jewish community:
   a. Jewish communities in the Diaspora: Whence? Where? Whither?

6. Questions that relate to Judaism:

    a. How shall we understand Judaism?
    b. In what direction shall it move?
    c. What shall be my role in the ongoing life of the Jewish people? American Jewry? The State of Israel?

7. Questions that relate to individual fulfillment:
    a. What hope for individual fulfillment and national redemption unifies and guides Jewry now and always?

The author, Aharon Kessler, writes of the challenges and confrontations in Jewish Education as follows:

Jewish schools operate within the larger context of the fact that our community continues to grow only insofar as each new generation takes its rightful place as knowledgeable and committed Jewish adults.

V

The Image of the Historic Jew

1.
Why This Bulletin?

A study of professionally trained and full-time teachers in three school systems revealed that a substantial majority have limited time to devote to continuing study of the subjects they teach. In a similar study of teachers in Jewish congregational schools, which I conducted a long time ago for the American Association of Jewish Education in the New England states, the information indicated that a majority who were employed as part-time instructors were neither diplomated nor licensed. With the exception of a small number of "student teachers" in the larger cities, the others found it unnecessary to devote time to continuing study. The conclusion reached by the surveyors of both studies was that teachers who do not engage in continuing study rely on the knowledge they acquired in earlier years and on the students' textbooks.

In the course of years, numerous efforts to change conditions in Jewish education are evident. At the present, most Jewish teachers in congregational schools are graduates from American teachers colleges or are teachers who specialized in education in their respective universities. There are those who are familiar with and quite expert in the latest educational techniques. However, due to the absence of Jewish teachers colleges, many had no opportunity to study the sources of Judaism, such as the Talmudic period, the medieval philosophy, and contemporary Jewish history, philosophy, and literature.

Barry Chazen, of Brandeis University and the School of Education of the Hebrew University of Jerusalem, writes of the crisis and the hope for the Jewish school. He characterized Jewish education as being seriously ill. Contemporary Jewish education is all too often neither contemporary, Jewish, nor education. He calls on the Jewish community to harness its resources to meet the challenge of constructing a new Jewish educational system truly appropriate for twentieth century Jewish life.

Unfortunately, this problem is not clearly understood by educational administrators, boards of education, and parents. When children complain of boredom in the classrooms, it is generally attributed to faulty methods of instruction rather than to unchallenging materials that should arouse curiosity and interest in young people who are searching for the answers that Judaism can provide.

When the College of Jewish Studies was accredited by the University of Pittsburgh, Professor Lawrence Little, Head of Courses in Religious Education in the Graduate School at the university, invited Dr. Aharon Kessler to organize a Department of Religious Education for the two faiths—Judaism and Christianity. The objective was to provide courses of study to fill the need of history, pedagogy, and religious education for both faiths.

Dr. Kessler joined the faculty of the graduate school and established several courses dealing with the history and philosophy of education. The Jewish and Christian clergy welcomed these courses. Principals and teachers in the Jewish schools enrolled in these classes, as well as students and faculty members from the Pittsburgh Theological Seminary.

This bulletin contains an outline of the first introductory lectures given in Jewish education. The title of the lecture series is "The Image of the Historic Jew." Each lecture is structured in the problem-solving method. It raises issues, explores the issue, and provides solutions for further consideration.

2.
Lecture I:
Introduction to the Image of the Historic Jew

The subject under consideration in this series of lectures was suggested by a student at Oberlin College. Following a lecture I had given at that school on "Jewish Contributions to Civilization," based on Joseph Jacobs' classic by the same title, a student asked for a private meeting.

"Your lecture disturbed me," he began. "I had never heard this approach to Jewish history and I can't help but wonder how authentic your thesis is."

I then asked: "How intensive is your formal Jewish education?"

He responded: "I was raised in a conservative Jewish home and attended Hebrew school for five years. After my Bar Mitzvah, my parents insisted that I continue in the congregation's high school, which I did for two years. Since I entered Oberlin, I have had no contact with Jewish culture. The image of the 'historic Jew,' which I perceived in my mind during these four years, did not motivate me to seek further knowledge of Judaism."

I interrupted him. "Could you describe your own perception of the image of the Jew to me?"

He replied: "An ancient people, living in ghettos, persecuted for their religion, but holding on to their beliefs and rituals, many of which are out of place and out of time in the modern world. I feel some pride about Jewish contributions in the ancient world, but neither do I have a clear understanding of the nature of those contributions nor any hint as to what the Jewish people contributed to civilization during the past two thousand years. If your lecture is based on authentic knowledge of history, then I have lived the four years at Oberlin with a wrong image of the Jewish people."

His use of the term "image," which I did not employ in my lecture, intrigued me.

"What do you mean by image; an apparition which is an unusual sight, or a specific experience?" I asked.

He replied: "As a science major, I mean a set of values or character traits that would typify the historic Jew in my mind."

As our discussion continued, he became more specific and posted three questions? "I believe that many young American Jews are concerned with the following questions: What does it mean to be Jewish? Who is the most qualified authority to give an accurate answer to this question? What is the secret of Jewish survival?"

My explanations:

I take it that your use of the term "being" is in the philosophical sense, which means "existing." In that case, your question really is, "What makes a person Jewish?" The same question may be asked of an American, "What makes a person an American?" In the latter query, the answer is "American law." According to American civil law, a person born to American parents is automatically an American. In addition, a foreign-born person who is admitted to American citizenship is an American. In a similar manner, "being Jewish" is determined by Jewish law. Since the Jewish people have no civil law to guide their Jewish lifestyle, they are guided by religious laws in matters that pertain to their Jewishness. The religious law is known by the Hebrew term, *halakhah*. According to *halakhah*, a person born to a Jewish mother is automatically Jewish. A non-Jew who converts to Judaism by accepting the Jewish religion is also Jewish. No authority can rid a Jew from his Jewish people.

In another respect, however, Jewish law is different from American law. According to American law, a person may give up his U.S. Citizenship or exchange it for citizenship of another country. Jewish law permits no authority, even the person himself, to relinquish his/her membership in the Jewish people. This includes a Jew who converts to another religion. In the eyes of the *halakhah*, the convert remains Jewish pertaining to certain matters.

There is another aspect to membership in the Jewish people that may be of interest to you. It is what sociologists designate as consanguinity, which means "relationship by common ancestry." Jews trace their origins to the patriarchal family of Abraham, Isaac and Jacob. A convert to Judaism is therefore required to adopt Abraham and Sarah, the first Jews, as their ancestors. Thus, a male convert adds the name Abraham to the name that was given him at birth, and a female convert adds Sarah to her given name.

This should answer your first two questions. For an answer to the third question in which you seek an explanation of "the secret of Jewish survival," you would have to turn to history. As "a science major," you probably would ask what kind of history I have in mind, or go a step further and require a definition of history. In anticipation of both questions, I shall begin my explanation with definitions.

What Is History?

The Italian historian, Benedetto Croce, gave the following definition of history:

> All history consists essentially in seeing the past through eyes of the present in the light of its problems, and the main work of the historian is not to record, but to evaluate; for if he does not evaluate, how can he know what is worth to record?

What is meant by evaluate? It is to appraise, to estimate the value or worth of the information which the historian collects in order to judge reliability and effectiveness of the recorded events. Such information, however, is not limited to facts or specific events; it also contains ideas, ideals, and concepts that are the products of the human mind. The latter are thoughts, explanations and interpretations related to cause and effect of what has happened to a people or groups of peoples. History is not a self-contained science. It makes use of a variety of other sciences to arrive at its conclusions. Among the sciences which history draws upon are archaeology, anthropology, psychology, religion, political science, social science, and literature. In these disciplines, the image of the people, their ways of thinking and life styles are reflected.

What Is Jewish History?

Jewish history is no exception to this rule. But when Jewish history is compared with the histories of other contemporary nations, the competent historian must include in his evaluation certain elements which the others do not have. I shall mention three of these unique elements. One is what the leading historian Simon Dubnow calls "The Range of Jewish History." A second is what Prof. Nicholas de Lang, of the University of Cambridge, describes as the "Mystery About Jewish Existence." The third is what the sociologist, Robert E. Park, designates as "The Status of the Jews As a Marginal People."

The Range of Jewish History

The history of the Jewish people is like an axis crossing the history of mankind from one of its poles to the other. As an unbroken thread, it runs through the ancient civilizations of Egypt and Mesopotamia, down to the present-day cultures of modern times. Its divisions are measured by thousands of years.

The Mystery about Jewish Existence

There is a mystery about the very existence of the Jews: a people dispersed through the countries of the world, without (until recently) a land of their own or a common language, and yet possessing a strong sense of unity and common identity. Jewish identity is an enigma even to Jews themselves, impossible to capture in a single phrase; the only way to approach it is through history. To be a Jew is . . . to acknowledge an attachment to a past. Individual Jews are connected to one another in a way that the leaves of a wide-spreading tree are connected to one another: some leaves clustering close together or brought into momentary contact by the passing winds, others located far away, yet all similar in kind and linked by a complex structure of branches ramifying outwards or crossing in an apparently haphazard way, but all attached to the same trunk through which they draw their nourishment from the invisible roots. A Jew in Philadelphia or Frankfurt may have little in common, on the face of it, with a Jew in Kiev or Casablanca, in Tel Aviv or Tashkent. The only thing that unites them all is a feeling, however faint or unformulated, that they share the same origins, perhaps the same historic destiny which might, almost at random, have placed the one here and the other there.

The Jews are a small, scattered people. With one exception they are a tiny minority of the population of every country where they live, and the majority of Jews almost everywhere are immigrants or the children or grandchildren of immigrants.

He concludes:

> To understand the contemporary Jewish world, it is essential to know of the upheavals of the past hundred years. But the story must be traced further back than that.

The Jews as a Marginal People

People belonging to a specific ethnic group are known in sociology as marginal people. Marginal people live in two cultures—in their own culture and in the culture of the dominant majority. Living in two cultures creates tension derived from dual loyalties or commitments to conflicting values and standards of either group. In some instances, living in two cultures may cause mental conflict. Another characteristic of a marginal people is ethnocentrism, which is an "attitude that one's own cultural legacy (heritage) is a vital condition to a satisfactory life."

From the beginning of their long history, the Jews have been destined to live in more than one culture. Abraham, Isaac, Jacob, and their families, the progenitors of that nation, certainly faced the dilemma resulting from their participation in the conflicting Canaanite cultures. The same was true of their descendants, the Israelites, who lived in Egyptian bondage and their descendants who conquered and occupied the land Canaan. The Book of Judges gives a full account of their struggles with paganism. In the sixth century B.C.E., the Judeans, who were exiled to Babylonia, had to accommodate themselves to Babylonian and later to Persian cultures. During the Second Commonwealth, as a distinct nation in their own land, they could not escape the challenges from Hellenism and later from Roman culture. A similar fate befell the Jewish communities outside of Palestine, both in the Mediterranean and other Near Eastern countries. Since 70 C.E., Jews have been living as marginal people under Christian and Islamic rule in all parts of the world.

Sociologists point out that the marginal person's response to the dilemma of living in two cultures is not always the same. In some instances he is not fully loyal to the values and standards of either group, nor is he fully acceptable to either of the groups with which he identifies. At other times, he is fully committed to both cultures. The latter statement (but not the former) applies to the Jews. The Jewish capacity for loyalty to their own culture and adjustment to foreign cultures has always been exemplary. In addition, says Robert E. Park (who introduced the concept of "marginal man"), the marginal man living in two cultures "absorbs much greater experience of life and a more flexible capacity for adjustment than the man who lives in normal conditions." He suggests further:

> The marginal man occupies the position which has been, historically, that of the Jew in the Diaspora. The Jew has everywhere and always been the most civilized of human beings.

The Problem with Jewish Survival

Some sociologists express deep concern with the Jewish preoccupation of survivalism. Prof. Steven M. Cohen writes:

> Jewish survivalism has its unhealthy, even neurotic side... The Jewish world would be a very different place were we to put aside our obsession with survivalism and worry less about whether we'll manage to survive as Jews. it would be better were we to be concerned about how to live as Jews and about what Jews think of Judaism.

The reasons for our preoccupation with survivalism are easily explained. Speaking of our own Jewish community in the United States, we are an ethnic minority among a majority population which is Christian. The laws of this land guarantee us the right to exist as a subgroup, but within our Jewish community we lack the immunity to resist the debilitating forces that could lead to our disintegration as a distinct people. I am referring to the forces that weaken the very qualities which have kept our unique Jewish distinctiveness alive in previous generations. In other words, the greatest threat to Jewish survival comes from assimilation.

Assimilation has occurred to numerous ethnic minority groups in the United States. A variety of reasons, some social and economic, others political and cultural, have been responsible for their disappearance. Underlying all such reasons, however, is the critical problem of a lack of ethnocentrism. Ethnocentricism is an attitude or conviction that one's own culture is a vital condition to a satisfactory life.

Why does an ethnic group cherish its own culture? One reason is that legacies of that culture had benefitted previous generations. The people's culture credits these legacies with having made previous generations strong, wise, or moral. Religious legacies are considered supernaturally inspired or revealed as immutable and everlasting.

The British historian, Arnold Toynbee, speaking about certain distinctive spiritual features of human nature which he characterizes as "marks of being human," describes such spiritual features as "encounters."

> Encounters between ourselves and human beings alive or dead, about whom we know something through visual or oral or written information. Indirect relations may affect us more deeply and more dynamically than any personal relations because they have made, or at least are believed to have made, some impact on our lives.... The founders of the higher religions and schools of philosophy have influenced hundreds of millions of human beings who were still unborn during their lifetime.

But when a legacy of the past meets with a contemporary culture, either the culture may challenge the legacy or the legacy may challenge the culture. When a modern person is confronted by such challenges, three alternatives are open to him:

1. One alternative is to ignore the challenges that come from the past legacy.
2. A second is to accept the legacy and ignore the challenges that come from modernity. This attitude is based on the assumption that "what was good for my ancestors is also good for me."
3. The third is to establish a *modus operandi*, a form of compatibility or accommodation between the past and the present. To quote Mordecai M. Kaplan: "The past has a vote, not a veto."

The first response may be expected from people who lack a cultural perspective of evolution and of the human condition. The second response is to be expected from strict traditionalists. The third alternative is the one which the intellectual, who is knowledgeable of his heritage, would choose. On what basis would this intellectual choose accommodation of the two extremes—on the psychological, or the philosophical/sociological basis?

The Psychological (Freud):

> Mankind never lives completely in the present. The super-ego perpetuates the past, the traditions of the race and the people, which yield but slowly

to the influence of the present and to new developments in mans' life.... The child's super-ego is not really built up upon the model of the parents, but it takes over the same content, it becomes the vehicle of tradition and of all the age-long values which have been handed down in this way from generation to generation. You may easily guess what help is afforded by the recognition of the super-ego in understanding the social behavior of man in providing us with some practical hints upon education.

The Philosophical/Sociological (John Dewey):

The mind contains within itself a multitude of habits and impulses, memory of action, a glance backward.

The Jews as an Ethnocentric People

Sidney Goldstein and Calvin Godsscheider (*Three Generations in a Jewish Community*) have stated: "The Jews are an intensely social and *ethnocentric* people who tend to feel that group preservation is a vital condition in life. Jewish religious tradition is group centered in many of its important rituals, first in the family, then in the synagogue and community. Even when religious interests are not involved, Jews are known to seek the company of other Jews, want their children to marry other Jews and be part of the Jewish community."

From this standpoint, a Jewish child is not born a *tabula rasa*, a clean slate, but is heir to at least 100 generations of Jews. Each generation has imprinted in the child's super-ego: moral standards, religious values, social habits, and ideals.

Who of the past generations transmitted this heritage? It would be a gross error to think that they were only authors, legislators, religious, political, or intellectual leaders. In each generation, it was handed down by fathers, mothers, grandparents, teachers, and whole families to their children, and grandchildren. Each child born to Jewish parents is a link in a chain that goes back to ancient times and is a legitimate heir to the legacy transmitted to him/her from that past.

The three elements: the *psychological*, super-ego; the *historical*, continuance of the past and the present; and the *sociological*, ethnocentric, combine in promoting Jewish communal survival through involvement in Jewish communal life.

In other words, when the psychological, philosophical, and sociological influences are applied to Jewish identity, we arrive at one plausible reason for Jewish survival.

But heredity alone does not explain why one hundred generations of Jews, always living as marginal people (in at least two cultures and in some instances in more than two), had chosen to remain loyal to their traditions. Ethnocentricity, the feeling of satisfaction in being Jewish, does not satisfactorily answer the question, "What kind of satisfaction have Jews who lived during the past two millennia under Christian and Islamic rule, derived from being Jewish?"

The only logical and perhaps scientific answer I can give is to examine the image which those Jews who survived as Jews had of themselves. For example: In 1883, the Jewish population of Berlin consisted of 2,472 Jews of whom 1,236 converted to Christianity. In other parts of Prussia, an additional 1,182 Jews converted. Another example is found in the thirteenth century where one million Jews flourished in all of Europe. What does this show? Here I come to the theory in my thesis about the image of the historic Jew.

For further readings:

1. de Lange, Nicholas, "The Jews And Their History," in *Atlas Of The Jewish World*. (Phaidon, Oxford 1985.)
2. Dubnow, Simon, "An Essay In The Philosophy of History," in *Nationalism and History*, edited by K. S. Pinson. (Jewish Publication Society 1958.)

3.
Lecture II:
The Image of the Historic Jew

What is meant by the "Jewish image"? In this context, image is a picture in the mind that reveals ways of thought, patterns of behavior and strivings of the Jewish people for unity and perfection in the world. The Jewish image is a product of Jewish culture and the culture is a product of the image. Has the self-image of the Jew played a role in Jewish history? I believe that it always has been a factor in Jewish survival and assimilation. I shall explain assimilation first. A sociological definition of assimilation is a one-way process in which an individual relinquishes the culture of his own group and takes over the culture of another, generally a larger group. A major reason in an individual's determination to assimilate is depreciation of his group's culture. In other words, the Jew who severs his ties with his historic people either has a negative image of Jewish culture or no image at all.

When I presented this view in a course, "The Religion and Culture of the Jews," at the University of Pittsburgh, a student asked that I "describe a positive image of the Jew." This being early in the term, I had preferred to delay an explanation until the students had an opportunity to read some of the assigned basic literature in Jewish thought. But realizing the need of an immediate reply to a student's inquiry, I gave the following response: In the nineteenth century, a Jewish historian, Edward Gans, compared the Jews to the "Jordan River that empties into the Sea of Galilee and is not lost within it, in spite of the difficulty in specifying its unique character." The Jordan, I explained, originates in the mountains of Lebanon and Hermon, flows down to the Sea of Galilee, enters the Sea and then emerges from it, flowing down to the south. Jewish uniqueness is similar in the sense that the Jews having emerged from their ancient homeland, entered into the universality of mankind and, in spite of difficulties, maintained their uniqueness.

A contemporary Jewish historian, Prof. Jacob Talman, commenting on the "Jewish uniqueness within the universality of mankind," pointed out that "The Jewish tradition has viewed Jewish dispersion as the grounds on which a bridge is erected to the world of perfection, the better world of tomorrow, a sort of messianic destiny."

The philosopher Herman Cohen explains "messianic destiny" as the goal of world history. "The goal of world history," he wrote, "is not ruled by blind chance. It is *the establishment of a moral order for all mankind—a messianic age*." This concept is clearly formulated in the Torah, developed by the Prophets and interpreted by the rabbinic sages.

Jews have always understood their "destiny" as a mission to bring this world goal into realization. In the Bible, Israel is described as "a nation that shall dwell alone." This challenge, as the historic Jew understood it, is for Israel to live among peoples, yet its distinction, its religion, is to have universal significance. Israel's mission became its vocation, a summons to bring the messianic world goal for all mankind to all mankind. The strict traditional Jew interprets the realization of the messianic ideal through a personal messiah. Other Jews understand it for Israel to be a model in universal history. In other words, their contact with the world is a mandate for the Jews to align themselves with those people and causes that seek justice and freedom from evil for all humankind.

A statement of the Christian theologian Prof. Rosemary Ruether is of interest. She said: "Christianity needs a Christ-image to give it redemption; Judaism needs no Christ-image because it has the Exodus."

The First Image Which the Historic Jew Has of Himself

When the historic Jew looks into the mirror of history, he sees himself as elected by God to live as an ethical people and rise above any environment in which he happens to find himself to new moral heights. Jews who lack knowledge of biblical history, in which the foundations for Israel's missions were laid, may encounter difficulties with the conceptions of "chosen people" and "to rise above the environment to new moral heights." In specific terms: The biblical period in Jewish history produced the idea of "ethical monotheism." What is this concept? "*One God who is concerned with the way man lives out his life on earth.*" Man is created in God's ethical image which means, "considering all our differences, you are like me and I am like you and both of us are like God in the Creator's eyes. Hence, one rule of equality and justice must govern us all."

How does this conception differ from pagan conceptions? Paganism taught that the gods and man are subject to decrees of a blind fate which, in Greek, is *moira* and in Latin, *fatum*. Paganism denied ultimate freedom to the gods and to man. Jewish monotheism *knows of no fate*. It knows of God's will which He revealed through a system of law that acts with a moral purpose and whose fundamental attributes are goodness, freedom, equality, and "rational choice in which there is the possibility of rebelling against God Himself." God presented His system of law to Israel's ancestors for their acceptance or rejection. He sent apostolic messengers, known as prophets, to teach His system of law to them and to all future generations of mankind. What kind of teachers were these prophets? In an essay titled, "Moses," the Jewish philosopher Ahad Ha'am describes the prophets:

> The prophet has two fundamental qualities which distinguish him from the rest of mankind. First, he is a man of *truth*. He sees life as it is, with a view unwarped by subjective feelings; and he tells you what he sees just as he sees it, unaffected by irrelevant considerations. Secondly, the prophet is an *extremist*. He concentrates his whole heart and mind on his ideal, in which he finds the goal of life, and to which he is determined to make the whole world do service, without exception. He can accept no excuse, can consent to no compromise, can never cease thundering his passionate denunciations, even if the whole universe is against him. From these two fundamental characteristics there results a third, which is a combination of the other two; namely, the supremacy of *absolute righteousness*. As a man of truth, he cannot help being also a man of justice or righteousness, for what is righteousness but truth in action. And as an extremist, he cannot subordinate righteousness to any irrelevant end. The prophet then is in this position: on the one hand, he cannot altogether reform the world according to his desire; on the other hand, he cannot cheat himself and shut his eyes to its defects. Just as the prophet will not bow to the world, so the world will not bow to him, will not accept his influence immediately and directly. The influence must first pass through certain channels in which it becomes adapted to the conditions of life.

Have the Prophets Failed?

Have the prophets failed because the world would not accept their teachings?

Here, I wish to introduce the philosopher Martin Buber. In an essay titled, "Plato and Isaiah," he wrote:

> Plato was about 75 years old when he traveled to Syracuse in the hope that his disciple Dion would found the ideal republic. Dion was assassinated and Plato realized that he failed in his attempts to establish the perfect state. In his *Republic*, Socrates is asked whether the philosophic man would be at all apt to concern himself with affairs of state. Socrates replied that in his own state, it certainly will concern him with such matters, but the state which he conceives and which is suitable to him would have to be one other than his native land, unless there is some divine intervention. Because the man who is blessed with spirit and yet confronts a furious mob feels like one who suddenly finds himself surrounded by wild beasts. Such a man will henceforth keep silent, attend to his own work, become a spectator, and live out his life without doing any wrong to the end of his days. When his listeners say to Socrates, "Such a man will have accomplished great work by the time he dies," Socrates replies, "But not the greatest, since he has not founded the state which befits him." This is the gist of Plato's resignation.
>
> Isaiah does not share Plato's resignation.
>
> When Isaiah hears the divine message tell him to go to the people and tell them that they are faithless to God and call on them to return to faithfulness, he is also told that his message will be misunderstood, misinterpreted and misused. From the very outset, the prophet is told that he must fail. Being a prophet means being powerless, and being powerless he must confront the powerful and remind them of their responsibility. Isaiah failed, as predicted. The people and the king opposed him. But his failure is quite different from Plato's. Our very existence as Jews testifies to this difference. We must yet experience an era in history which refutes history. The prophet fails in one hour of history, but not so far as the future of his people is concerned. For his people preserve his message as something which will be realized at another time, in another hour, under other conditions, and in other forms. The prophet cannot withdraw to the role of silent spectator, like Plato did. He must speak his message. The message will be misunderstood, misinterpreted, misused; it will even confirm and harden the people in their faithlessness, but its sting will rankle within them for all time. This is the true meaning of the messianic destiny of the Jewish people.

The British scholar, Joseph Jacobs, wrote: "The prophets, it is true, found no successors in Israel for their remarkable amalgam [mixture] of rhapsody [lyric poetry] and politics, but their spirit informed all the higher thought of all nations and continued to the higher spirit of the Jewish people ever since."

How did the prophets' messages reach the masses of Jews of post-biblical generations? The answer is that the Jews have always been a most literary people. The Torah commands Jewish fathers to teach their children. In the Second Commonwealth, each morning as part of the Temple service, priests publicly read portions from the Torah and following the services, priests, scholars, and common people went to the synagogues to study. The Talmud relates that there were 100 synagogues in Jerusalem and similar places of study in many other cities.

The following quotation by the anthropologist Raphael Patai, from the writings of Ernest van den Haag, gives a more elaborate answer to the preceding question.

> ... Jews are human, we all are, but Jews are in a sense more human than anyone else: they have witnessed and taken part in more of the human career, they have recorded more of it, shaped more of it, originated and developed more of it, above all, suffered more of it, than any other people. No other nation has witnessed so much, argued and bargained so much, and yet clung to its own inner core as much as the Jews have...

For further readings:

1. Kaufmann, Yehezkiel, *The Religion of Israel*, Translated by Moshe Greenberg. (The University of Chicago Press, 1960)
2. Buber, Martin, *The Writings Of Martin Buber*, Edited by Will Herberg. (A Meridian Book. The World Publishing Co. 1956)
3. Ahad Ha-Am, *Essays, Letters, Memoirs*, Translated by Leon Simon. (Oxford-East and West Library. MCMXLVI)
4. Jacobs, Joseph, *Jewish Contributions to Civilization*. (The Conat Press, 1919)

4.
Lecture III:
The Jew and History

This is perhaps the place for a brief return to Prof. Talman's expression "Jewish uniqueness" and to my question, "How did the prophets' messages reach future generations?" I call your attention to explanations by leading historians of the unique place of the Jewish people in history.

Simon Dubnow writes:

> The Jews are the historical nation of all times, a description bringing into relief the contrast between it and all other nations of ancient and modern times, whose historical existence either came to an end in days long past, or began at a date comparatively recent.... Jewish history, then, in its range, or better, in its duration, presents a unique phenomenon.

Prof. William Foxwell Albright writes:

> Hebrew national tradition excels in its clear picture of tribal and family origins. In Egypt and Babylonia, in Assyria and Phoenicia, in Greece and Rome, we look in vain for anything comparable. There is nothing like it in the traditions of the Germanic peoples. Neither India nor China can produce anything similar, since their earliest historical memories are literary deposits of distorted dynastic tradition, with no trace of the herdsman or peasant behind the demigod or king with whom their records begin. Neither in the Indic historical writings (the Puranas) nor in the earliest Greek historians is there a hint of the fact that both Indo-Aryans and Hellenes were once nomads who migrated into their later abodes from the North. The Assyrians, to be sure, remembered vaguely that their earliest rulers, whose names they recalled without any details about their deeds, were tent dwellers, but whence they came had long been forgotten.
>
> In contrast with these other peoples, the Israelites preserved an unusually clear picture of simple beginnings, of complex migrations, and of

extreme vicissitudes, which plunged them from their favored status under Joseph to bitter oppression after his death.... There is scarcely a single biblical historian who has not been impressed by the rapid accumulation of [archaeological] data supporting the substantial historicity of patriarchal tradition....

The British historian Edward Hallet Carr (Cambridge University) writes:

Like the ancient civilizations of Asia, the classical civilization of Greece and Rome was basically unhistorical. Herodotus as the father of history had few children, and the writers of classical antiquity were, on the whole, as little concerned with the future as with the past.... Poetic visions of a brighter future took the form of visions of a return of a golden age of the past—a cyclical view which assimilated the processes of history to the processes of nature. History was not going anywhere: because there was no sense of the past, there was equally no sense of the future.... It was the Jews, and after them the Christians, who introduced an entirely new element by postulating a goal toward which the historical process is moving—the teleological view of history. History thus acquired a meaning and purpose....

Prof. Denys Page (Cambridge University) writes:

Sometime about 2000 or 1900 B.C., Greece was invaded and permanently occupied by a new people, the first speakers of the Greek language. After some hundreds of years...these Greek invaders came under the spell of Minoan Crete, and the fusion of two cultures resulted in one of the most brilliant periods of civilization in the whole history of Greece.... The Mycenaeans disappeared from the scene in a rather sudden and mysterious way during the twelfth century B.C., and from then onwards all is darkness or dimness for about four hundred years, until the founding of the Olympic games in 776 B.C. At that time, the Greeks themselves knew nothing whatever about their past, except that a large body of epic poems had somehow survived—and this was almost the only record they had of their own history.

In teaching young people, the term unique should be used with caution for it might be confused with chauvinism, which is belief in superiority. I am, therefore, careful to define unique prior to quoting a phrase in which it is used. Generally, I explain that in history and psychology, uniqueness is referred to as an unusual or singular trait in the personality of one individual or social group. Jewish history has a uniqueness which other histories lack. As an example, I compare the above statement by Prof. Page with the literary and historical knowledge that was extant in ancient Israel in the same eighth century. I recall Page's statement that "in 776 B.C.E., the Greeks knew nothing whatever about their past" and ask: "What did the Jews know about their past at that time and previously to that time?" Let's look at the following:

In the eighth century B.C.E., Amos and Hosea prophesied in Israel and Isaiah and Micah in Jerusalem. Their prophecies are a combination of knowledge of the past and promises of a better future. The history of the biblical period spanning 1,500 years is preserved in great detail in the Bible. What motivated the Jews to commit their historical experiences to writing? Foremost is the way the Jews viewed history. The historian, Prof. Abraham A. Neuman, points out: "Judaism views theology through the eyes of history in contrast to Christianity, in which theology is primary and history is secondary." That is to say the Jews believed that God's will and presence are revealed in the historical events of the world. When the revealed historical events are committed to written words, the written words become sacred and are cherished, preserved and transmitted to future generations. Another explanation to consider is from the psychological standpoint, which George Orwell describes as "motives that impel people to write history." Orwell identifies the desire to write as "the historical impulse which aims to seek out things as they are, find out true facts and store them up for the use of posterity." Correlated to this desire "is the desire to push the world in a certain direction and alter our ideas." To this, I wish to add Carr's analysis of the philosopher Francis H. Bradley's definition: "For the historian, the end of progress is not already evolved. It is something still infinitely remote, and pointers towards it come in sight only as advance. . . . The content of history can be realized only as we experience it."

The views of the two preceding authors point to special traits which have existed in the Jewish character from early beginnings in Jewish history and earned for them the accolade of "a people strongly dominated by a sense of history" and the title, "the People of the Book," given to them by Muhammed. The following comment by Raphael Patai deserves our attention: "What is of special interest for us . . . is that whatever language the Jews acquired or developed was used without delay as a literary medium."

For further readings:

1. Albright, William Foxwell, "The Biblical Period" in *The Jews: Their History, Culture and Religion*, Edited by Louis Finkelstein. (Harper & Bros, 1949)
2. Carr, Edward Hallett, *What Is History?* (Vintage Books, 1961)
3. Jones, Hugh Loyd, *The Greeks*. (World Publishing Co., 1962)

5.
Lecture IV:
The Image of the Historic Jew in the Second Part of History

In the first part of history, Simon Dubnow characterized the Jews as "a people that developed under the influence of exceptional circumstances and finally attained to a high degree of spiritual perfection which eventually gained universal supremacy, but neither exhausted its resources nor ended its creativity. Not only did it continue to live upon its vast store of spiritual energy, but day by day increased its store."

The Image of the Jews:

> Dubnow begins the second part of history with the year 70 C.E. He describes the Jews as "thinkers and sufferers."

> The extraordinary mental energy that had matured the Bible and the old writings in the first period, manifested itself in the second period in the encyclopedic production of the Talmudim, in the religious philosophy of the middle ages, in Rabbinic [literature] in the cabala, in mysticism, and in science.

The Jew as "Thinker":

> The spiritual discipline of the school [of learning] came to mean for the Jew what military discipline is for other nations.... Jewish history presents the chronicle of morality, religion, and social converse.

> The Jew thinks and writes.
> Prof. Solomon Zeitlin's characterization of writing in the Second

Commonwealth may be applied to many other Jewish generations: "Jews who couldn't write well did not write at all; those who could, wrote prodigiously." Thus we have the warning by the author of Ecclesiastes: "My son, be warned: of making many books there is no end...."

The following statement by Prof. Walter Kaufmann (philosopher at Princeton) describes the image of the Jews as "thinkers":

> The persistent concern with social justice from the Law of Moses and the Hebrew prophets down to the twentieth century, the disproportionate presence of Jews in movements of social reform and the central place of philanthropy in Jewish traditions are not likely to be questioned.... The ancient insistence that no Jew should remain illiterate, and the medieval love of learning, bore abundant fruit whenever opportunities arose — in Spain during the age of Maimonides, and then again after the emancipation. In utterly disproportionate numbers, Jews crowded into colleges and universities, obtained professorships and Nobel prizes, and left their mark in almost every field of learning. To have such a history is marvelous. To have such ancestors is unbelievable, and to have ready access to such a tradition and such a syndrome is a great blessing.... Not all national heritages are equally rich. Not every nation has a great literature. I am glad I am a Jew.... The Jews certainly do not have a monopoly on everything good. But the sense of history and the syndrome I have described are worth preserving and developing.... Nobody has any right to ask the Jews to go on demanding more of themselves than other nations do — nobody, except the Jews.
>
> Do we want the Jews to have a future and to live, if possible, another few thousand years? As an individual, I certainly should not want to live that long. But the Jewish people show no signs of aging or becoming feeble. Far from living on their memories of ancient glory, they have added to their past achievements in the present century. Having survived immense ordeals with undiminished vitality, most Jews naturally want to have a future, and I share that wish.
>
> The most obvious answer to the question of what kind of future do we desire for the Jewish people in the diaspora, is this: The kind of future I desire for the Jews in the dispersion is that they should continue to be in the forefront of humane endeavors, enriching humanity.

The Jew as "Sufferer":

Dubnow describes Jewish suffering as "the thrilling drama of Jewish martyrdom.... It gives heartening expression to the spiritual strivings of a nation whose brow is resplendent with the thorny crown of martyrdom. It breathes heroism of mind that conquers bodily pain." In a word, Jewish history is sublimated (refined; one that is considered more culturally acceptable).

"Martyrdom" derives from the Greek "martyr," meaning "witness," and is applied to sufferers for belief, faith, or adherence to a cause. In the ancient world, people suffered and died for economic and political causes, not for intellectual or spiritual ideals. Of interest may be the Hebrew word for war, *milkhamah*, which combines the meanings of *melakh*, "salt," and *lekhem*, "bread." In paganism, a conquered people that worshiped five gods could freely adopt another five gods that were worshiped by the conqueror. Judaic monotheism worshiped one God and had no room for other gods, particularly when any other gods were no-gods. The Prophet Isaiah drew a distinction between pagan idolatry and Jewish monotheism:

> To whom, then, can you liken God,
> What form compare to Him?
> The idol? A woodworker shaped it,
> And a smith overlaid it with gold,
> Forging links of silver.
> As a gift, he chooses the mulberry—
> A wood that does not rot—
> Then seeks a skillful woodworker
> To make a firm idol,
> That will not topple.
>
> Do you not know?
> Have you not heard?
> Have you not been told
> From the very first?
> Have you not discerned
> How the earth was founded?
> It is He who is enthroned above the vault of the earth,
> So that its inhabitants seem as grasshoppers;
> Who spread out the skies like gauze,
> Stretched them out like a tent to dwell in.
> He brings potentates to naught,
> Makes rulers of the earth as nothing.
> Hardly are they planted,

Hardly are they sown,
Hardly has their stem
Taken root in earth,
When He blows upon them and they dry up,
And the storm bears them off like straw.

To whom, then, can you liken Me,
To whom can I be compared?
—says the Holy One. (40:18–25)

For further readings:

1. Kaufmann, Walter, *Existentialism, Religion And Death*. (A Meridian Book, New American Library, 1976)
2. Kaplan, Mordecai M., *The Future Of The American Jew*. (Reconstructionist Press, 1967)

6.
Lecture V:
The Jews—First Martyrs in History

I. The Greek Period

The Jews were the first people in history to suffer martyrdom. They invented martyrdom by suffering and dying for the ideas of belief and faith.

Their first experience with martyrdom occurred in the Greek period. That experience Josef Kastein describes as:

> A clash between a world where religion was falling to bits and a world in which religion was being consolidated. These differences produced a disparity between their spiritual and material forms of life. The Greeks certainly felt that their world of gods exercised a definite influence on what they did and what they did not do, but they failed to receive any guidance from them. The gods were so threadbare, so disunited, and too much like themselves in all they felt and did! The lives of the Judeans, whether in their private or communal lives, was an attempt to prove themselves true to the divine mission.

The conflict between Greeks and Jews as a clash of two distinct cultures is fully illustrated by the rebellion which commemorates the Hanukkah festival.

The Hanukkah Story

At that time, Antiochus IV, known as Epiphanes (174–164 B.C.E.), aimed at Hellenizing all lands under his rule. Judea was of particular importance to him because it served as a buffer state between his empire and Egypt, the seat of the Ptolemies. He sought to make Jerusalem a Greek *polis* (city) and introduce into the city the various forms of Greek social life. But the king realized that the Jewish religion, which he regarded as superstition, resented Greek influences.

The historian Prof. Solomon Zeitlin writes:

> He decided to destroy the Jews and their Judaism by force. He abolished the daily sacrifices, defiled the Temple, and decreed that swine be brought on the altar as sacrifices.... He prohibited the Jews from keeping the Sabbath. To circumcise their sons was punishable by death. The Books of the Law were put to flames; the people of foreign countries were settled in Jerusalem.

The Jews responded to Antiochus with a declaration of war. The Jews who died in that war were the first martyrs in history. Their deaths were for belief and faith.

For a broader understanding of the friction between the Jews and the Greeks, and later the Romans, Prof. Rosemary Ruether's analysis deserves our attention. She quotes Marcel Simon's explanation:

> The Greeks and Romans regarded Orientals with a certain contempt and looked on them as a degenerating influence. But this prejudice was cultural rather than strictly racial. That is to say, it disappeared as the Oriental assimilated into the Greco-Roman culture. The special polemic against the Jew was a consequence of religious sociology; that is, it was a reaction caused by special social consequences of Jewish religious law. Since Hellenistic society regarded Greek culture as the standard for human existence, such a group of "barbarians" would refuse assimilation into Hellenistic culture on the grounds that its gods were false and its manner "unclean" was a cultural affront of no small proportions. The stage was set for a *kultukampf* [clash of cultures] between Jewish and Greek society that took the form of forced attempts at Hellenization, such as that under Antiochus Epiphanes, and the struggle for Palestinian independence from the Maccabees to the Jewish wars.
>
> So the Jewish reaction to its Greek environment was not merely one of antipathy, but a complex dialectic of assimilation of the best elements and transformation of these into Jewish terms. Judaism could thus present itself to the Hellenistic world as the original version of that higher philosophy for which the Gentiles were seeking. This took the form of an active and highly successful missionary stance of the synagogue within Hellenistic cities. Judaism in the Greco-Roman period was an evangelical religion that was in the process of breaking its ethnic boundaries to become a uni-

versal faith. The Septuagint, the Greek translation of the Scriptures created in Alexandria in the third century B.C.E., is the sole example in Jewish history of a scriptural translation that was allowed (for a time) to enjoy the same status as an inspired text as the Hebrew Bible. The doctrine of the Noachian laws gave Judaism a rationale for accepting the "righteous pagan" as a child of God who had a place in the promised Kingdom. Rabbinic teaching urged the full equality of the proselyte with the born Jew and indeed a special solicitousness for the proselyte, since his faith was presumed to be weaker than that of the born Jew. This missionary period of Judaism created around the Hellenistic synagogue a circle of "God-fearers" who were attracted to Jewish monotheism and ethics. It was this universal dimension of Judaism, created by the Jewish mission to Gentiles in the Diaspora, that the Christian Church took over and appropriated. It is impossible to understand the rapid spread of the Church in the Diaspora without recognizing that it built upon and fell heir to this work of Jewish mission and Hellenistic Jewish apologetic.

II. The Roman Period

Jewish martyrdom in the Roman period lasted almost a century and resulted from a variety of political and religious conflicts. Politically, it was the demand of liberation of Judea from Roman rule. The historian M. Stern writes:

The powerful clash between the Jews and the Roman Empire at the end of the Second Temple era was the result of an accumulation of several factors, some specific grievances, others imponderables. In the ideological sphere, there was a sharp conflict between the Jewish conception of Israel as the elect, with a glorious political and spiritual future, and the reality of the all-powerful Roman Empire, in which Judea was merely one of many subject provinces. This contrast found release in messianic hopes and the anticipation of heavenly salvation, which would bring eternal sovereignty to the Jewish nation as the heir of the Roman Empire.... The ideology of messianism and of the elevation of the Jewish people had borne a clear activist overtone among certain circles ever since Roman rule had begun. They regarded the duty to fight against Rome as a positive commandment, which should compel even the hesitant among the nation to take up arms, for the Jews had no master but God....

... there were also specific aspects of Roman rule that severely offended Jewish sensitivities. Roman control of the Temple and of the Temple cult and the imposition of harsh taxes and duties, which placed a heavy burden on the population, all caused the masses to hate the foreign rulers.

III. The Heroic Age

Kastein describes this period as "The Heroic Age." He traces this age from the rise of the Hasmonian family, the Maccabees, to the destruction of the Jewish state by the Romans in 70 C.E. He explains that the "heroism of the Jews in that period which manifests the resolution of sacrifice for an idea is unparalleled and unexemplified in history." It teaches:

> ...that nothing in the Jewish heritage forces the Jew to an attitude of renunciation and weakness, to bow before foolish humiliation at the hands of his environment.... When they declared war on Rome, their resistance took its root in religion.... Even those among the people who might be described as passive or moderate Pharisees had only lost their faith in the technique of resistance, in resistance with violence; their belief in life, in the future, in the permanence and immortality of the nation was much stronger than ever. But, as the prophets had intended, they wanted their resistance to be spiritual resistance. They wanted to save their nation by means of religious discipline, by spiritual measures of segregation, when the struggle demanded it even at the cost of sacrificing the existence of the state itself if it could not achieved any other way.... The Messianic idea, universally held by the Jews, was conceived as capable of realization. Some saw in the Messiah God's ambassador who could free them from the yoke of Rome and restore the theocracy. For others, the real importance of the idea lay in the belief that God, through the Messiah, would at last establish justice on earth. He would hold a great court at which the whole world would be judged, after which the Empire of Peace and the brotherhood of mankind would be founded on earth. This Messianism was still of this earth and was awaiting the moment when disaster of the age would be swept away in one great act of retributive justice and national vengeance. The people all felt that they could no longer deal with the situation with their own strength alone, but that God must come to their help....

Thus, Dubnow's characterization of the Jews as "thinkers and sufferers" amply applies to the martyred Judeans of the Roman period in history.

For further readings:

1. Zeitlin, Solomon, *The Rise and Fall Of The Judaean State, Vol. I.* (The Jewish Publication Society of America, 1962)
2. Ruether, Rosemary, *Faith and Fratricide: The Theological Roots Of Anti- Semitism.* (A Crossroad Book, The Seabury Press, 1974)
3. Stern, M., "The Period Of The Second Temple" in *A History Of The Jews*, Edited by H. H. Ben-Sasson. (Harvard University Press, 1976)
4. Kastein, Josef, *History and Destiny of the Jews.* (The Viking Press, 1933)

7.
Lecture VI:
Christian Theological Anti-Semitism

The Theological Roots of Anti-Semitism

The theological and political roots of anti-Semitism that sprouted in the early period of Christian history have never dried up.

Kastein writes:

> The Christian religion, whether in the form of Catholicism, the Orthodox Church, or Protestantism, has been a factor perennially hostile to Judaism ever since the time of Paul.... Ever since the days of Constantine, the opposition of the Christian state to the Jews has been the primary manifestation of its being.

Kastein cites as an example a statement by the leading historian Theodore Mommsen: "Mommsen regarded the solution to the Jewish problem as lying in the conversion of the Jews to Christianity." He also calls attention to an event that occurred late in the 19th century. "In 1898 Belgium, having been infected by French anti-Semitism, held a solemn procession of its clergy commemorating the trial [based on a false accusation of the Jews] for desecrating the Host which had taken place in that country in 1370—proof that the church had a long memory...."

Ruether traces the roots in greater detail:

> We must recognize Christian anti-Semitism as a uniquely new factor in the picture of antique anti-Semitism. Its source lies in the theological dispute between Christianity and Judaism over the messiahship of Jesus, and so it strikes at the heart of the Christian gospel. It was this theological root and its growth into a distinctively type of anti-Semitism that were responsible for reverting the tradition of tolerance for Jews in Roman law.... it was

only when Christianity, with its distinctively religious type of anti-Semitism based on profound theological cleavage within the fraternity of biblical religion, entered into the picture that we begin to have that special translation of religious hatred into social hatred that is to become characteristic of Christendom.

Antipathy of Judaism in the New Testament

In tracing the antipathy of Judaism in the New Testament, we must pause to examine the views of the Apostle whose influence has been lasting on Christianity. This was Paul, a Greek Jew from Tarus in Asia Minor, whose Jewish name was Saul. For a time, he was a student of the sage, R. Gamaliel, but he acquired his general education from Hellenism. At first, Paul was a strong opponent of Jesus and the Christian movement, but on a journey to Damascus on a mission from the Sanhedrin, he saw a vision of Jesus and became a devoted convert. The following quotation is from a letter he wrote to the Galatians:

> Those who rely on the keeping of the Law [Torah] are under a curse.... The Law will not justify anyone in the sight of God.... The Law is not even based on faith, since we are told: "The man who practices these precepts finds life through them" [You shall therefore keep My statutes and My ordinances, which if man shall do, he shall live by them: I am the Lord. Lev. 18:5] Christ redeemed us from the curse of the Law by being cursed for our sake.... (Gal. 3)

Dr. Gregory Baum comments:

> Paul, himself, from whom Vatican II has taken its language about Israel's ongoing election [chosen people concept] had no intention whatever of recognizing the Jewish religion as a way of grace. Israel had become blind, according to Paul; it was a way of death, of spiritual slavery. Despite this blindness, the Apostle taught God did not permit Israel to disappear; the election remained with it, not however as a source of present grace, but as a divine promise guaranteeing the conversion of the Jews at the end of time and their integration into the Christian church, the one true Israel....

Ruether comments on Paul's attitudes toward the Jewish people and Judaism:

For Paul, the reign of Torah is equivalent to the reign of these demonic powers and principalities of the finite realm. This allows Paul to equate the Torah as the guardian spirit of the people of the Old Covenant with elemental spirits of the universe, the "false gods" of the pagans ... while under the Torah the people were "slaves to the elemental spirits of the universe," but now, as free sons of God in Christ, "how can you turn back again to the weak and beggarly elemental spirits, where slaves you want to be once more," by submitting to the ordinances of the Torah?

Christian Policy Beginning with the Fourth Century C.E.

A description of Christian-Jewish relations beginning with the fourth century, when the Roman Emperor Constantine (312–337) converted to Christianity, is discussed by Kastein:

The conversion of Constantine to Christianity changed the position held by the Roman state toward the Jews as a *religio licita*, a lawful religion. Christianity became the state religion in accordance with the fundamental principle *cujus regio ejus religio*, "the religion of the ruler is the religion of the state." When the conversion of the emperor was officially established, hundreds of thousands of Christians suddenly made their appearance.... Jewish history is not concerned with Constantine's change of religion, but it is concerned with his change of attitude toward the Jews. So long as he remained pagan, he respected other religions, but as soon as he became a Christian, he persecuted the Jews for no other reason than that they believed something different from what he believed.

He did not adopt his attitude of his own accord; it was forced upon him by the Christian priesthood, who disapproved of the freedom of conscience he had intended to make the basis of his rule.... The clergy could no longer be satisfied with Christianity being placed on an equal footing with Judaism. The open and secret struggle in which, ever since its foundation, it had been engaged against Judaism must now be brought to an end, and nothing could be simpler than to use the power of the state to this end. Thus they assumed the same attitude of overbearance and intolerance as their predecessors, the pagan priests of Rome, had done in defense of the state religion and their own position of power. As soon as Christianity became the recognized religion of the state, the hostility of the clergy became too active and determined to be explained on the grounds of religious fanaticism alone; it was much more the attitude of those who regarded themselves as successors of the state priests of pagan Rome; and the sect which but a short time previously had been the object of persecution inaugurated its career as a state religion by immediately adopting an attitude of intolerance and persecution in its turn. It did not feel called upon for the moment to supply the world with a practical proof of its religious spirit.

As time progressed, the early roots of antipathy toward the Jews in the Christian world sent out spores that produced new forms of conflict. When speaking of the Middle Ages, Prof. Jacob Katz wrote:

In the Middle Ages the conflict was concentrated in three main areas: dogma, exegesis [interpretation of biblical sources], and morals. In the field of dogma, the Jewish doctrine of the absolute unity [oneness] of God, as opposed to the [Christian] trinity, was the main point of contention. Next in the order of importance in this area is the argument about the advent [the coming] of the Messiah, whether the advent had already occurred in the past or was expected to take place at some future date. Exegesis was concerned with the claim that certain Christological references [to Jesus] were contained in the Hebrew Bible. As for the controversy over moral teachings, this resulted mainly from the Christian attack on Jewish morality as having, among other faults, particularistic trends.

Particularism means distinctiveness and refers to Jews having remained a distinct people after the rise of Christianity which regarded itself the universal fulfillment of the messianic hope. Ruether explained: "Christianity having become the established religion of the empire, Christian theologians came to imagine that the religion of the biblical God had literally conquered all the people and all the lands." Christianity, this belief maintained, became the universal religion of all mankind and no room was left for the religion of the particular group, the Jewish people. Actually, Christian particularism versus universalism was also based on another assumption. The Church postulated the theory that God, who elected Israel as His chosen people long ago and entered into a covenant with them, had, with the coming of Jesus, broken that covenant, made the Christians the new Israel, and entered into a new covenant with them. Based on this theory, the Church designated the Hebrew Bible, the "Old Testament," and the Gospels as the "New Testament."

Katz continues:

While the old areas of conflict receded, new issues now came to the fore. Which of the two religions conformed more closely to rational criteria? Which was burdened more heavily by mysteries? Such were the questions posed during the Age of Enlightenment. With the rise of romanticism, the question assumed something of this nature: Which of the two religions is more capable of satisfying the urge for religious emotion? When positivism became dominant, religion appeared almost entirely discredited. Only the moral issue remained as the deciding factor in assessing the relative merits of the two traditions. Was Christianity to be preferred because of its universalistic ethic, or must it be discarded because of its unrealistic demands upon the individual to forego his just rights, in contradistinction to Judaism, which had, as its point of departure, the insistence on objective justice? The two religions were weighed against each other....

For further readings:

1. Baum, George, "Introduction to *Faith And Fratricide*." Op. cit.
2. Katz, Jacob, *Emancipation and Assimilation: Studies In Modern Jewish History*. (Gregg International Publishers Ltd., 1972)

8.
Lecture VII:
Rehashing Ancient Prejudices

In the preceding lectures, I have discussed the attitude of the Church toward the Jews.

A student raised the question: "Of what value is it to rehash ancient prejudices?" I inquired: "Are you addressing your question to the Jews or to the non-Jews?" He replied: "To both. Why dwell on the past? The past is dead and cannot influence our lives." My answer, I told him, would consist of three brief statements to which, I hoped, he would give serious thought:

1. The prejudices from which Jews have suffered in the past did not die with the past; they are very much alive in the present and may continue in the future unless we remember the past.

2. The philosopher Sidney Hook wrote: "The past world and the present are so continuous that there are few problems which can be intelligently understood without transcending the immediate context in which they are discovered."

3. The philosopher George Santayana wrote: "Those who cannot remember the past are condemned to repeat it. . . . This is the condition of children and barbarians in whom instinct has learned nothing from experience."

Another student posed a question: "How did the policy of the Church affect the Jews?" I suggested that he search for a reply to his question in historical sources and promised to make some of the sources available to the class. At the next session, I distributed copies of quotations from a manuscript which I later published as a book, *The Fate of the Jews In the European Society*, and invited the students to read and discuss them. The following are excerpts from this work.

"The Codex Theodosianus and the Jews"

In 438 an important document was compiled known as Codex Theodosianus or the Theodosian Code. Edicts from the reign of Constantine in 315 to Theodosius II (408–50) were systematized and brought up to date. Four categories of edicts concerning the Jews were included, some favorable insofar as they sought to protect the Jews from Christian violence, and others detrimental to their welfare. Every edict is introduced by a theological preamble of a damaging nature. M. Safrai points out: "Every edict to protect the Jews began with the comment that it intended to suppress the power and insolence of the contemptible Hellens, Jews and heretics."

The Theodosian Code and edits that followed its publication, as Baron points out, "underscored the new legal inferiority of Jews with respect to all positions of power and prestige." His comments on the conditions of the Jews in "the Christian Empire" are pertinent.

> The Christian empire... excluded the Jews from rights enjoyed by all other citizens. The old principle of equality of rights, never formally proclaimed and hence never formally abrogated, was in practice dishonored more and more. The *De altercatione ecclesiae at synagogue dialogue*, written after 404, speaks of the elimination of Jews from the *militia armata* and from several other offices. In 439 Theodosius II proclaimed the general exclusion of the Jews from all civil and military posts of honor....

Among the statutes in the Code that were unfavorable to the Jews, the following may be mentioned:

a. Conversion to Judaism was forbidden, while Jewish conversion to Christianity was favored;
b. Christians who answered to Judaism were declared "intestate";
c. Jewish children who converted to Christianity were to be disinherited by their parents;
d. Jews were forbidden to own Christian slaves.

In 408, before the Code was promulgated, Theodosius issued a law forbidding Jews to celebrate the festival of Purim because the clergy had accused them of burning images of the cross on that occasion. In 415, the Jewish patriarch, Rabbi Gamliel, was deposed, which led to the disappearance of the Jewish Patriarchal Office, and a new tax was imposed on the Jewish community. Existing synagogues were ordered destroyed and new ones forbidden to be constructed. Father Flannery writes:

> Other restrictive legislation...curtailed the Jews' civil status. They were barred from public functions, like the army, administrative posts, and off and on from the legal profession. Marriages to Jews, seen as "shameful" and "adulterous" unions, were prohibited under the penalty of death.

Louis I. Newman points out:

> The presence of Jews in Christian countries forced the Catholic Church and later Protestant theologians to explain the reason for their survival as a people in Christendom.... The explanation of (Pope) Innocent III was a favorite one in an important group of Christian theologians. The Jews had been preserved in serfdom and inferiority in order to testify to the truth of Christian doctrine; their sufferings throughout the centuries and their future career were decreed as punishment for their rejection of Christ.

For a further understanding of the Church's attitude toward the Jews, the following quotation from James Parkes deserves our attention.

> (The Church) turned consistently on...the prevention of Jewish influence or authority over Christians, and the relegation of the Jews to the status of social inferiority befitting a deicide people. Instead of the protection which had been guaranteed by Roman Law, and which remained effective in principle, even if practice sometimes transgressed it, the Jew had to be satisfied with an ineffective ban on excessive persecution.... Only against his murder would the Church, the guardian of the oppressed, lift up her voice. If an order went out for his expulsion, the Church approved, for Christian society was better without his presence; if his property were confiscated, the Church rejoiced; if his children were baptized by force, the Church regretted it, but doctrine forbade any attempt to restore the child to the home and the religion of his fathers.

The Black Death and Inquisition (1347–1350)

The Black Death

The fourteenth and fifteenth centuries brought new calamities upon the Jews of Europe, which Father Flannery describes as follows: "For Jews it was a tragedy to which, after the fall of Jerusalem, only the horrors of 1096 and 1939 were comparable."

A Bubonic Plague, known as the Black Death, was transported from India and swept throughout Europe, killing one-third of the population. "Before long," writes Flannery, "the inevitable scapegoat was found. Who else but the archconspirator and poisoner, the Jew?" Rumor spread that in order to destroy Christendom, the Jews poisoned the wells with such ingredients as lizards, frogs, spiders, and Christian hearts mixed with dough from the sacred wafer of the host.

Father Flannery continues:

> The story that Jews in Spain had circulated the death-dealing drug... spread like wildfire. It was first believed in Southern France, where the entire Jewish population of a town was burned. From there the deathly trail led into Northern Spain, then to Switzerland, into Bavaria, up the Rhine, into Eastern Germany, and to Belgium, Poland and Austria.... Charles IV made efforts to protect "his" Jews, but half-heartedly. As often as he offered aid, he granted immunity to the attackers or conceded Jewish property to favorites even before a massacre took place. The emperor was to all practical purposes, a broker in Jewish property.
>
> In the high Middle Ages, the Church's struggle to reassert the theologically required status of "misery" upon the Jews was rewarded a thousandfold. The medieval period ended with the Jewish community reduced to political servitude, social ignominy and ghettoization, economic ruin, vulnerability to violence from below, and arbitrary exploitation and expulsion from above until finally the Jewries of England, France, Spain, Portugal, and much of Germany had been disseminated, expelled, or forced to practice their religion in hiding. Above this whole development, there reigned the theological image of the Jew, both shaping developments and then serving as the explanation and excuse for them, the image itself growing constantly more evil, until it culminated with the virtual identification of the Jew with the Devil....

Special attention to the history of anti-Semitism must be given to the twentieth century. Grosser and Halperin characterize this century as follows:

> Anti-Semitism was so pervasive that Jews living anywhere outside the Far East were affected by it.
>
> Mob attacks, pogroms, expulsions, economic and political restrictions, pillage and slaughter plus minor iniquities of discrimination, social

ostracism, insults and racial slurs combined to shape the experience of Jews in this century....

Anti-Semitism permeated the Western world. The anti-Semitic cultural traditions perpetuated over centuries by religious teachings and beliefs—Catholic, Orthodox and Protestant—expanded in scope by racial anti-Semitism of the 19th century and had its impact in the 20th century.... Anti-Semitism, in the 20th century, includes virtually all beliefs, attitudes, and tactics that have developed from the first century. The only anti-Semitic practices that do not occur are compulsory baptism and forced attendance at conversion sermons....

The twelve year period of Nazi power, especially the last six years of their regime, was the most precarious period in Jewish history. In contrast to other periods of anti-Semitic excesses, such as the Crusades and the Black Death, no havens were available and virtually no escape was possible for Jews under Nazi control. The very survival of Jews was never more seriously threatened than during this period....

The anti-Semitism of the 20th century... is tied to nationalism, racism, and ideology. And as if to underline the irrational quality of political and social behavior, anti-Semitism survives with vitality.

The religious factor has played a central role in anti-Semitism since the advent of Christianity. It will continue to be a basis for antipathy and prejudicial actions against the Jews so long as the Church, both Catholic and Protestant, does not change its attitude and make a sincere effort to establish a healthy relationship with the Jews. Such a relationship calls for repudiation of the belief that the Jews are evil and deserving of condemnation by God and Christendom.

James Parkes voices a similar and more detailed call to Christendom. In "Judaism and Christianity," he writes that the process involved in establishing mutually satisfying, compatible and equitable religious interrelationships between Christianity and Judaism will take time. He cautions Christians on the need for realistic expectations and warns them that Jews will not quickly accept Christian protestations that they are now ready to support the notion that Jews may remain Jews and still be thought of as religious equals to Christians. Although both Christians and Jews may point with pride to their record of common work for social and political betterment, this is but one step in the long and rocky path toward total harmony. Should we look closely at even this specific area of endeavor, we find that Christian missionary societies viewed the partnership formed in working for social and political good with hostility and derision.

In addition to the effort required to overcome deep seated personal antipathy, there are other staggering difficulties. As Parkes explains, at the very foundation of Christianity is the acceptance of the teachings of the Christian Bible. Since the Bible cannot be rewritten, how would it be possible to counteract those portions of the Christian sacred writings which foster old prejudices? Parkes suggests that in Christian churches and Sunday schools they try to omit completely from public use those portions of the Bible which teach and encourage negative attitudes toward the Jews. While this might only be possible to a limited extent, it could be coupled with instilling in the church membership an instinctive awareness that "the Bible contains interpretations of past generations" and that while "such was an interesting view," we have progressed beyond that thinking; or that "it is a pity that on such a point there was so much prejudice or misunderstanding in the mind of the writer."

Parkes thus recognizes that while few churches could be accurately labeled as actively anti-Semitic, their nonselectivity in presenting biblical passages to their congregants, and in their services and the general unwillingness to amend their teaching in religious education classes, they predispose adherents to viewing their "Jewish neighbors with an unfriendly eye." When young Christians continue to use "Christ killers" in hurling an epithet at Jewish classmates, it is all too plain that the seeds of anti-Semitism are still being sown in Christian religious education.

For further readings:

1. Kessler, Aharon, *The Fate Of The Jews In The European Society: Theological Negations Of The Jewish People*. (Pittsburgh, Pa., The School of Advanced Jewish Studies. 1981)
2. Flannery, Edward H., *The Anguish Of The Jews*. (Macmillian Publishing Co., 1904)

9.
Lecture VIII:
Jewish Martyrdom Challenged

At the conclusion of one of my public lectures on "Dramatic Moments in Jewish History," a "Minister of the Gospel," as he introduced himself, raised two questions: (1) "Do Jews ask themselves whether God approves their suffering?" and (2) "How do Jews explain their people's suffering to children in their religious schools?"

In my response, I pointed out that the first question is inaccurately phrased. First, the Jews are not the only people in history who have suffered from persecution in the past nor who are suffering from persecution in the present. Those who are concerned with God's attitude toward human suffering should ask themselves why God permits all his children to suffer? I include as "God's children" Jews, Christians, Muhammadans, believers and non-believers. Until one arrives at a satisfactory answer to this question, all explanations are fantasy logic.

The second question has merit. Before I suggest a concrete explanation, however, I wish to pose a similar question to you as a Christian educator: "How does Christian education explain the suffering of the early Christians who were fed to the lions by the Romans?" The minister replied, "Those were Christian saints who chose martyrdom for their belief in Christ. Had they chosen life instead, Christianity would have died."

My reply: You identify the early Christians as saints and martyrs. Their sainthood, according to you, consisted of their belief in an ideal and their martyrdom resulted from their resolve to maintain the ideal, even at the penalty of dying for it. I grant you that that was a noble choice. But martyrdom is not a Christian invention. Long before the rise of Christianity, the Jews in Judea fought the Greeks, also for ideals. Their ideals were belief in ethical monotheism, in the Siniatic revelation, in prophetic morality, in national freedom, in democratization of religion and in the ideal of spiritual peoplehood. The historian Simon Dubnow writes: "To think and to suffer became the watchword of the Jewish people, not merely forced upon it by external circumstances beyond its control, but chiefly because it was conditioned by the very disposition of the people, by its national inclinations." When their "national inclination" was challenged by foreign powers and their spirituality was endangered by outside political authority, the nation, small and weak as it was, responded with a declaration of war on the mighty Syrian-Greek empire and later on the Roman empire. That was before the Romans fed the Christians to the lions.

How do Jews explain their people's suffering to their children? Jewish tradition has coined a term for it: *Kiddush Ha-Shem*, means "sanctification of the [Divine] Name." *Kiddush Ha-Shem* requires the willingness to die for an ideal and since the Greco-Roman period, it denotes martyrdom. In brief, when a person willingly suffers persecution rather than violate the Divine commandments, he achieves *Kiddush Ha- Shem*, the status of a martyr to whom the appellation of *Kodosh*, "holy," is applied.

Dubnow writes: "It gives heartening expression to the spiritual strivings of a nation whose brow is resplendent with the thorny crown of martyrdom. It breathes heroism of mind that conquers bodily pain. In a word, Jewish history is history sublimated."

In the nineteen hundred years since the rise of Christianity, the Jewish people neither engaged in conquest of other people's lands, nor sought to impose their religion, culture, or economic or social ambitions on other people. Dubnow writes:

> The originality of Jewish history consists, indeed, in the circumstance that it is the only history stripped of every active political element. There are no diplomatic artifices, no wars, no campaigns, no unwarranted encroachments backed by armed force upon the rights of other nations.... Jewish history presents the chronicle of an ample spiritual life, a gallery of pictures representing national scenes. Before our eyes passes a long procession of facts from the fields of intellectual effort, of morality, religion and social converse.

10.

Teaching Methods: Teaching Jewish Suffering as Martyrdom in the Jewish Secondary School

The Jewish secondary school cannot and must not ignore the perennial problem of Jewish suffering in any form of discrimination. The social psychologist, Kurt Lewin (late Director of the Center for Group dynamics at M.I.T.), urged parents and teachers not to keep the problem of anti-Semitism away from the Jewish child. In the introduction to Lewin's book, *Resolving Social Conflicts*, Prof. Gordon Alpert writes:

> In Lewin's judgment, it is not safe to assume that the discrimination he [the child] will encounter in later life constitutes so many hard knocks that he can adjust to when the time comes. The social ground of an individual's life is too important a matter to be left to chance development. The Jewish child needs to know from an early age that his conditions of security are in some respects unlike those of an average child. To be clear about one's membership is the only way for the child and adult to avoid the ravages of anxiety, self-hate, and debilitating environment.

To quote from Lewin's book:

> We may conclude that in regard to the Jewish problem the action of Jewish parents should be the same as in matters of sex or any other education; namely, true, open, and realistic. These are considerations to act on... The basic fact is that their child is going to be a member of a less privileged minority group and he will have to face this fact.... The attempt to keep this problem away from the child as long as possible, and soft pedal it, will in all likelihood make for greater difficulties in adjustment later on.
>
> A better understanding of the sociological problems involved is of particular value to the Jewish adolescent. For it can help him to solve one of the most bewildering puzzles, what kind of a group the Jews are, whether

he personally belongs to them. He will often feel himself more like some gentile friends than some Jews, and he is apt to make this feeling of similarity or dissimilarity his measuring-stick for group belongingness.... He will see that the main criterion is interdependence of fate, with the rest of the American Jews and, indeed, with the Jews all over the world.... A strong feeling of being part of the group and having a positive attitude toward it has to be built up on the basis of active responsibility for the fellow Jew, as one of the outstanding policies in Jewish education.

In our contemporary society, the only place where children receive a Jewish education is the Jewish school. In past centuries, the home and school shared equally in the responsibility of educating the child. The home provided experiences in Jewish living and the school taught the reasons and meanings of these experiences. Kurt Lewin writes:

> Historically, the Jews living in the Diaspora were kept together partly by the inner cohesive forces of the group and partly by the pressure of hostile majorities.

In the United States, hostile pressures from outside, in whatever form they may occur from time to time, are not strong enough to cause the young Jew to realize "that his own fate depends upon the fate of his entire group, which should make him eager to take a fair share of the responsibility for its welfare."

There is also another aspect to this problem that must be considered by the Jewish school. The Jewish minority in this country is protected against the various types of overt pressures which, in previous generations, forced the Jews to become a compact society. Children are aware of anti-Semitism but rarely feel its sting. When, in their study of Jewish history they are introduced to "Jewish suffering" as a constant recurrence, it is not unusual for some to become utterly bewildered about why this has been the fate of the Jewish people and in what respect it is their own obligation to remain Jewish. Kurt Lewin comments:

> To preach Jewish religion or nationalism is not likely to have any deep effect. To speak about the glorious history and culture of the Jewish people will not convince them either.

I believe that most Jewish educators would agree with Lewin's theory as it relates to the Holocaust and to other devastating episodes of Jewish suffering that are commemorated in history. The difficulty, however, is finding the links that tie together the causes, means, and consequences. This is necessary if we are to help the students understand their moral significance both as Jews and human beings. In other words, how do we present the information as historic truth and as a lesson of moral concern in a way in which students do not become disillusioned with their people's fate and their own Jewish identity.

The terms "causes," "means," and "consequences" require definition. Cause is the process of reason that produces the event. Means is the course of action or the instrument by which an act can be accomplished. Consequence is the relation of a result to its cause. When these terms are applied to a teaching-learning situation, the first two, cause and means, can be achieved through a didactic method of teaching the basic information about the historical phenomena. Consequences, however, require understanding of the rationale for the ideology to persecute the Jews by the Gentile world and the reactions to the persecutions upon the Jews. Without going into detail, I shall quote from my own classroom experience in teaching one chapter of Jewish history to students in a college class and, in a simplified form, to high school students. The lesson was divided into three parts: Introduction, Lecture and Reading From the Text, and Discussion.

Part One: Introduction

In the past weeks, we have talked about wars among nations and conflicts between the Church and the Jews. We have also discussed the Mohammedan invasions in the second half of the 7th century and the "Pact of Omar," which contained the following declaration: "Members of another religious group are inferior to Mohammedans. No new synagogues or churches could be built. Members of another religion could not ride on horses but only on mules, nor could they carry swords. In general, non-Moslems were to be so dressed as to be easily distinguishable from Moslems." I raised the fallowing question: "The Pact of Omar was promulgated in lands already conquered by the armies of Islam. Therefore these decrees were not strategies of war. What motivated the Moslems to decree them?" The students responded: "To conquer the minds of the Christians and Jews for the Mohammedan religion."

I continued: "Now, let us turn to the conflicts that exist in our time between the Soviet Union and the United States. What are these conflicts about?" The students responded: "About communism and democracy." I commented: "In other words, each people wants to conquer the minds of the other people for their ideals. What definition have we given to 'suffering for an ideal'?" The students: "Martyrdom." I: "Would you say that the Jews who suffered in conflicts with the Christian Church throughout the ages have been martyrs?" The class agreed.

Part Two: Reading from the Text

"We are now ready to talk about a series of events in history which the author of our textbook describes as: 'The Crusading age stimulates piety and commerce among the Christians and brings poverty and heroic martyrdom to the Jews.'" (A *History Of The Jews* by Solomon Grayzel, Book III, Chap. IV, p. 339.)

Before we read the text, I should like to make a few introductory comments. In your study of medieval European history in high school, you will come across very few references to the Jews. One reason is that the authors of the textbooks had little, if any, knowledge of Jewish history. Another reason is that Jewish suffering at the hands of Christian kings, popes, and the masses would be unpleasant to the sensibilities of many people. In addition, the world history which you learn in school gives only a broad review of major events and ideas without great detail. Therefore, for a basic knowledge about the Jewish people, one must look to Jewish history for accurate information. You can contrast this with the material I found in a high school textbook giving the following explanation of the Crusades: "The Crusades were wars undertaken by European Christians between the 11th and 14th centuries to recover the Holy Land from Islam. In the 7th century, Jerusalem was taken by the caliph, Omar. In the 11th century, the mad caliph, Hakim began to persecute the Christians and profaned and despoiled the Holy Sepulcher in Jerusalem. In 1095, Pope Urban II called upon Christians to go to war for the Holy Sepulcher. From the crosses that were distributed to the people, the Crusaders took their name." The details that followed gave no inkling of what happened in the European countries through which the Crusaders made their way to the Holy Land.

Let us now open our textbooks to Chapter IV, p. 340:

The Church Finds Its Strength—After many centuries of internal weakness the Catholic Church finally established its unity and its power. By a slow process, the local clergy monks obtained a firm hold on the minds of the population of Western Europe. Through them the popes exercised stronger power than any ruler of their day. Toward the end of the eleventh century, Pope Urban II could undertake an international policy for the Church such as his predecessors might have dreamed of but could not have thought possible. He called for a crusade, an attempt by the Christians of the West to take Palestine away from the Mohammedans and to make of it a province of the Roman Catholic Church. He offered to forgive the sins of anyone becoming a soldier of the Cross and to guarantee admission into Paradise to anyone who fell in battle fighting for Christianity. The response was remarkable. Every parish church became a recruiting station and every monk with a loud voice and the ability to stir the emotions of the populace urged the men to abandon mere earthly occupations and join the army of the Lord.

The Crusaders—They started a tremendous emotional movement. Even children enrolled and set out on the perilous journey, certain that God would guide them on the road. On the whole, it was as sincere a religious movement as was to be found anywhere. These people were horrified, now that it was insistently called to their attention, that the sepulcher of Jesus should be in the hands of unbelieving Mohammedans, and they were willing to sacrifice themselves for its redemption. But there were a great many who had other motives. Some of the nobility among the crusaders were nothing more than fortune hunters, looking for lands to rule over. Some of the ordinary crusaders were serfs, peasants of the lowest mental type, who sought a chance for adventure and for freedom from a dull and servile life. Even worse was the fact that the First Crusade was poorly organized. Armies of peasants marched off without proper leadership and without adequate provisions. Unrestrained, they were bound to become a danger where there was not enough force to hold them in check. The fact that many Jews had wealth which could be taken as booty was a constant temptation, and a reason for taking it away from them was not hard to find. Before long the crusaders began to argue that it was ridiculous to go forth to kill God's enemies in a distant land while the Jews close at hand, equally opposed to Christianity, were left behind unharmed. Soon the cry was heard, "Kill a Jew and save your soul!"

The historian Hugo Valentin (University of Upsala, Sweden), writes about Jewish suffering at the time of the Crusades:

The Crusades mark the turning-point in the history of Western Jewry. Their consequences, it has been said, extend even to our own day. Before them the persecutions of the Jews had not only been relatively rare, but were also, generally speaking, more marked by the desire of the spiritual and temporal authorities for religious conformity than by hatred of the Jews. Popular feeling had not been inordinately anti-Semitic, and neither in France nor in Germany had the Jews on the whole occupied an exceptional position politically or economically. But now, under the stress of the general heresy-hunt, the masses were filled with a hatred of the Jews which in greater or less degree has survived to our day. The Jews' prosperity was broken up, partly by pogroms, partly by enforced canceling of the crusaders' debts, partly by anti-Semitic legislation the practical effect of which was to expel the Jews from the community, and partly by the fact that Christendom, which now owing to the Crusades came directly in contact with the Levant, no longer required them [the Jews] as intermediaries. Congregations with proud traditions and important Jewish centres of learning were annihilated, whereby the level of Jewish culture was reduced....

Valentin quotes a statement by Count Coudenhave-Kalergi, whom he described as "the convert from anti-Semitism, exclaiming admiration and amazement that there is no people in the history of the world that surpasses the Jews for courage."

Part Three: Discussion

Educational psychologists point out that not all teaching methods are equally appropriate for helping students attain instructional objectives. This is true in many learning situations and particularly when the subject matter requires analysis, synthesis and evaluation. The subject for which I prepared a lesson plan in Jewish history is a typical example. After I decided on the content of the information to be presented to the students, I searched for a method to help them attain certain instructional skills by means of the analytical discussion method. The instructional skills were:

1. Fostering critical thinking in the appraisal of ideas. To achieve this objective, students must learn to support their opinions with reasoning based on facts.
2. Fostering democratic skills in the free and rational examination

of ideas. This calls for the ability to listen to others, to evaluate their arguments, to formulate one's own views in the heat of give and take, and to continue to focus on the problem at hand despite emotional arguments and influences.

Suggested Topics for Discussion:

1. Hostility toward the Jews in the medieval period was influenced by religion as it was conveyed by Christianity. In the 19th century, antipathy of the Jews throughout history was given the name "anti-Semitism." The religious cause and means of anti-Semitism persisted to our own day. But there is also another way of viewing hostility of one group toward another group. Social scientists who study the structure of society in terms of individual and group interaction explain attitudes of prejudice by majorities toward minorities as problems in social life. Let us analyze the social aspect as it applies to anti-Semitism.

2. The Jews are not the only people who have been and still are suffering from discrimination by individuals and groups in society. Characteristics of discrimination vary with the kind of prejudices people harbor. Researchers have found that "feelings of prejudice do not necessarily originate through contact with the people to whom it is directed. An individual needs only to be exposed to the prejudices of those around him to become infected himself. Another consideration is that prejudice is learned behavior. When children observe their elders' prejudices, they imitate them and develop prejudices of their own." One theory that explains the reasons for prejudice is "scape-goating." This is "when people place the blame for one's troubles, frustrations, or sense of guilt on some convenient but innocent person or group." For example: Some people blame ethnic or minority groups for whatever unpleasantness they themselves experience. Hitler blamed the Jews for Germany's loss of World War I. In response to the question why he selected the Jews, he replied, "Because they are there."

Discrimination of minorities, such as ethnic, racial, and religious groups by the dominant majorities among whom they live, is based upon biological, social, cultural or religious differences between the respective populations. Specifically, "racial minorities differ biologically in skin color, hair texture, head shape, and eye color. Ethnic minorities differ culturally in language, customs, religion, food habits, child rearing practices, values and beliefs from the dominant group."

Religious differences have been the major cause of Jewish suffering since Christianity became the official religion of Rome in the 4th century C.E. In a similar manner, Jews also differed from many majority populations and also from other ethic groups in social and intellectual characteristics such as literacy, moral and educational values, customs, habits, and appearance. Considering, however, the nature of the hatred, its consistency and duration over two millennia which the Christians felt for the Jews, the roots of the malady go deeper in the souls of the perpetrators than, as some sociologists and literati attribute it, to "an instructive feeling of hostility which exists in the embryo in every group of persons in relation to a group differently constituted." Another way of putting it is the "dislike of the unlike."

3. An examination of the many theories that have been advanced by historians, social scientists, literati, and sociologists about anti-Semitism should lead to the conclusion that there is a certain element of truth in most of them but none ignores the major role that religion has played in the past and still plays today in fostering prejudice against the Jews. Let us return to the Swedish historian Hugo Valentin's conclusion. Quoting Count H. C. Kalergi, he writes:

> The ultimate cause of anti-Semitism is religious fanaticism.... In classical antiquity, the Jews irritated the non-Jewish world by denying all gods but God and by severing themselves from the pagans. During the Middle Ages, the cause of anti-Semitism was Christian intolerance of the Jews, who were regarded as the murderers of the Saviour. But modern, ostensibly a-religious anti-Semitism has also a similar cause, though this appears under the protective disguise of racial antipathy. At the same time, as children learn to love Christ, the Saviour and the friend of children, they are naturally seized with indignation against those whom they deem to have hated, tortured and killed him.... As a rule, no doubt the youth or the grown man drops the faith of his childhood, but not his anti-Semitic antipathies, which, in ignorance of the history of their genesis, he supposes to be "innate." He then looks for an explanation of them and finds in pseudo-scientific articles and books in which the Jews are depicted as an inferior race. The radical anti-Semites gain a new supporter. Religious prejudice is primary, antipathy secondary, racial prejudice tertiary.

11.
Martyrdom as Kiddush Ha-Shem

Jewish education on the elementary level has kept pace with general education in many aspects of educational practice. This includes consideration of the students' chronological and maturational levels, overall intelligence and instructional methods that are most suitable to the students' individual and group characteristics according to the subjects they are studying. Much less attention has been given to the secondary level on matters of educational objectives, the choice of subject matter and the intersections between the objectives, students' characteristics, and the teaching methods. This is gradually being remedied in general education but has received scant, if any, attention in Jewish schools, particularly beyond Bar and Bat Mitzvah.

The primary thrust of this essay is how to explain Jewish suffering to teenagers while taking into account their intellectual and personal needs in the most suitable manner. In a previous lecture, I suggested the idea of martyrdom and pointed out that Jewish tradition has given martyrdom the concept of *Kiddush Ha-Shem*, "Sanctification of the Divine Name." The literal meaning of Kiddush Ha-Shem is neither easy for young people to interpret nor to comprehend. It is, therefore, necessary to bring it down to the students' levels through three steps: (1) I begin the lesson with a definition of martyrdom. The one that I feel is most comprehensive is that: "Martyrdom is submission to suffering, persecution or death for the sake of a principle, cause or faith"; (2) I follow the definition with the explanation by Rabbi Abba Silver: "Personal sacrifices are often involved in pursuit of the good life. Sometimes even martyrdom is called for. The Jewish people gave the first religious martyrs known to mankind, and through many dark and weary centuries of exile and persecution, its noblest sons and daughters never denied God the supreme tribute of martyrdom"; and (3) The Jewish conception of martyrdom is the integrating last phase of instruction.

The Value Concept of Kiddush Ha-Shem in Martyrdom

In rabbinic literature, martyrdom is not conceived as suffering for every principle or cause. It is related to the idea of holiness, *kedushah*. The implication of holiness is that by human action man can sanctity life and death. Life is sanctified through morality that consists of perfection and rules that regulate all other purposes. Sanctification of death is a willingness to make the sacrifice of giving up one's life to the honor of God. The idea of Kiddush Ha-Shem means self-sacrifice when God's name is profaned or when the Torah is in danger of being abolished. When a Jew gives up his life under such conditions, his death produces a holy action. Rabbi Max Kadushin explains this concept as follows: "Any act which produces a consciousness of God's holiness in the person who performs it, sanctifies God. Any worthy action performed by a Jew in public which enhances the prestige of Judaism sanctifies the name of God." In brief, the rabbinic sages raised the concept of martyrdom to the heights of morality and holiness.

The sources upon which they built their concept of Kiddush Ha-Shem are biblical verses, "You shall faithfully observe My commandments: I am the Lord. You shall not profane My holy name, that I may be sanctified in the midst of the people Israel—I the Lord who sanctify you" (Lev. 22:31–2). The sages interpreted this verse to mean, "God said, if you sanctify yourselves, I esteem it as though you had sanctified Me" (Sifra Kedoshim, Ch. 1). Another verse was also interpreted to convey the meaning of martyrdom as Kiddush Ha-Shem: "Love the Lord your God with all your heart and soul" (Deut. 6:6). The sages read "your soul" to mean "even though He takes your soul."

The following quotations from rabbinic and modern literature shed light on the Jewish attitude toward martyrdom as Kiddush Ha-Shem. *Talmud, Sanhedrin 7a*. The rabbinical council that met in the 2nd century in Lydda laid down the principle that a man is required to give his life rather than transgress the laws pertaining to idolatry, incest, and murder. Prof. Epraim E. Urbach points out:

> These three offenses were singled out, not on account of the punishment they involve, but because they rest on fundamental principles the abolition of which could undermine the entire existence of Judaism. The source treating of this is the teaching of R. Johanan.... When Rav Dimi came back (from Eretz Israel to Babylonia) he said in the name of R. Johanan:

This was only in regard to a time when there is no religious persecution, but at a time of persecution a man should suffer death rather than violate even a minor law.... Thus the dicta of these Amoraim [Sages of the Gemora] add considerably to the stridency of the principle, in that one should suffer martyrdom and not transgress even a minor precept in public.

It should be realized that the Halakhah of Kiddush Ha-Shem as martyrdom originated at a time of religious persecution in the Second Commonwealth. To quote Kadushin:

The following rabbinic tribute to contemporary martyrs reveals martyrdom for matters of law: "They that love Me and keep My commandments" (Ex. 20:6), says R. Nathan, "refers to those who dwell in the land of Israel and give their lives for the sake of the Mitzvot [commandments]." "Why are you being led out to be decapitated?" "Because I circumcised my son (that he be) an Israelite." "Why are you being led out to be burned?" "Because I read the Torah." "Why are you being led out to be crucified?" "Because I ate unleavened bread [i. e. observed Passover]."

The ethical philosopher, M. Lazarus, described Kiddush Ha-Shem as "the most exalted thought."

The sanctification of God through man may be called the most audacious, the most exalted, ecstatic, and useful of thoughts. The expression, "I am sanctified" (Lev. 22:32; Ezek. 20:41), conveys the sublimest notion conceived by the mind of man — it is the noblest word framed by the human tongue!

Prof. Robert M. Seltzer explains the rabbinic concept of Kiddush Ha-Shem as follows:

Israel was the only nation that has taken on the "Yoke of Heaven" by honoring the unity of God.... This is by accepting God's decrees in the Torah. Israel's act at Sinai is a crucial moment of cosmic history because it was, so to speak, the beginning of Torah's incarnation in the world.... By assuming the yoke of the commandments, Israel became a holy people. Holiness means not just abstaining from fusion with other nations and from following their ways, but imitating God's attributes through acts of mercy and through study.... Because Israel has accepted the Torah, its actions either sanctify God's name or profane God's name on earth.

From *The Encyclopedia Of The Jewish Religion*:

During the Middle Ages, mostly in connection with the massacres which accompanied the Crusades, whole communities underwent self-immolation at the behest of their leaders rather than submit to baptism (the example of the Jewish community of York 1190 is outstanding). These tragic episodes are usually regarded as the classic example in Jewish thought and history, and to this day a prayer is recited on Sabbath for "the holy congregation who laid down their lives for sanctification of the Divine Name" and Sephardi communities recite a special memorial prayer (*Hashkavah*) in memory of the Inquisition.

My suggestion to explain Jewish suffering and all forms of discrimination as martyrdom exceeds pedagogic needs. The historic Jew saw in Israel's suffering the purpose of their destiny as the eternal people, God's people. In a letter which Moses Maimonides wrote in 1172 to the Jews of Yemen, who confronted the choice of conversion to Mohammedanism or exile, he counseled them: "Hold fast to the Covenant, fulfill the statutes of your religion.... Should ever the necessity of fleeing for your lives to a wilderness and inhospitable regions arise — painful as it may be to sever oneself from dear associations, or to relinquish one's property — you should still endure all."

In the 19th century, Rabbi Samuel Hirsch described the destiny of the Jewish people as spreading the true knowledge of God, which it received, to all humanity.

> This vocation is the mission of the Jewish people. They did not receive truth only for itself, but for humanity as a whole; and the Jew must testify to this faith not by words alone, but through their existence, and must prove the power of their faith through its realization in their own lives. The sufferings of Israel also serve this purpose. Israel is the suffering servant of the Lord, through whose ordeals the impotence of evil becomes manifest. (See Julius Gottmann)

12.
Jewish Attitudes Toward Christianity in Light of Christian Anti-Semitism

In a seminar at the Graduate School of Education at the University, Christian ministers frequently asked, "In light of Christian anti-Semitism, what has been the Jewish attitude toward the Christian religion?" In my reply, I quoted from a marvelous essay by my teacher, Prof. Abraham A. Neuman, at Dropsie College:

> Notwithstanding the inhospitable spiritual atmosphere of the Middle Ages, Judaism, although oppressed by its own daughter religions, recognized its spiritual kinship with them. It regarded these dynamic conquering faiths as carriers of divine truth to the nations of the world. Without deviating from its uncompromising monotheism and consequent opposition to the trinitarian conception of God, the divine nature of Christ, the worship accorded to saints and images, and other Christological features of the Church, Judaism freely acknowledged the divine mission of Christianity, and equally that of Islam, whose theism was pure and unblemished. According to Jewish teaching, they were unconsciously—but by God's design—Israel's apostles to the heathen nations. They were the active agents spreading the basic truths which God revealed to Israel in forms which were more readily assimilable to the heathen nations because if their pagan background. The very elements in Christianity which separated it from the mother religion—the conception of God in human form, the priest as the intermediary between God and man, the profusion of images with supernatural attributes, the worship of saints, the dogma of mysteries or sacraments—were interpreted as pedagogical means for drawing pagan multitudes to the true God who revealed Himself to Israel as the One God, the Creator of the Universe, the Father who created man in His image, who inspired him to a life of holiness through compassion, love, and justice. Precisely during the period of medieval scholasticism, when Christian dogma was being crystallized in rigid concepts, Jewish philosophers inter-

preted sympathetically, as means to an end, Christian teachings which were unacceptable to them but which were effective psychologically in bringing about the mass conversion of heathen nations to Christianity. This enlightened attitude impressed itself also on Jewish canon law.

For further readings

1. Lewin, Kurt, *Resolving Social Conflicts* (Harper & Bros. 1948).
2. Grayzel, Solomon, *A History Of The Jews* (Jewish Publication Society 1968).
3. Valentin, Hugo, *Anti-Semitism Historically And Critically Examined* (Viking Press 1936).
4. Silver, Abba Hillel, *Where Judaism Differed* (The Macmillan Co. 1956).
5. Kadushin, Max, *Worship And Ethics: A Study In Rabbinic Judaism* (Northwestern University Press 1964).
6. Urbach, Ephraim E., *The Sages: Their Concepts And Beliefs* (Hebrew University 1975).
7. Encyclopedia Of The Jewish Religion, Ed. R. J. Zwi Werblowsky and G. Wigdor (Adama Books 1986).
8. Guttmann, Julius, *Philosophies Of Judaism* (Jewish Publication Society and Holt, Rinehart & Winston 1964).
9. Neuman, Abraham A., "Judaism" in *The Great Religions Of The World*, Ed. E. J. Jurji (Princeton University Press 1967).
10. Gage, N. L. and Berliner, David C., *Educational Psychology* (Rand McNally 1979).
11. Perry, John A. and Perry, Erna K., Contemporary Society: An Introduction To Social Science (Harper & Row Pub. 1980).

About the Author

Aharon Kessler was awarded his Ph.D. from Dropsie College for Hebrew and Cognate Learning in biblical and rabbinic literature. He has been active in Jewish education since 1940, when he was invited to join the Zionist Youth Commission, established by the Zionist Organization and Hadassah.

In 1941, Dr. Kessler established the first Young Judea Study Camp in New Hampshire with the aid of Justice Louis Brandeis. The late Dr. Shlomo Bardin established within this camp the Brandeis Institute Camp. Both institutions were sponsored by the Zionist Youth Commission.

In 1945, Dr. Kessler joined the American Association of Jewish Education as National Consultant. In that year, Mrs. Eleanor Roosevelt established a White House Advisory Youth Committee and invited Dr. Kessler to join this committee that she had established. In 1950, he was delegated by the Jewish Agency for Israel to study Jewish education conditions in five South American countries: Brazil, Argentina, Uruguay, Chile, and Peru.

In 1951, he was appointed by the American Association of Jewish Education to join Dr. Uriah Engelman, Director of Research, to conduct a study of Jewish education in Pittsburgh, Pennsylvania. The study recommended the establishment of a communal system of education under the supervision of a newly created council of Jewish Education. The Council immediately invited Dr. Aharon Kessler to serve as its Executive Director. Dr. Kessler soon established the College of Jewish Studies, which later became the School of Advanced Jewish Studies.

When Dr. Kessler arrived in Pittsburgh to assume his responsibilities in Jewish education, he was invited by the chairman of religious education in the Graduate School of Education at the University of Pittsburgh to become a member of the graduate faculty. Thereafter, he was also invited to join the faculty of the university's Department of Arts and Science to teach the religion and culture of Judaism.

Over the years, Dr. Kessler has written more than sixty works on Jewish education, which include the subjects of history, literature, religion, philosophy, and pedagogy. Many of these books were published by the College of Jewish Studies, the School of Advanced Jewish Studies, and the Nadiv Fund for Jewish Culture.

Dr. Kessler retired in 1985 and continues to devote himself to writing new works.